Born Under the Gun

BORN UNDER THE GUN

A History of Kamerun, WW I, Christian Missions and the Internment Camps of Fernando Po

ROBERT J. O'NEIL

The Crossroad Publishing Company
New York

The Crossroad Publishing Company
www.CrossroadPublishing.com

© 2018 by Robert O'Neil

Crossroad, Herder & Herder, and the crossed C logo/colophon are registered trademarks of The Crossroad Publishing Company.

All rights reserved. No part of this book may be copied, scanned, reproduced in any way, or stored in a retrieval system, or transmitted, in any form or by any means, electronic, mechanical, photocopying, recording, or otherwise, without the written permission of The Crossroad Publishing Company. For permission please write to rights@crossroadpublishing.com

In continuation of our 200-year tradition of independent publishing, The Crossroad Publishing Company proudly offers a variety of books with strong, original voices and diverse perspectives. The viewpoints expressed in our books are not necessarily those of The Crossroad Publishing Company, any of its imprints or of its employees, executives, or owners. Although the author and publisher have made every effort to ensure that the information in this book was correct at press time, the author and publisher do not assume and hereby disclaim any liability to any party for any loss, damage, or disruption caused by errors or omissions, whether such errors or omissions result from negligence, accident, or any other cause. No claims are made or responsibility assumed for any health or other benefits.

Book design by The HK Scriptorium

The title *Born under the Gun* was inspired by a name given to Godfred Buma Langmia in the Bali language. He was born in a Fernando Po internment camp in 1919.

Library of Congress Cataloging-in-Publication Data

Names: O'Neil, Robert J., 1939- author.
Title: Born under the gun : a history of Kamerun, WW I, Christian missions and the internment camps of Fernando Po / Robert J. O'Neil.
Description: New York : The Crossroad Publishing Company, [2018] | Includes bibliographical references and index.
Identifiers: LCCN 2018039101| ISBN 9780824599621 (trade paper) | ISBN 9780824599904 (mobipocket) | ISBN 9780824599898 (Epub3)
Subjects: LCSH: World War, 1914-1918¬—Campaigns—Cameroon. | Missions, German—Cameroon. | World War, 1914-1918—Equatorial Guinea—Fernando Po. Germans—Cameroon—History. | Refugees—Germany—History—20th century. Refugees—Equatorial Guinea—Fernando Po—History—20th century. | Concentration camps—Equatorial Guinea—Fernando Po. | Cameroonians—Equatorial Guinea—Fernando Po—History. | Germans—Equatorial Guinea—Fernando Po—History. | Fernando Po (Equatorial Guinea)—History.
Classification: LCC D576.C3 O64 2018 | DDC 940.54/72460967186—dc23 LC record available at https://lccn.loc.gov/2018039101

Books published by The Crossroad Publishing Company may be purchased at special quantity discount rates for classes and institutional use. For information, please e-mail sales@Crossroad Publishing.com.

To my father
John J. O'Neil, Sr.
1912–1992

Fighters for Germany's Honor! The Imperial Protection Force for Kamerun.
Monument, Malabo, Equatorial Guinea

This monument to African troops in the German colonial *Schutztruppe* of Kamerun was recently rediscovered in the city of Malabo on the island of Bioko, Equatorial Guinea. With permission of the German Ambassador to Equatorial Guinea.

Contents

Foreword *by Professor Victor Julius Ngoh* — ix

Acknowledgments — xi

Preface — xiii

Introduction — 1

1. The Imperial German Colony of Kamerun in West Africa and Christian Missions to 1914 — 7

2. World War I in Kamerun — 40

3. Retreat to Spanish Territory and Transportation to Fernando Po — 71

4. The Internment Camps on Fernando Po, 1916–1919 — 87

5. Repatriation to the Mainland and a Divided Kamerun, 1919–1920 — 107

Conclusion — 127

Appendix 1: Testimony of Cameroonians — 133

Appendix 2: Stories of Kamerun and Fernando Po — 150

Notes — 159

Index — 179

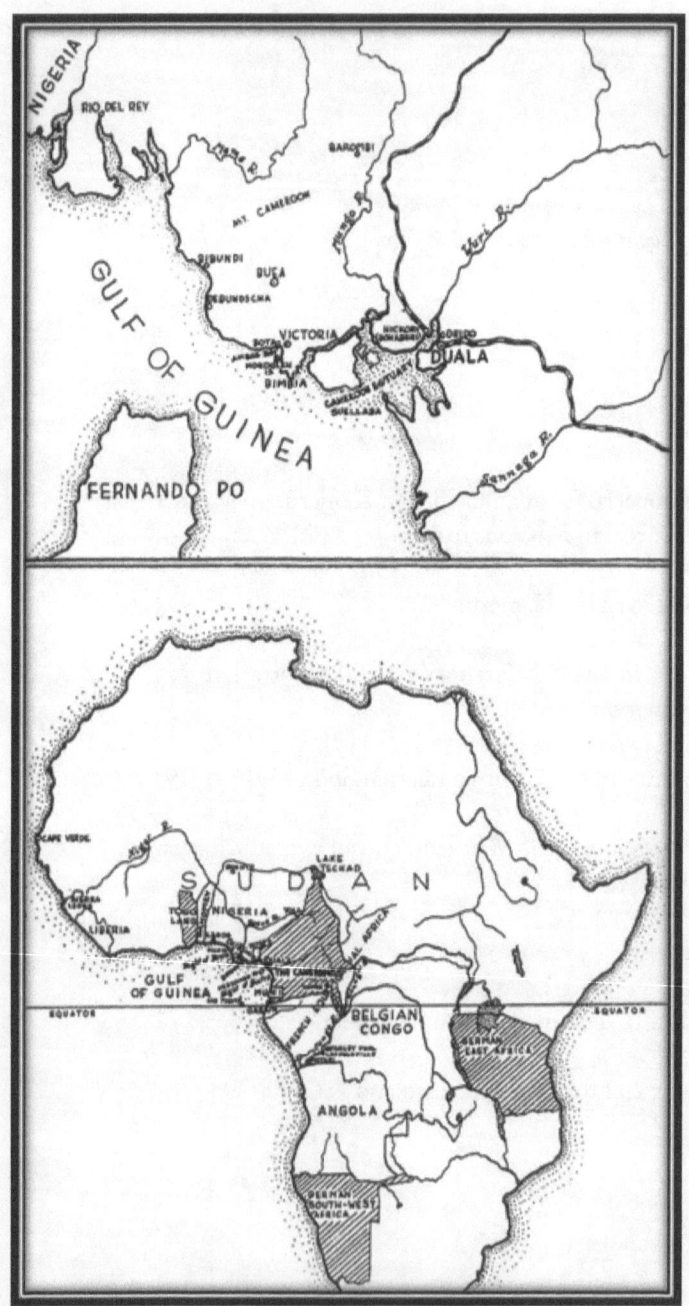

From *Germans in the Cameroons 1884–1914*,
by Harry R. Rudin, Yale University Press, 1938.

Foreword

Reverend Fr. Robert O'Neil is no stranger to Cameroon, more especially with regard to the history of missionary activities in Cameroon, given that he was a Mill Hill missionary priest in Cameroon for some years; his love and passion for Cameroon and its people bring him back to Cameroon ever so often.

His latest publication on Cameroon, titled *Born under the Gun*, is based largely on interviews and memories of Cameroonians, men and women from the Bamenda grassfield (present-day North West Region of Cameroon) and writings of missionaries. The belief in God and Christianity that runs through most of the narratives, testimonies, and memories of most of the Cameroonians is an added religio-historical uniqueness of this publication.

The author has succinctly examined World War I in Kamerun; the retreat of German colonial troops and Cameroonian soldiers and porters to Fernando Po (now Equatorial Guinea); the internment camps in Fernando Po; and the partition of German Kamerun. This makes the publication a welcome relief to scholars on Cameroon history and Cameroon sociology. The retreat of German troops from Kamerun to Fernando Po definitely created the first "refugees" of Europeans, Germans, in Africa.

Born under the Gun is a well-researched, well-written and a much-awaited valuable contribution to the historiography of Cameroon. The history of Cameroon, especially its political history, is becoming more and more popularized, and a better understanding of the 1914–1919 story in Cameroon is indispensable for an objective comprehension of the totality of the country's history. This publication is highly recommended for scholars of all disciplines and those interested in understanding the socio-political complexity of Cameroon history.

Professor Victor Julius Ngoh
7 August 2017

Acknowledgments

Collecting material for this book began more than thirty years ago. The idea came from Peter Logue, then guest master at the Cistercian Monastery, Mbengwi, in Cameroon. Conversations with Professor Harry R. Rudin of Yale University and his book were an introduction to the topic of German Kamerun. Graham Irwin, Professor of African History at Columbia University in New York, a mentor and friend, showed me how to write it. Paul Verdzekov, scholar and archbishop of Bamenda, provided the opportunity to collect the life histories quoted throughout. All are of blessed memory.

In addition to the Cameroonians who shared their stories I am most grateful for the help of others.

In Cameroon: Primus Forgwe of the National Archive in Buea; Cornelius Esua, current archbishop of Bamenda; Professor Victor Julius Ngoh of the National University; Gabriel Nkweti, an old friend in Moghamo country; and also Fr. Joseph Akem and Philip Akanji Mbah.

Outside of Cameroon there were many who helped in various ways, especially in their generosity. They include: J. Ball, J. Bike, J. P. Gallagher, E. Kozlowski, J. P. Roach, W. K. Walsh, archivist T. O'Brien of the Mill Hill Missionaries, and M. Faulkner of SOAS in London.

Five people deserve special thanks.

The late Miriam Luciano, who translated from the Spanish J. Vincent's booklet on the internment.

Publisher Gwendolin Herder.

Hollis Lynch, Emeritus Professor of History at Columbia, read and commented on the manuscript. Without his wisdom and clarity the book could not have been completed.

Father James Lloyd of St. Paul's in Manhattan, who, for more than twenty years, was untiring in his encouragement. I am grateful for his persistence and friendship.

And finally, there is one person in Cameroon, living with his wife and five children at Mile Four in Limbe, SW Region, who was a right hand when collecting oral testimony in Cameroon. During 1984 and again in 1988–89 Benard Forkwa was my research assistant. It was he who set up the tape recorder and transcribed all the interviews. Without his assistance, there would be no record of the "splendid sources" Professor Irwin praised. He helped to rescue from anonymity the life stories of many of his countrymen and women.

Preface

Karl Rahner "reminds us that the Holy Spirit is revealed as the divine power in the deepest heart of each person and of this earthly world. This power is the graced centre of creation...." And Pope John Paul II explained that "the presence and activity of the spirit are universal, limited neither by space or time... affecting society and history, peoples, cultures and religions."
—Daniel J. O'Leary[1]

Following the defeat of the Germans in Kamerun... a... unique refugee situation occurred. German troops sought refuge in Rio Muni and Fernando Po. Probably the only large group of Europeans to ever become refugees on the African continent, the Germans were followed by their planters and businessmen and by some 60,000 African soldiers and villagers.
—Ibrahim Sundiata[2]

The internment of Germans, their troops and their supporters on the island of Fernando Po during World War I "constitutes an important yet hitherto largely neglected episode in Cameroon colonial history."
—Jacqueline de Vries[3]

In these pages there are the characters you'd expect to find in a history of colonial West Africa. Explorers, soldiers and traders, missionaries and planters and a few prominent Africans coopted into the expansion of colonial control over new areas and peoples. And there are the events that brought Africans into a cash economy, a world religion, and the Great War between the European nation states. But here you will also find others often not heard from.

This is a time in our collective history when we ask about all those left behind, the anonymous men and women of history. We have become more and more aware that we are connected to one another as individuals with hopes and ambitions, whether one is a governor of a German colony or an elder in a small village of the African interior. Even an unbeliever can accept that we flow from a common origin and continue to move and grow more dependent on our connection with one another and the care of our environment to survive. A believer can go beyond and recognize the Spirit moving through the story told in this book, especially in the words of the many Cameroonians who shared their memories with the author. It is in their words that the image of God is revealed present in the heart of each one of them.

And so we can be curious about the historian Harry Rudin traveling through Cameroon in 1932 and equally so about the life of a plantation worker from a village in the grassfields, or a servant to a German army officer who lived out his life in a town on the Mamfe–Bamenda road. You will find them and more in the following pages.

Among them, Peter Vewesse in Babanki Tungo village is as important to this incomplete story as missionary Bender at Soppo, General Dobell, the Allied commander in World War I, and Karl Ebermaier, the last governor of Kamerun. But the story is incomplete because we know very little about thousands of others; the porters used by the colonizers, the members of the *Schutztruppe*, and the plantation workers who never returned to their villages. We try in the following pages to recall a few, often in their own words. We also use the writings of missionaries who describe their uprooting during the war to give a voice to those Christian eyewitnesses.

The story begins in the North West Region of Cameroon in 1965. Almost all the interviews with Cameroonians in this book are from that area. It moves back in time to Germany and colonial Kamerun, the arrival of Christian missions, through World War I, the removal of missionaries and the retreat of German forces to Spanish territory and asylum. The history is told of Spain's presence in Muni and Fernando Po. The camps of internees on Fernando Po are described along with life there for Cameroonians and some Germans, and finally repatriation to the mainland. A postwar Kamerun is divided, and men and women return to their homes. With the repatriation and division of Kamerun the book returns again to the North West where it started, completing a circle of events. Throughout the book, oral testimony used is from men, and some women, in what was, during post–World War I, called the Bamenda Province of the British Southern Cameroons.

A Trip to West Africa

In 1999 while traveling to West Africa to continue a research project in Cameroon history and collect material for this book, I had a room at the Bota Catholic Mission on the coast of Cameroon in Limbe. From there one could look across the sea to the island of Bioko, part of Equatorial Guinea. One hundred years earlier, Bioko was known as Fernando Po.

The Republic of Cameroon is a West African country of more than 20 million people. It is 5 degrees north of the equator with an Atlantic coastline, and in the interior, boundaries with six other African countries. The name Cameroon comes from the Portuguese, who visited the coastal settlements as early as the fifteenth century and called the Wouri River estuary the River of Prawns,

Rio dos Camaroes.[4] Later, English traders used the name for the mountain nearby. In 1884 Germany annexed the coastal area and then extended the name "Kamerun" to the entire territory, much of which is modern Cameroon.

Cameroon's neighbor, Equatorial Guinea, became independent of Spain in 1968. In the nineteenth century it was part of the Spanish Territories of the Gulf of Guinea. Later Spain united the island of Fernando Po, now called Bioko, with its mainland possession, Rio Muni, into the colony of Spanish Guinea.

Entries in an old notebook describe that journey: On November 2nd 1999 Swiss Air flight 272 left Zurich for Douala in Cameroon. Passing over the Sahara Desert, the savannah and the great forests of West Africa, it was to make a brief stop at Malabo on Bioko.

It was still rainy season. When we crossed the West African coast one could see clearly the Bota Islands near the Cameroon town of Limbe. We approached Bioko, the island that in times past was called Fernando Po when it was part of Spain's overseas empire. Bioko was covered by clouds, but at about 800 ft. the plane broke through. I was surprised at how dense the forest was. Very few houses were to be seen. As we approached the runway one could see a dirt road and a small town with a church and square at its center, in the way of Spanish missions.

The Airbus landed at 5 pm and remained for 45 minutes before continuing the short distance to the African mainland. It was a hard landing on the one air strip. From the window one saw a sign: "No photographs." A small anti-aircraft gun was under a raffia shed. There were two soldiers. A white pick-up with yellow blinking lights guided the aircraft to a small terminal area. I thought of an old airport at Bali in the North West Region of Cameroon: bush, rusted out machinery, and weather-beaten buildings. At least three-quarters of the passengers left the plane. A European seated nearby suggested that Mobil Oil was drilling off shore and a new airport was being constructed and that was one reason so many deplaned: to work in construction. Others getting off were timber workers from Indonesia. "Housing," he continued, "was a problem but despite the difficulties the people were very friendly and the place as yet was unspoiled."

In 1916 housing was also a problem on the island. But in that year it was because of the thousands of Cameroonian soldiers in the German colonial army and their retinue who were given asylum by the Spanish governor. They had retreated with their German officers and some civilians, pursued by British and French columns, across the border between the German colony and Spanish territory during World War I. The German colony in those days was called Kamerun. The Spanish held the territory of Rio Muni on the mainland and the island of Fernando Po. From Rio Muni many were transported to the island where they were to be interned until the end of the war in Europe. Most were repatriated to the mainland in 1919.

Germany hoped that the Kamerun *Schutztruppe* could be kept intact after the collapse of their defenses in January 1916. If the soldiers of the colonial protective force were kept together on Fernando Po they could return quickly to the mainland after the war. The thinking was that a peace agreement would restore Germany's colonial empire.[5]

The war and the internment are key events of this story. But more than the political success in keeping a German colonial army intact, it is also a story of the survival and growth of the Christian church in Cameroon. More than once it appeared that the church faced disaster, but each setback led to something unexpected. Even before Germany annexed Kamerun this happened with the failure of a Baptist mission on Fernando Po. This setback led to the opening of a station on the Cameroon mainland. The politics of German colonialism in turn forced out the Baptist missionaries. This led to a young independent congregation. World War I saw the destruction of much of the work of Catholic and Protestant missionaries and the deportation of all German missionaries, but a few local leaders came forward to continue the work of evangelization. The internment itself allowed a few missionaries and Christians to evangelize many hundreds in the camps and send them back as missionaries to their own people. At each step what seemed a loss became a gain. According to one recent report, 53.4 percent of the current population is Christian.

The plane took off in the twilight and banked around slowly eastward toward Cameroon. It was getting dark. From the window I could see much bush and little signs of life on Bioko. Near what may have been an oil refinery there was the glow of burning gas brought from the sea bed. The glow of similar flames on oil drilling platforms could be seen far out to sea in the Bay of Biafra as we continued toward Douala.

As the flight approached the mainland of Cameroon on that dark night I recalled my first contact with this area of the world in December 1965 while a passenger on a freighter. We passed the island of Fernando Po and then were piloted up the Wouri estuary to the port of Douala. Douala was then part of French-speaking East Cameroun. I was a Catholic missionary, appointed by the London-based Mill Hill Missionaries to the English-speaking West Cameroon. Mill Hill Missionaries had arrived in 1922 to take up the work left behind by German missionaries during World War I. There was a short plane ride over creeks and swamps to Tiko in what was then West Cameroon. In all directions were oil and rubber plantations established many years before by German planters, the first sign that Cameroon was once part of German Africa, from 1884 to 1916. The second night there was a bed in what had been the old German officers' quarters in Soppo on the slopes of Cameroon Mountain, an active volcano.[6]

Christmas that year was in the northwest of the country at one of the early Catholic missions called Njinikom. On the way to the mission station the lorry

Preface xvii

The North West Region and surrounding area. Wikimaps.

passed through the provincial capital, Bamenda, where there is a former German fort overlooking the town and surrounding countryside. The old Bedford picked its way along the rough laterite and gravel road, much of which was traced by the Germans before World War I.

Among the first visits to an outstation of Njinikom was to the village of Fuanantui. After the service an elder by the name of Michael Timneng introduced himself. Others explained that he was one of those who had brought the Catholic Church from the island of Fernando Po after World War I.

For many years the German times were a mystery to me. In the 1980s, especially in 1984, when doing research for a dissertation on the Moghamo area, and again in 1988, there was opportunity to ask elders about the past and record their life histories. Some spoke about the time many spent on Fernando Po during World War I. This book is a direct result of those interviews, many of which are used in this story.[7]

To know the full story one must reach back to the annexation of the Cameroon by Germany in 1884 and the arrival of Protestant and Catholic missionaries. Baptist missionaries arrived first, from Spanish Fernando Po, 32 km off the coast of Cameroon, where they had been since the 1840s. World War I brought a setback to the missions as all German missionaries were considered to be prisoners of war. A few continued to work until early 1916, when the last were finally deported or retreated with a German army into Spanish Rio Muni.

The story of Imperial Germany's Kamerun includes a description of World War I as the Allies and German *Schutztruppen* fought over the territory. It is also a tale of the Christian mission to this part of West Africa. The war and the Allied treatment of German missionaries damaged the relationship between churches of the mission movement but did not contain the gospel.

James O'Connell worked as a missionary in Kenya. He described the movement of the Spirit as being like the wind that fills the sails and drives the settled ship of life out of the harbor into the great expanse of sea beyond the horizon. That is what we may discern in the story of the Christian church of those years until 1919 and beyond in Cameroon.[8]

It is hoped that this study will contribute to the record of an early colonial period of Cameroon history and rescue the names and stories of some of the participants from anonymity. This is especially true of the Cameroonians who remembered German Kamerun and shared their memories with me.[9]

Introduction

> *Ich bin ein Bub' von Kamerun.*
> *Der deutschen Kolonie;*
> *Fürst Bismarck hatte viel zu tun*
> *Bis er erworben sie.*
>
> *The young Negro schoolboy in German Cameroons who years ago composed these lines and declaimed them at a school celebration had no idea of the difficulties that confronted Bismarck at the time he acquired this German colony. Even less did he realize what turn of fate had kept his land from becoming an English colony and himself from singing England's praises in English.*
>
> —Professor Harry Rudin, 1932[1]

The names of current West African countries may be familiar to some, but few of us know about the colonies that have disappeared. One was Imperial Germany's Kamerun, which existed between 1884 and 1916. Its demise was brought about by World War I and the final stages of the "scramble for Africa" initiated by European powers.[2]

Someone who influenced several generations of those interested in Africa and German Kamerun was Professor Harry Rudin of Yale University in the United States. Reading his 1938 book, *Germans in Cameroon*, and meeting with him several times in the mid-1980s at his home in Hamden, Connecticut, encouraged my own interest. From our conversations his journey to Cameroon in the early 1930s is imagined.

Far out at sea on a moonless night Fante fishermen looked up from their fishing lines to watch a small steamer, about five miles away, sail southeast with all her lights on and the sound of music reaching out to them across the sea. It was April 1932.

Among the passengers on board the SS *Wahehe* that night were Harry Rudin of Yale University in the United States and A. Victor Murray, a lecturer in education in the Selly Oaks Colleges in Birmingham, England. Rudin was on his way to Cameroon to continue his research for a book that was later published as *Germans in Cameroon*. Murray had already toured Africa in 1927 to study native education and especially the training of teachers in the colonies. He had published a book in 1929 titled *The School in the Bush*. On this journey he gave Rudin a signed copy of his book.³

On the same journey Rudin purchased a *History of Nigeria* by A. C. Burns in Lagos for 15 shillings. Burns, a colonial official, had been deputy chief secretary of the government of Nigeria. He first arrived in Nigeria in 1912 and over the years collected material for his book, published in 1929. He hoped to help residents who were missionaries, traders, or colonial officials with a short history of the local people and their relations with the British government. Nigeria governed the British Cameroons after the end of the German colony in World War I under a League of Nations mandate.

Rudin, Burns, and Murry were of a time that has long disappeared. But each has left a written legacy in their observations and the testimony of people they met. Even the ship that carried Rudin and Murray, typical of many that sailed the coasts of colonial Africa from Europe, had its own story. It is linked to the one in this book. Although German Kamerun had ceased to exist thirteen years before at the Treaty of Versailles, the SS *Wahehe,* a merchant ship of 4,683 tons, built in Hamburg in 1922, was owned by the Woermann Company and flying a German flag. One port of call was Douala in the former Kamerun, then under a League of Nations mandate and divided between Britain and France. Douala was Rudin's destination in 1932.⁴ His research helped him to become a pioneer in the study of German imperialism. He was to have a long career at Yale University where he was a scholar of European diplomatic history and among the first to promote the study of African history.⁵

Rudin's book became a classic work of the period of 1884 to 1914, stopping short of World War I and the retreat of the German forces and thousands of Cameroonians into Spanish Rio Muni in 1916.

The obelisk on the cover, dedicated to African members of the Kamerun *Schutztruppe* and especially those who died during World War I, is in the Santa Maria district of Malabo. Malabo was called Santa Isabel when the island was Spanish Fernando Po. The memorial, neglected and covered with vines, was rediscovered a few years ago by visiting Germans. On the plaque is written in German: "The Brave Defenders of Germany's Honor. The Imperial Protection Force for Cameroon."⁶

In November 2014, on Germany's "Volkstauertags" or Remembrance Day, the German ambassador to Equatorial Guinea, Rainer Munzel, gave a brief speech at the monument to remind everyone of the grief and pain inflicted by all wars and totalitarian regimes. The monument "commemorates the internment of German forces in Equatorial Guinea in the first world war," he said, and also "reminds us that humanitarian action is possible during war." His words were a reference to the thousands who were given refuge by Spain and the governor at the time, Angel Barerra Luyando.⁷

According to Ambassador Munzel, there had been a cemetery in Malabo

Schutztruppe monument before its restoration.
With permission of the German Embassy, Malabo.

with a German section with six graves and a Cameroonian section where several hundred soldiers were buried. The cemetery no longer exists. Unfortunately, he wrote, "It is today part of the international airport of Malabo."[8]

The Cameroonian soldiers remembered were part of the Imperial Protection Force, or *Schutztruppe,* in the Kamerun. This was the name given to all colonial troops in the German Empire from the late nineteenth century. It was established in 1895 and existed side by side with a police force begun in 1891. The official purpose of the troop was to ensure the safety and the maintenance of public order in the colonies and combat the slave trade. A unit model was to have two officers, three German NCOs, one respected African officer, four indigenous noncommissioned officers, and one hundred and fifty indigenous soldiers. In reality it could be quite different. In Kamerun perhaps one half of the recruits came from nearby French and British colonies.[9] The *Schutztruppe* was never part of the German Imperial army but a force responsible to the Colonial Office. In Kamerun the governor was in command. The Kamerun troop before the war in 1914 had its headquarters in Soppo on the slopes of

Mt. Cameroon. It staffed 49 garrisons with 61 officers, 23 physicians, 23 civilian administrators and technicians, 98 German noncommissioned officers, and 1,650 Africans.

Such troops of Africans served in units that were set up and equipped for the purpose of holding down the African population and maintaining control of the colony. This was the practice not only in Kamerun but in Germany's other African colonies as well.[10] Their lives, and that of their wives and families and other workers for the Germans, remained linked with their experience in the military.[11]

In the 1980s there were only a few who could speak of those days of German Kamerun and Fernando Po. There was an opportunity to interview some of them in 1988 when I recorded the testimony of two Cameroonians, Benedict Mukom and Peter Vewese. Their village is in the North West Region about one hour from Bamenda.

The two men shared their memories about the days of Imperial German Kamerun. One told the story of his father, Aloysius Mukom, while the other, Peter Vewesse, was an eyewitness.[12]

Benedict Mukom was waiting in the old stone presbytery at Babanki Tungo Catholic Mission. He sat quietly in the sitting room on one of the colonial-style arm chairs. It was a bright afternoon, but little light entered the room because of small windows shaded by a wide verandah.[13] Mukom had retired from public life to his home in the village. He began to tell his story beginning with his father, Aloysius Mukom, who was a young man during the "German time."

Aloysius made contact with Germans at the Bamenda station in what is today the North West Region. He used to cut plantains on Babanki land in Bambui and sell them to the soldiers at the fort. One day an African soldier wanted a steward and offered the job to Aloysius; he took it. From Bamenda he followed his new employer to Bota near Victoria on the coast. The soldier was a Catholic, and so the boy began to "learn doctrine" at the Catholic Mission. After some time he was sent to St Mary's School at Sasse, and later to the first Catholic Cameroon seminary founded by the Pallottine Missionaries, also at Sasse. When World War I came to Cameroon in 1914 he was sent by the German missionaries to Dschang, a military station in northwest Cameroon, where there was a Catholic Mission.

Benedict's father had never been to Fernando Po, but he did know someone in the village who had. He led us to a compound and a modest house nearby.

Peter Vewesse welcomed us to his home. He was ill and had been resting. Peter was almost ninety years of age in 1988. Rereading the book of interviews twenty-five years later, I found that Vewesse's page was marked with a copy of his baptism record. It recorded that Peter Vewesse was born in 1900 and baptized on Fernando Po on 15 April 1918 by Fr. Baumeister, one of the German missionaries interned on the island. His sponsor that day was Joseph Monye.

Peter Vewesse, Babanki-Tungo, North West Region, 1988, © Robert O'Neil

A few weeks later he received his First Communion. He was confirmed on 8 August. Vewesse was one of the few remaining survivors in the Bamenda grassfields of the thousands of Cameroonians who had spent the years 1916–1919 on Fernando Po.

Missionaries who arrived after the war were often surprised to meet Christian communities led by returnees like Michael Timneng in Kom and Agathe Koigni, the first Tikar Christian who evangelized Bandam village, in Bamum. They had been instructed in their Christian faith while on the island. There were also groups of ex-soldiers who continued to turn up at the funerals of comrades in Bali-Nyonga and elsewhere.

Africans in the colonial wars most often died in anonymity. They were buried in a pauper's grave and their names and stories wiped from memory and history.[14] A few graves are marked along with those German soldiers who also died in Kamerun. There is such a grave site in Bamenda in the North West Region. A retired British colonial officer recalled his first visit to Bamenda, Cameroon, when it was administered under a League of Nations mandate. He admired the old fort built with burned bricks before the Great War. Bamenda was a German station. "Hard by," he wrote, "I found the inescapable cemetery and pointers to a troubled past. Colonial powers had inevitably had garrisons of troops in strategic locations." There were graves of German soldiers who had died of illness and others who had been killed "in some bloody local encounter probably unrecorded." "One wondered what the driving force had been and whether it had been worth the cost. Did Kaporal Moeller who fell in some battle or other, have time to contemplate his past or have the last rites? Did the people back home have any knowledge of what was going on in their name?"[15] Somewhere, unmarked, there are also graves of the carriers pressed into military service and the hundreds of soldiers in the Kamerun colonial army. One reminder is the monument in Malabo.

Members of the Kamerun *Schutztruppe*. Buea Archive.
A 1937 history of the fighting by German troops in Cameroon reported that during the war 25 officers and 78 European servicemen "fell at the hand of the enemy"; 9 officers and 60 servicemen died of their wounds or sickness. Of the *Schutztruppe* "one thousand two hundred black soldiers gave their lives for the German cause."[16] Reprinted with permission.

The hope for a swift end to the war in Europe and returning to life in a German colony is seen not only in the designs of military planners but also in the testimony of missionaries, administrators, and Cameroonians. On Fernando Po an organized force was ready to return to administer the colony. But the Treaty of Versailles failed them all. Kamerun was taken from Germany and divided between Britain and France. Some saw this as a setback for "civilization" while colonialization continued.[17]

CHAPTER ONE

The Imperial German Colony of Kamerun in West Africa and Christian Missions to 1914

> In 1883 few would have believed that in five years the Baptist missionaries would have packed their bags and left, and that a German flag would fly, not only over the independent chiefdoms of Douala, but over Victoria also, the very creation of the English Baptist Missionary Society.
>
> —Shirley Ardener [1]

> In 1889 the first European found his way on to the grasslands. This was the German Doctor Zintgraff who, starting from Sabes, passed through Banumbat and emerged on the Plateau at Bamungwen. From here he went to Bamessong and thence to Bali.
>
> —Arnett, Resident, Cameroons Province, 1925. [2]

Germany's Arrival in West Africa

The year 1884 was a turning point in the history of Cameroon. In 1883 independent chiefdoms along the coast of Cameroon had enjoyed a political freedom limited only by their trade interests. The most important foreign cultural influence was English. The Baptist mission was still important, and there was optimism about its future, especially at Victoria. German traders were a growing presence, but the British had a consul and naval vessels in the area. But this changed in 1884. German traders began to do much better than their more numerous British rivals, and sickness and death had weakened the presence of Baptist missionaries. In July 1884 the position of the British traders began to decline.[3]

On Monday, 14 July 1884, a German flag was raised at the coastal settlement of Douala on the Cameroon River. Under instructions from German Chancellor Bismarck, Gustav Nachtigal aboard the gunboat *Moewe* had made a treaty with kings Bell and Akwa. Across the river at Hickory Town, the ruler, Lock Priso, raised no flag and refused to sign a treaty with the Germans. In a few short years Germany annexed the coastal area of Cameroon but extended its influence over a wider and wider area of the interior. Despite initial local resistance, for the next thirty years the coastal settlements and the interior grew into the German colony known as Kamerun.

The arrival of Germany was part of what is called the "scramble for Africa." It began with the French occupying Tunisia in 1881 and the British invasion of Egypt in 1882. Tunisia and Egypt were the two richest territories of the Ottoman Empire. From North Africa it spread to the mouth of the Congo River, where the French and agents of King Leopold of Belgium competed for control of the Congo River Basin. Germany made claims in 1884 to coastal areas of East Africa, South West Africa, Togo, and the Cameroons.[4]

A meeting of fourteen countries took place in Berlin between 15 November 1884 and 25 February 1885. The major participants were France, Germany, Great Britain, and Portugal.[5] The Berlin Conference formalized the claims of European states to territory in Africa.[6] Claims were negotiated between the major powers and territory mapped. At no point did Africans have a part to play in the decision making. The General Act of the conference of 26 February 1885 was a treaty drawn up by representatives of the major European powers and the United States. It became the legal document that regulated the claims of sovereignty over territory along the African coast. According to the General Act whatever country claimed the coast of Cameroon, for example, it would need show that they had power enough to administer and defend the area and that the other signers of the General Act were informed.

Five years later, representatives met again in Brussels and drew up an agreement concerning claims of the interior. By the end of the nineteenth century based on these documents, European states had claimed all of sub-Saharan Africa and divided the continent into fifty irregular territories.[7] During the nineteenth-century the industrial revolution in Europe and America and the need for raw materials found in West Africa was a major reason for the competition. There were other reasons: European powers were richer than they had been, new technology was available, for example, the breech-loading magazine rifle, and there was the self-assurance, a feeling of superiority of Europeans to Africans. In addition there was a growing consciousness of Africa due to regular steamship service, the increased activity of missionary societies, geographical societies, and the expansion of trade.[8]

Searching for the raw materials to feed their growing economies, Britain, France, and Germany established small settlements along the coast of West Africa, where they competed for influence and business with local rulers. Coastal settlements like Douala were often visited by Portuguese, Spanish, and British traders and explorers, but it was Germany that succeeded in making a permanent claim.[9]

The products that first attracted traders to the area were palm oil, palm kernels, ivory, and slaves. With the end of the slave trade, for many years palm products and ivory were the only products of value traded. Ivory was in great demand in Europe. It was used for billiard balls, carvings, piano keys, and trimming for pipes, canes, crutches, and furniture.[10]

But Germany was not among the early commercial interests to set up trading posts on the Cameroon coast in order to exploit local products. British traders were already active among the Duala people. The English government made an agreement in 1842 with two kings in the area of the Wouri River to encourage trade in palm oil and ivory provided they stop trading in slaves. Trade was carried on from "factories," the name given to their trading stations on the beaches, or from hulks of dismantled ships anchored in the river.

Although the Carl Woermann Company of Hamburg traded along the West African coast from 1837, it was not until 1868 that Woermann opened a trading post at Douala on the estuary of the Cameroon River. Adolf Woermann, son of Carl, was to become an important figure in the development of trade on the Cameroon coast. His company cooperated with British traders in doing business with the Duala people.[11]

The Duala, a coastal Cameroon people, had a long history of trading with Europeans, especially with the British. Since the early nineteenth century, British traders had been in the area, and they used hulks moored in the Cameroon River as their stores. To the west, at the foot of Cameroon Mountain, was an English Baptist mission station, Victoria, founded by missionaries who had crossed from the Spanish island of Fernando Po. Victoria was described as a "miniature theocracy."

In order to settle disputes between European and African traders Britain helped to set up a court of equity in Douala. In support of the British presence, a consul was appointed to the Bight of Biafra and Benin. He visited regularly on a gunboat. And so by the 1870s Cameroon was clearly within the sphere of Britain's "informal empire" despite the presence of rival traders. It seemed that Cameroon would easily establish a more permanent relationship with Great Britain. In 1879 some Duala chiefs, realizing the usefulness of British support for their unstable local authority, wrote to Queen Victoria asking for her help in what has been called "strong English": "We wish to have your laws in our towns. . . . Plenty wars here in our country. Plenty murder and plenty idol worshippers." Their petition was rejected by a government not wanting to commit any more financial support to British trading interests. But by the early 1880s, mainly due to fears that France, not Germany, might act ahead of Britain, opinion in London began to turn in favor of a British protectorate over the Cameroons.[12]

In the meantime the Swedish explorers Knutson and Valdau were trekking the area of Mt. Cameroon and at the end of 1883 they discovered wild rubber. A German journalist and explorer, Hugo Zoller, assisted by the Swedes, began making trade agreements with local village heads near Douala and toward the mountain.

It was not until November 1883 that the British cabinet finally agreed to the establishment of a protectorate along the Niger Delta–Cameroons coast. It took six more months to work out the financial and legal problems caused by the decision. And so it was not until May 1884 that E. H. Hewett, the British consul, was instructed to make treaties with the coastal chiefs. By June he was signing agreements with chiefs of the Niger Delta, but when he reached Douala in mid-July he "found to his astonishment that the German flag had been raised there a few days earlier."[13]

Hewett has gone down in history as "Too Late" Hewett, but Rudin did not believe that his treaty would have been accepted by the local chiefs even if he came earlier. Article 6 of the treaty was to deprive the local people of their trade monopolies with the interior. As the British and the Germans tried to get written agreements with the local chiefs, the advantage was with the Germans who were willing to recognize the trading rights of locals. In addition, many treaties were needed because there was no one central authority in Cameroon. Even at Victoria, where the British thought they were well established, they found that the local king of Bimbia had already signed an agreement with the Germans. For the expansion of trade, Bimbia was considered an excellent starting point for an overland route to the interior.[14]

In Europe the initiative to set up a German protectorate in Cameroon had come from a small group of German businessmen. German traders had objected to the French practice of charging heavy duties on non-French goods imported into their colonies. It was seen as a threat to the commercial activities of other Europeans. The British were also criticized. German traders in Douala had many grievances against the British-dominated "court of equity." And so, in July 1883 the Hamburg Chamber of Commerce presented Chancellor Bismarck with a memorandum urging the government to acquire a strip of territory in the Cameroons before it was lost to the British or the French. Bismarck was opposed to colonial expansion, but the merchants had a powerful spokesman in Adolf Woermann, the head of the trading company and a close friend of the chancellor. Moreover, a treaty between Portugal and Great Britain in February 1884 was seen as a threat to German interests. By May, Bismarck accepted some measure of responsibility for German commercial interests in West Africa as a necessity. In July, Commissioner Nachtigal, who had been signing agreements along the Togo coast, arrived in Douala. A few days before his arrival, the local German traders, acting on instructions from Adolf Woermann, concluded a treaty with "the independent Kings and Chiefs of the Country called 'Cameroons.'" Under the treaty the local leaders agreed to surrender "our rights of Sovereignty, the Legislation and Management of our Country" to the German firms under certain conditions. One condition was that when setting up an administration "our country's fashions will be respected."[15]

Shirley Ardener described the annexations. Captain Moore, one of Hewett's naval escorts, was suspicious of German intentions and so went ahead of Hewett, arriving in Douala on 11 July. King Bell was advised to wait for Hewett, but Bell warned that the British must come quickly. As Moore sailed out of the estuary he met Nachtigal and Dr. Buchner on their way to Douala. The Germans thought that the British had signed treaties ahead of them. "While Moore had been talking to King Bell, Woermann, Schmidt, and Schultz were in Bimbia where they were able to obtain signatures to a treaty.... On the same day, Voss and the chief of Dido Town, Douala, signed a treaty on board the hulk *Louise*." King Bell wanted to wait a week as he promised Captain Moore.

On the 12th, Nachtigal sailed upriver in his warship, the *Moewe*. It was bigger than the British gunboats, and its presence alarmed the local chiefs. They called a meeting and drew up a statement that they gave to the Germans. "The Duala terms confirm the contention that these chiefs, inexperienced in international politics though they may have been, certainly did not hand their territory away in the thoughtless greedy ways" some later commentators implied.

The treaty was finally signed between King Bell and King Akwa and a number of their Duala subordinates on the one hand, and four German traders: Schmidt, Voss, Woermann, and Busch on the other. Ceremonies were held on Monday, 14 July 1884, at Bell, Akwa, and Dido Towns. Voss, the senior German citizen on the river, handed the treaties over to Nachtigal, "accompanied by pipes, drums and volleys and the hoisting of the German flag."

When Hewett arrived three days later on the H.M.S. *Flirt* he found six English trading agents of Bristol trading companies living in hulks. They came aboard and informed Hewett what had happened. English traders and missionaries had been taken by surprise, thinking that the land was under British protection.[16]

Nachtigal raised the German flag over a trading station on 14 July 1884 and installed his assistant, Dr. Buchner, on 19 July as temporary imperial representative. He then sailed on 20 July and claimed five other trading posts for Germany along the Cameroons coast.[17] Nachtigal was to die at sea. He was buried on 20 April 1885 in Cape Palmas, Liberia.

German colonialism in Africa differed from that of Britain and France in important ways. Germany lacked a historical model for the administration of overseas territories, and so its parliament, the Reichstag, became more active in colonial affairs. Chancellor Bismarck expected the traders who asked for a protectorate to pay for the cost of administration, but they were not willing to do so. Events soon forced Berlin to become more involved. The only representative of Germany in the first months after annexation was Dr. Buchner, who lived in a room he rented from the Woermann Company.[18] Buchner "found himself in immediate conflict with British merchants and missionaries, most of whom refused to accept German rule,"[19] and with many of the local people.

As Germany worked to consolidate its authority, a Polish officer in the Russian army, Stefan Rogozinski, who had come to West Africa with a scientific expedition, was encouraged by British traders to begin making treaties on their behalf with village heads around Mt. Cameroon. Then at Hickory Town, one of the Duala leaders, Lock Priso, led a violent demonstration against German authority. Buchner called in German warships under Admiral Knorr to put down the uprising with gunfire and a detachment of marines. One result was the destruction of the Baptist mission. Buchner was replaced by Admiral Knoor, who began issuing decrees that firmly established German authority and closed the Court of Equity.

The rebellion of Lock Priso, and Admiral Knorr's recommendations, forced Bismarck to ask the Reichstag in 1885 for money to set up a government in Cameroon, now called Kamerun. It was a humiliation for Bismarck because he had convinced the Reichstag to approve a protectorate by claiming it was necessary to safeguard German interests from their British and French rivals. Also it was understood that the main administrative costs would be paid for by the trading firms. The firm with the largest interest in Kamerun was Woermann of Hamburg.[20] In addition, Bismarck had to take action because Nachtigal had died and Buchner had returned to Germany due to illness.

Bismarck was angry with Britain over the uprising at Hickory Town. The news of Rogozinski, joined with England's demand for compensation and other disturbing reports, caused one German political leader to warn of "a grave danger of war over their differences."[21]

The British Foreign Office protested that it only wanted friendly relations with Germany. Therefore by February 1885, the British government adopted a less aggressive attitude than it had in December. Buchan, the agent of an English firm in the Cameroons, who had been appointed vice-council, was shipped home, and a number of small claims based on temporary treaties of Rogozinski and others were dropped. The British government asked its merchants to cease stirring up the local people against the Germans and rather to encourage them to accept the new government. By the end of 1885 some cooperation had been restored between British and German traders. The last obstacle to complete German control of the Cameroons was eliminated in 1887 when the English Baptist Missionary Society sold its holdings at Victoria to the Basel Mission. Basel missionaries were German speaking.[22]

Governors of Kamerun

From the annexation until World War I the story of German's Kamerun colony can be followed through the efforts of successive governors, commercial interests, and missionaries.

On 3 July 1885, Julius von Soden became Kamerun's first governor. He remained in office until 1891. By the end of 1886 the Germans had reached agreements with the British and the French over the colony's boundaries. In return for concessions elsewhere on the Nigerian coast the British abandoned Victoria and their claims to Mt. Cameroon, and agreed to a frontier going northeastward from the Cross River to the Benue. The Campo River was the boundary between Kamerun and French Gabon. In 1893 an agreement with Britain extended the western border from the Benue River to Lake Chad.[23]

While von Soden was governor, Germany consolidated its hold on the coastal region, and commercial companies began to expand their trading contacts with the interior. A number of explorers reached markets controlled up to that time by local traders from Douala. To reach what is now the North West Region of Cameroon the German explorer Eugen Zintgraff had worked out a plan to set up a line of stations from the coast to the "high plateau" beyond the escarpment that divides the forest from the grassfields. The Germans were attracted by some of the principle trading commodities and the potential manpower of the area and wanted to by-pass local traders. The aim was direct trade to German companies at the coast and away from rival trade routes to the Benue and Calabar. But despite the eagerness of traders to expand into the interior, Germany was reluctant to take on new responsibilities when there was little money available.

The slopes of Mt. Cameroon were explored and German authority established over the Bakweri people. The German flag was raised at Buea. Buea later became the capital of the Kamerun under Governor von Puttkamer. The governor established the Botanical Gardens at Victoria, where experiments in agriculture could be carried out. Plantations were begun on the slopes of Mt. Cameroon. By 1913 the plantations owned about 100,000 hectares in the Victoria area.

Under von Soden's successor, Eugen von Zimmerer, the first determined attempts were made to open the interior to trade and administration. Also under his tenure the most serious scandal in Kamerun history took place. While Zimmerer was away in Germany, his chancellor, von Kleist, mistreated soldiers whom the explorer Gravenreuth had rescued in Dahomey. Von Kleist's cruelty and immorality led to an uprising among the soldiers. In 1894 he was tried and convicted of misconduct by a special disciplinary court in Potsdam.[24]

Zimmerer was succeeded in 1895 by Jesko von Puttkamer, who was governor until 1907. He is considered "the real architect of German hegemony." When he took over the office the total budget of the Kamerun colony was only 600,000 marks. Its only armed force, the *Polizeitruppe*, most of whom were ex-slaves purchased from the independent king of Dahomey, had been weakened by their mutiny under von Kleist. German authority was almost nonexistent in the interior. But by 1907, the colonial budget had risen to six million marks, of which half came from imperial grants. By 1914 the police force, *Polizeitruppe*, had about 1,200 police and 30 white officers. The *Schutztruppe* had 1,550 men under 185 white officers.[25] German authority had been established by a large number of small military expeditions into almost every district. Von Puttkamer believed that consolidation and conquest had to take place before the colony could be economically exploited in the interests of Germany. He established concession companies with a monopoly over the rubber, ivory, and other wild produce of two vast areas, one in the south and the other in the northwest. Neither proved as profitable as was hoped. More significant for the future was the development of large plantations of cocoa, rubber, palm oil, and bananas on the fertile volcanic soil of Mt. Cameroon. Von Puttkamer's plantation policy was an economic success. In 1898 he was instrumental in starting a private trading company, Gesellschaft Sud-Kamerun, to exploit the forests of the southeast. A German monopoly was established in rubber and ivory. The activity of French, Belgian, and Dutch traders was stopped. In 1899 another company, the Gesellschaft Nordwest-Kamerun, was set up to exploit Bamun and Bamileke. The colony's exports, which never exceeded five million marks in value during the 1890s, grew to fifteen million marks by 1907.

It was von Puttkamer who moved the civil and military administration of Kamerun to Buea and Soppo respectively.[26] Puttkamer arrived in Douala from German Togoland, where he had been commissioner, on 11 December 1894. He was not yet forty years of age. At that time German government officers were stationed in both Douala and in Victoria, locations that required crossing of the creeks between both places. The climate was not good in either location, and many officers fell ill, especially with malaria.

In 1894, after two weeks of military action, the Buea area was "pacified." Then plans went forward to move the headquarters to Buea and Soppo. The chief reason for the move to Buea was the health of his European staff. He was sure that Buea, high up as it is, would be a much more favourable climate, despite the heavy rain it experienced each year. The workers who helped build the governor's house, the *Schloss*, were from Togoland. Construction of the residency was finished on the 1 June 1902.

Economic development accelerated under Governor von Puttkamer. However, his attitude toward the local population was harsh. He was in favor of corporal punishment, was unwilling to improve the working conditions of plantation laborers, and approved of keeping local girls as what was termed "semi-concubines." Under his administration, exploitation of the economy came first.

In 1906 the Akwa chiefs in Douala sent a long list of complaints about the governor to the Reichstag. Von Puttkamer was recalled, convicted, and dismissed in 1907. The behavior of von Kleist, Puttkamer, the explorer Dominik, and Judge Wehlan, who was convicted of cruelty toward people of Douala, were but "a few of the many cases of bad administration" that went before the Reichstag between 1901 and 1907.

From the beginning of Germany's ventures in colonialism there was vigorous criticism in the Reichstag, particularly from the Social Democrats and the Catholic Centrists. Since every budget for the colonies had to be submitted to the Reichstag, anti-imperialists had an opportunity to express their opinion. Some criticized the government on principle, accusing it of producing nothing but "murder, robbery, syphilis and the curse of liquor."[27] But other Social Democrats supported their criticism with information supplied by missionaries and traders working in Kamerun. According to Rudin, Germany had an undeserved reputation for poor colonial administration. Less well known was the effort to improve administration from 1907 to the beginning of World War I.

The reported abuses in Kamerun angered many in Germany and led to protests by the general public and by anticolonial groups in the Reichstag over the administration of Kamerun and the mistreatment of local people. Since 1890 there had been a section of the Foreign Office—*Kolonialabteilung*—to administer the colonies. Germany's colonies were an important issue in the election of 1906. This was a victory for the supporters of a German colonial empire and led to the creation in 1907 of a permanent Colonial Office—*Kolonialamt*. A man with "liberal and humane views on the treatment of natives," Bernhard Dernburg, was chosen to head the office. He and his successors "took an intelligent, often enlightened view of colonial administration. The excesses of the pre-1906 era were largely eliminated, and a series of able administrators were appointed to fill key colonial posts."[28]

A serious problem in Kamerun was the constant demand for labor not only for the plantations but also as porters, or carriers, between the coast and the interior. Almost 100,000 men were needed constantly to supply a labor force for traders, planters, and administrators. Almost 80,000 of them were carriers. In addition to very harsh working conditions, recruiting practices were often oppressive and the death rate very high. The expropriation of land and the death rate for grassfields' laborers on plantations and as carriers were among the "most serious problems of the entire German colonial empire."[29]

After the dismissal of von Puttkamer in 1907,[30] Dr. Theodore Seitz was appointed governor. Unlike his predecessor, he is known for his "vigorous protection of native rights." In this he was supported by the colonial minister, Bernhard Dernburg.Governor Seitz was in office until 1910. He was determined to remedy the mistakes of the previous administration especially when it concerned native welfare. He encouraged local representation on local councils, restricted the sale of alcohol, addressed the control of certain kinds of domestic slavery, tried to eliminate forced labor, flogging, and other abuses on the plantations, and was sympathetic to complaints about the misuse of the head tax system.

It was while he was in office that Germany and France negotiated the handing over to Kamerun of a large territory. As a result of the Agadir crisis in Morocco, France agreed to give part of the French Congo to Kamerun in return for recognition by Germany of French claims in Morocco. Germany surrendered her claims in Morocco and, as compensation, according to the Anglo-French Convention of 4 November 1911, received 107,000 sq. miles of French Congo. The area became known as Neu-Kamerun and allegedly had a population of one million. Germany also gave up some territory between the Longone and Shari Rivers. The transfer gave Kamerun an outlet to the Congo River and virtually doubled the size of the protectorate.[31]

Dr. Otto Gleim followed Seitz. He was governor until 1912 when he was replaced by Karl Ebermaier, who was governor until the occupation by Britain, France, and Belgium in 1916 during World War I.

King Rudolf Manga Bell of the Duala

Both Gleim and Ebermaier faced increasing resistance to their authority by the Duala people. The Duala trade monopoly as middlemen for the interior had been largely replaced by European traders. One source of income for the Duala became the sale of land that Europeans wanted to buy for later speculation. Serious resistance began with the government's attempt to remove Duala people to outside of the city and appropriate some of their land. The government's motive was alleged to be the improvement of sanitary conditions and to control land speculation by some of the local people. Among the complaints, one concerned the sale of 722 acres along the river. The Duala argued that according to the terms of the 1884 treaty the land was not to be taken from them. Despite their protests and that of their King, Manga Bell, the support of some missionaries and traders, and with the sympathy of Governor Gleim, their protests to the Reichstag failed. The "natives" began to be removed from the land in 1912. On 20 February 1913, King Manga Bell submitted a formal protest and hired a German lawyer to represent the Duala people in Berlin. The Colonial Office refused to change its decision and defended its policy to critics in the Reichstag. Manga Bell then sent a letter to other Cameroon chiefs looking for support. He was later accused of treason by the German administration at the start of World

Proposed flags for Kamerum. Wiki Commons.

The Imperial German Colony of Kamerun

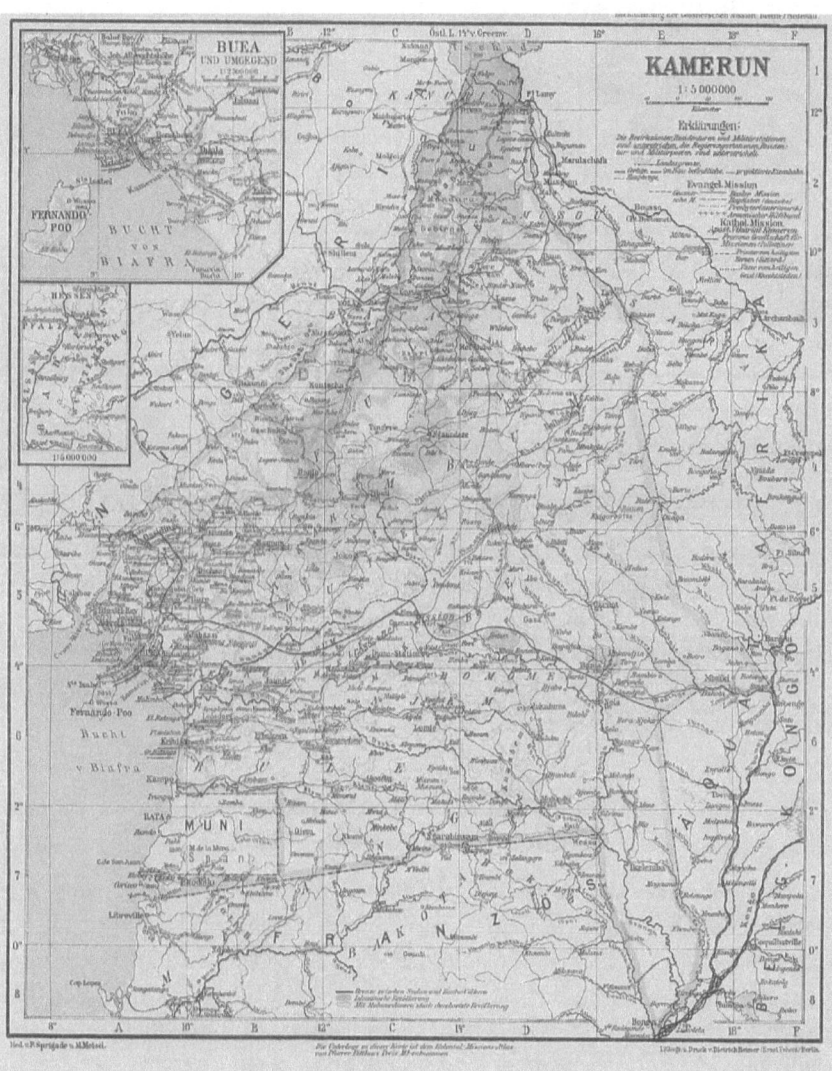

Map of Kamerun 1914. By Paul Sprigade / Max Moisel, Staatsbibliothek zu Berlin–Preußischer Kulturbesitz. Moisel was a pioneer mapmaker in Kamerun. Wikimedia.

Rudolph Manga Bell
in Germany, 1902.
Service Protestant de Mission-Défap.

War I. During his trial he admitted that he sought the help of other countries in the controversy. He looked for any means to help his people to keep their land. This letter was used as evidence against him. He was tried and executed for treason.[32]

In the years immediately before World War I, Germany increased investment in the development of Kamerun. Between 1908 and 1914 Berlin gave the colony 20 million marks in grants and 50 million marks in loans. At the same time Kamerun continued to be explored in a search for natural resources, largely financed by the economic committee of the *Kolonialgesellschaft*.

Important to the story of the Kamerun colony and the future of the people of Cameroon was the presence of Christian missionaries.

Christian Missions and Missionaries, Catholic and Protestant, to 1914

Many times, years ago, in the North West Region of Cameroon, elders told stories about the coming of Christianity to their tribal area. They always spoke of the arrival of a trader or of a countryman who had worked at the coast, or someone who had been employed by the Germans, often ending up on Fernando Po during World War I. It was often a story of individual conversion, someone touched by the story of Jesus for the first time in what often was a cruel environment: A small boy listening outside a hut to singing and Gospel stories or a young man hearing about Jesus at a time his village was being tortured by deadly accusations of witchcraft. The message they heard was usually brought to the coast by a Christian missionary who belonged to a Catholic or Protestant group that sent people to evangelize the people of West Africa.

When Kamerun was claimed for Kaiser Wilhelm I on 14 July 1884, the government showed a "reasonable impartiality" toward the work of Christian missions.³³ In the Reichstag Protestant Christians were in the majority, but Roman Catholics also had influence. The *General Act of Berlin*, of 26 February 1885, promised protection of an individual's freedom of conscience and free and public worship. On 2 July 1890 the *General Act* and declaration of Brussels repeated the promise "to protect, without distinction of creed," the existing missions and those about to be established. On 10 September 1900, a German colonial regulation assured missionary freedom in Kamerun. Missions representing religious societies were not to be "legally hindered or restricted." However, it can be argued that the German government's "consuming interest" in protecting commercial firms did affect the government's attitude toward certain missionary activity. This meant that any missionary challenge, for example, to the abuse of Africans by traders, was difficult to pursue.³⁴

Before World War I Germany and France also signed an agreement that guaranteed the freedom of missionaries in all of their territories.

The Baptist Missionary Society

From Fernando Po to the Cameroon Mainland

Baptist missionaries were the first Western Christian missionaries to establish a permanent station in Cameroon. But before arriving on the mainland of Africa they first went to Fernando Po, the island of this story.

The history of the Baptist mission to West Africa and Cameroon can be traced back to midnight, 1 August 1838. On that date slavery was ended in the British Empire and nearly 800,000 black men, women, and children throughout the British Empire officially became free.³⁵ Adam Hochschild in his book *Bury the Chains* describes a church thanksgiving service in Jamaica the night of 31 July.

> Its walls were hung with branches, flowers, and portraits of Clarkson and Wilberforce. In a coffin inscribed "Colonial Slavery, died 31 July 1838, aged 276 years," church members placed an iron punishment collar, a whip and chains. As midnight neared the congregation sang. . . . "The hour is at hand," William Knibb called from the pulpit . . . at midnight the monster is dead. . . ." An open grave lay waiting in the yard of the church school. Still singing, the parishioners lowered the coffin into it. At the graveside they planted a coconut tree, as a "tree of liberty"—a symbol from the American and French revolutions and now adopted by former slaves.³⁶

In the British West Indies, a "wave of fervor" swept over the island of Jamaica. Freed slaves and Baptist missionaries, of the London-based Baptist Missionary Society (BMS), proposed to return to Africa with the gospel and establish a mission in West Africa. The BMS had been founded in England in 1792, and its first missionaries, William Carey and John Thomas, were sent to Bengal, India, the following year. Later missionaries were sent to Jamaica. On the Jamaican mission William Knibb, a BMS missionary and two Jamaicans, Henry Beekford and Edward Barratt, traveled to London to attend a meeting of the BMS on 22 May 1840. At the meeting they made an appeal to open a new mission in West Africa. Knibb was a strong supporter of West Indian colonization of Africa.

The BMS decided to sponsor a journey of two missionaries to Africa to explore the possibility of opening a mission on the Niger River Delta. John Clarke, a BMS missionary in Jamaica since 1829, and George K. Prince, a medical doctor and former slave owner, sailed for West Africa in 1840.

On 1 January 1841 they arrived by trading ship at Clarence on the island of Fernando Po. Clarence was later named Santa Isabel by Spain, and today is called Malabo. Their plan was to join the Delta expedition when it stopped briefly at the island on its way to the Niger River. The expedition never arrived. On Fernando Po, the natives of the island, the Bubi people, who lived in the interior, had little interest in the mission, but at the coast they were well received. There they were welcomed by the commander of the British naval squadron station at Clarence along with freed slaves and African migrants. Clarke and Prince wrote to London recommending that the first mission be opened on Fernando Po and not on the Niger.[37]

The Home Board in London decided to send Thomas Sturgeon and his wife to join them at Clarence. When Sturgeon arrived from England in September 1843 Clarke and Prince returned home to their families and began to recruit volunteers in England and Jamaica. Among the new missionary volunteers were Joseph Merrick, Alexander McCloud Fuller, and his son, Joseph Jackson Fuller. The mission to Fernando Po was to work among Africans who had been freed from slave ships by British gunboats and settled on the island along with other liberated slaves and "colored gentlemen" from Sierra Leone.

When Prince and his wife returned with Merrick, his wife, Elizabeth Knowles Merrick, and Alexander Fuller, Prince and Sturgeon sailed to the Niger in July. There they discovered that Presbyterian missionaries from Scotland were already preparing to begin a mission.

The following year, in February 1844, Clarke arrived with his wife, Margaret, and several others from Britain, including Alfred Saker and Helen Jessup Saker. Thirty-seven Jamaican settlers came along with them. By March 1844 the Baptist congregation at Clarence had 44 members, 190 "inquirers," and 300 "Sabbath scholars" in nine classes.

The Jamaicans settled among the African residents. They were not happy because they did not consider themselves usefully employed. They saw themselves as classroom school teachers but were only considered as educators in a broader sense, and not in the schools, where management was kept in the hands of the Europeans.[38]

On Christmas 1845 the Spanish consul-general arrived. Representing Catholic Spain, he had instructions to send the Baptist missionaries away if they would not stop preaching. He gave them one year to prepare to leave the island. Some missionaries had already made a decision to leave. By 1847 many on the Fernando Po mission decided to return to Jamaica. Included in the group was John Clarke. Clarke spent the rest of his life as a missionary in Jamaica.

Despite their disappointments and the consul-general's order, one missionary and two teachers were allowed to remain at Clarence. They carried on until September 1856 when a Spanish bishop and several priests landed. Two years later, on 22 May 1858, Don Carlos Chacon, the governor-general, arrived in Clarence. He came with six Jesuit priests. The Roman Catholic religion was proclaimed to be the only religion tolerated on Fernando Po. On 27 May, the Baptist congregation met for the last time for public worship. After that they could only meet privately and in small groups.[39] The disappointment of Fernando Po was to become a blessing for the Africans of the Cameroon coast. The BMS began to negotiate the sale of the Clarence mission with the intention of moving to the Cameroons, where they had established mission stations.

Paul Dekar points to other reasons for the failure of the Fernando Po mission. Rather than having been expelled from the island by Catholic Spain, more accurately their work was "severely circumscribed." It is true that in February 1843, when Spain returned to the island and the British abandoned Clarence, Spanish authorities made it clear that Roman Catholicism was to be the official religion of Fernando Po.[40] The late Professor Martin Lynn, in an article about the "Creoles" of Fernando Po, describes serious problems that arose for the BMS.[41] Many had volunteered for the Clarence mission without realizing how difficult life was going to be in such an unhealthy climate. There were also the racial attitudes of the time. This led to discontent among the Jamaicans when they were treated differently than the Europeans. And finally it was the failure to realize the original plan to penetrate the interior of West Africa along the Niger River.

Ibrahim Sundiata adds that the poor climate was certainly a reason and another was connected with "racial attitudes" of the time. The settlers found that the African children were a bad influence on their own and asked to send their children home. Some who could afford it sent them to school in Sierra Leone. In 1846 the Jamaican leaders also asked to leave.

There were also serious disputes over property rights of the mission. Complaints were made about the mission through the counsel, Nicholls, to the Spanish ambassador in London. This was one of the reasons that led to an expedition from Spain in 1845 and the declaration about the Roman Catholic religion.

The departure of the Baptists did not mean that there were to be no Protestant missionaries on Fernando Po. The Baptists were followed by a mission of the Primitive Methodists. A Primitive Methodist mission group sailed for Africa in 1870 and settled on Fernando Po, where they worked under terms imposed by the Spanish government.[42]

To the Cameroon Mainland

From Santa Isabel on Fernando Po to the Cameroon coast at the village of Batoke it is 27.49 miles by sea. Douala is 58.22 nautical miles away. On a clear day the Cameroon coast and Mt. Cameroon are visible from Fernando Po.

While the Baptists worked on Fernando Po they also took an interest in the coast of Cameroon. Already in 1841 Clarke and Prince had crossed the sea and visited Duala chiefs along the Wouri River Estuary and King William of Bimbia. And then on 10 April 1844 Joseph Merrick sailed from Clarence to visit King William's Town, near the present town of Limbe. Merrick was a Jamaican of mixed African and European ancestry who had arrived on Fernando Po in 1843.[43] The Bimbia people—also called Isubu or Isurwa—were a small coastal group who spoke a language similar to Bakweri, another local language. The Bimbia were different from other groups because of their trading and contact with foreign ships. The leader was King William, called "Bile" by the local people. The missionaries were exploring the area. For example, on 23 April 1844 Merrick left Bimbia and reached Buea on the slopes of Mt. Cameroon.

By 1845 mission stations were opened among the Isubu of Bimbia and two other groups at Aqua Town and Bell Town on the Wouri River. Joseph Merrick is recognized as the pioneer in Cameroon. He formed churches and schools and learned Duala and Isubu. Alexander Fuller, a former slave, joined Merrick and settled near the village of Bimbia, where they started a mission with a school. It was the first mission station and school in what later became the British Cameroons.[44] Merrick died in 1849 on his way to Jamaica. What was later accomplished by Alfred Saker and other Baptist missionaries in Cameroon was built on foundations laid by Joseph Merrick.[45]

Other Baptists, including Alfred Saker and his family and Sierra Leonean Thomas Horton Johnson, had crossed from Fernando Po and settled in Douala on 19 June 1847.

Joseph Jackson Fuller

Pioneer Alexander Fuller died in April 1847. His place was taken by his son, Joseph Jackson Fuller. The young Fuller was born on 29 June 1825 in Spanish Town, Jamaica. He and his parents were both slaves of a Jewish family. They were set free by emancipation in 1838. Joseph had already been freed when he was eight years of age under the "apprenticeship act." The Baptist mission offered his mother reduced school fees for him and his brother Samuel. Paul Dekar

Joseph Jackson Fuller.
With permission of the
Baptist Missionary Society.

writes that much of the credit for securing a mission in Cameroon belongs to Fuller. According to Ardener, the agreement with King William to purchase a site at Bimbia was due to the "remarkable Fuller."[46] First he had a print shop and bindery at Bimbia, and later, on the death of Merrick, he moved to Douala. He remained in Cameroon until 1888 when he retired to England where he died in 1908 at Stoke Newington and is buried at the Abney Park Cemetery.

The story of Joseph Jackson Fuller illustrates the hardships the missionaries faced and the courageous dedication of some. He arrived with his father on Fernando Po in 1844. Joseph married Elizabeth Johnson of Sierra Leone, a schoolteacher on Fernando Po, on 15 June 1847. In a family record it remembers a daughter, Mary, who was born in March 1848 and died seven days later. A son, Alexander Merrick Fuller, was born at Bimbia on 26 June 1849. Another son, Samuel, was born 20 December 1852 and died in 1857. A daughter, Margaret, born 11 March 1858, died in June 1859. Fuller then writes that "My dear wife Elizabeth died at Bimbia at the Mission House, 18 February 1859." He married again on 1 January 1861 to Charlotte Diboll. She was a Norfolk-born daughter of one of the white missionaries, Joseph Diboll. Fuller worked for thirty years in Cameroon. When he retired to England, first at Barnes and later at Stoke Newington, he was known as an exceptional orator and spoke before large audiences on Baptist and missionary topics, "pleading the cause of his African brother," according to fellow missionary Thomas Lewis.

African converts were among the first Christians. One of them was Thomas Horton Johnson, the first person baptized by Alfred Saker. Johnson in turn baptized the first Duala Christian, Bekina Bile.

Despite the pioneering work of Fuller and others, Alfred Saker was the "key figure" in the Cameroon mission.[47] He was born in Kent, the son of a millwright and engineer. He left school at the age of ten to help support his family

Alfred Saker.
Wiki Commons.

and learned his father's trade yet continued to educate himself by his reading. Convinced he was called to the missions he volunteered to serve overseas. For thirty-two years, from 1844 to 1876, he worked first on Fernando Po and then in Douala and Victoria in Cameroon. Finally he returned to Britain where he died on 13 March 1880. In his last public speech to delegates of the Home Churches in Glasgow he said: "If the African is our brother, should we not give him some of our bread and a draught of our water? Oh that I had another life to go out there."

Saker's first task was to transfer the Baptist community from Fernando Po to the mainland. He had purchased a strip of land along the coast at Ambas Bay from King William of Bimbia. It was reported to be 10 miles long and 5 miles wide. The strip included the present town of Limbe. Saker wrote on 27 September 1858 that "we took possession of the bay and its wilderness." Much of the credit for obtaining King William's agreement to the purchase of land, and apparently, even for suggesting the particular site should go to the remarkable Joseph Jackson Fuller. For it was Fuller who had been living most consistently at the mission station at Bimbia on and off since Merrick's day.[48] A British ship was to help evacuate 100 to 150 persons, of which two-thirds were women and children, to Victoria. The majority of the Creoles of the BMS stayed behind on Fernando Po.[49]

The new Baptist station of Victoria was to be self-governing. Saker's aim was to create "a centre of civilization, freedom, and light ... a religious, enlightened community." The first settlers had arrived from Fernando Po on 9 June 1858. After 1860 the Baptist community expanded to include places like Bonjongo, Mapanya, and Bakundu. The stations at Bimbia, Bethel, and Victoria centered about a chapel, a residence, and a school. This became a pattern for other mission stations and missionary groups. The Baptist mission aimed at learning local languages, translating Sacred Scripture, and teaching in the vernacular. It was important for these Protestant missionaries to have a literate population that could study Sacred Scripture for themselves.[50]

The Spanish government agreed to pay 1,500 pounds compensation to the Baptist Missionary Society for the losses they had on leaving Fernando Po. Meanwhile the British government continued to maintain a presence on the island. Because the people of Clarence lived off shipping in the harbor they did not transfer to the mainland and Amboises Bay. It was expected that the British would move there. The slopes of Mt. Cameroon had been explored and a place found for a sanatorium for the crews of the British squadron and even a possible coaling station in the bay. Those prospects encouraged the missionaries to purchase land and lay out a township. A report of the annual meeting of the Baptist Missionary Society in 1862 concluded that if the British government followed through with its plans the Baptists of Clarence would also settle on the mainland. There they "will then enjoy that freedom to worship God which the Spanish authorities continue to deny them."[51]

Alfred Saker's life was complicated by controversy. Thomas Horton and sixteen others complained to the BMS about his harsh treatment of others. Later Alexander Innes, a Scot recruit from Liverpool, also complained about Saker. The BMS suggested to Saker that he "modify his treatment" of the local people. It was Innes who made a case that Saker's secular activities undermined the mission mandate of the BMS, a mandate that emphasized preaching, teaching, and translating.

Saker's approach was also challenged by other missionaries as "too secular and technical and not sufficiently spiritual." It was a criticism that threatened the mission's social and educational work by "those who felt these efforts should be secondary to the goal of evangelism."[52] Despite his shortcomings Saker was the architect of a model Christian village at Victoria. He was also its governor. Missionaries George Grenfeld and Thomas Lewis helped to carry Saker's vision of the mission to the interior, not through native evangelists but rather by missionaries.

One of Saker's achievements was to complete in 1872 a translation of the Old and New Testaments into Duala. Saker's unusual combination of single-mindedness, practical abilities, and courage has earned him a place in posterity and the story of the Christian mission.[53] David Livingston wrote that Saker's pioneering efforts in Cameroon "were the most remarkable on the African coast."[54]

The growing shortage of Baptists missionaries did not retard the growth of a local church but rather encouraged the development of an independent Baptist congregation with its own church and schools and its own leadership. By 1879 there were two churches and three chapels but with less than 140 full members at Bethel and its outstations, and 42 members at Victoria. By 1880 they were very much on their own.[55] The days of the pioneering Baptist missionaries were to be cut short.

The final blow to the Baptist mission came in 1884, when Germany annexed Cameroons. The mission at Victoria remained an independent colony until 1886. It was officially transferred from England to Germany in January 1887. The missionaries who remained saw that it was not possible for them to continue surrounded by Germans. Finally, the English Baptists withdrew to reinforce their work in Congo. Between 1842 and 1886 the Baptists had sent twenty-one British and Jamaican couples and nine single missionaries to the missions of Fernando Po and Cameroon. Many were buried in Cameroon.

When Germany annexed Cameroon and Britain abandoned her claims, the BMS concerns "shifted from maintaining a native ministry to recovering the investment in Cameroon." The Baptist Missionary Society had already turned to a new area on the Congo River. The London headquarters of the BMS decided to leave Cameroon because it was unprepared to work in a situation where religious liberty was not guaranteed. London was also unwilling to champion a self-governing Baptist church. Unfortunately the BMS did not adequately credit the efforts of Jamaican missionaries to undertake a mission of evangelization on their own.[56] Finally the German government decided that Baptist property in Cameroon should be taken over by a German-speaking Protestant missionary society.

German Missionaries: The Basel Mission

In October 1885 representatives of the various German Evangelical Missions met in Bremen to discuss their missionary work in the new German colonies. They were aware that the English Baptists were prepared to hand over their mission in the Kamerun to a German Protestant mission society. And so it was suggested that the Basel Mission step in. The Home Board of the Basel Mission was not very interested. They already had missionaries in Ghana, where some were soon to die. There were also other areas of the world in need of their help. But they were still sympathetic to the situation of the English Baptists and so agreed to send a delegation to see the place for themselves. Missionaries Rittmann and Bohner from Ghana were sent along with Rev. Binetsch from the North German Missionary Society. They arrived in Douala on 11 January 1886. In Douala they spent eight days with Rev. Thomas Lewis of the Baptist mission. After a visit to Victoria they left Cameroon for Europe at the end of January. In Europe they gave a positive report to the Home Board, which decided that the Basel Mission should replace the English Baptists. In a letter from the German Foreign Office dated 12 June 1886 the Basel Mission was given permission to begin their work.[57]

The Basel Mission Society—*Evangelische Missionsgesellschaft Basel*—was founded in the Swiss city of Basel in 1815. It was international and interdenominational, with its patrons drawn from Pietistic circles of Switzerland and southern Germany.[58]

Pietism was originally a German religious movement of the seventeenth and eighteenth centuries that emphasized heartfelt religious devotion, ethical purity, charitable activity, and pastoral theology rather than sacramental or dogmatic precision. The term now refers to all religious expressions that emphasize inward devotion and moral purity.[59] It was an effort to reform Protestantism. Some have seen it as "a source of powerful renewal in the church. It can point to the need of scripture for the Christian life, encourage the lay participation in ministry, stimulate a concern for missions, advance religious freedom and cooperation among believers, and urge individuals to seek a close relationship with God."[60]

All the Basel Missionaries in Kamerun (about 1892–94).
© Basel Missionary Society.
Standing (from left to right): Friedrich Autenrieth, Karl Friedrich Stolz, Jakob Keller, Jakob Klöti, Otto Schkölziger, Karl Wittwer, Konrad Walter. Sitting (from left to right): Luise Christine Schmid-Gebhardt, Wilhelm Gottlieb Schmid, Walburga Walker-Schmid, Gottlob Walker, Lydia Hanna Bizer-Josenhans, Johann Georg Bizer.

The founding of the Basel Mission was part of a trend in Europe toward the formation of mission societies among Protestants and the sending of missionaries to foreign lands. In the first half of the nineteenth century they extended their work to Africa in an effort "to rectify the harm done by centuries of slave trading." The early recruits were of modest backgrounds from rural areas or small towns in Switzerland and southwestern Germany.[61]

Negotiations began between the Basel Mission and the English Baptists over the sale of mission property in Kamerun. With the help of a private German citizen who gave 1,000 pounds and the intervention of the German government, the Basel Mission compensated the Baptists with 3,000 pounds for their land and buildings.

On 23 December 1886 the first Basel Mission missionaries arrived in Douala. They were Rev. Gottlieb Munz and his wife, Rev. Christian Dilger, Rev. Johannes Bizer, and Rev. Freierich Becher. Munz had worked in Ghana and was named superior. At Douala they were welcomed by the Rev. Joseph

Jackson Fuller, his wife, and the congregation. Four days later, Becher died of malaria. The Basel missionaries took over ten congregations, including the main missions at Victoria and Bethel. The Victoria mission was led by Rev. Wilson and the Bethel mission by Rev. Dibundu.

Two issues troubled the local Baptist congregations. One was about the language to be used in their schools and churches after the German annexation. The other was the question of infant baptism, which at first did not appear to be a problem. The Baptists did not baptize infants, nor did they baptize by pouring water on the head but only by immersion. Despite their differences Rev. Dibundu asked the missionaries to baptize his recently born twins, a gesture that helped the Basel Mission to gain a foothold in the Kamerun.

When the first Basel missionaries arrived in Kamerun, they found that the Baptists had 203 registered church members in all their congregations and 368 schoolchildren. But the 1887 census showed a drop in membership to 172 and of schoolchildren to 238.

At first the relationship between the missionaries and the local Baptists was good. But before one year passed trouble arose at Bethel Mission. Led by a church elder named Collins, and accustomed to their independence since the departure of Saker, they demanded separation from the Basel Mission. The Bethel congregation left the Basel Mission on 15 March 1888. The Basel Mission paid the local Baptists for the church but allowed them to stay until they built a new one.

Soon there were problems at Victoria, especially over the use of the Duala language, which the Basel Mission had adopted following the translation by Saker of the Bible into Duala. On 11 June 1889 the Victoria Baptists wrote a letter to the missionaries that they did not agree that anything be taken out of the hands of Mr. Wilson "by whom the church will be conducted and continued exactly according to the laws and the mood of the Baptist Mission, from which the church will not move one inch."[62] The church at Victoria belonged to the Baptists, and so the Basel Mission had to build a new one. At first the Baptists carried on with their churches and school without outside help.

The missionaries continued to care for the outstations they inherited. On 5 August 1888 at the dedication of a small church at Tokoto village, the first congregation was established according "to the order of the Basel Mission." It was led by the catechist Johannes Deibol, who was later ordained.

Over the years, as the Basel Mission expanded, missionaries often stood against the Kamerun government in defense of Africans on issues of land rights, forced labor on plantations, the tax system, and the sale of alcohol. At the same time, in 1898 the mission began to engage in trading in order to support their religious works. This made them competitors with commercial firms, which in turn led to intervention by the government against their commercial activity.

At the beginning of World War I in 1914, the Basel Mission in Kamerun had 129 missionaries, more than 300 catechists and teachers, 16 mission stations with 388 outstations and 1,500 "communicants and parishioners."[63]

The German Baptist Missionary Society

The local Baptist churches soon found they needed outside help since they were no longer connected to the English BMS and wanted independence from the Basel Mission. In 1889, at a Baptist church in Berlin, a young Cameroonian student, Alfred Bell, son of King Bell of Douala, appealed for help for the churches at Douala and Victoria that had separated from the Basel Mission. Pastor Eduard Scheve formed a mission committee for Kamerun with the Baptist Union in 1890. With the help of a sister Baptist church in the United States, August Steffens and his wife, Anne, were appointed to Kamerun. Tragically, after only eighteen months, Steffens died of black water fever. His wife continued her work in the schools. In 1891 this German group also tried to "supervise" the independent Baptists at Victoria and failed, as had the Basel missionaries before them.

The German Baptists remained in Kamerun and were officially established as the German Baptist Mission in 1898. The Mission advanced inland from the mouth of the Wouri near to where Saker began his work at Bethel. In five years they were at Ngamba on the Mbam River. By 1914 they had 1,500 Christian converts and 3,000 students in their schools. By 1915 there were 6 central stations, 49 outstations, 23 missionaries, 67 Kamerun church workers and teachers. There were also 3,124 Cameroon Christians and 3,623 schoolchildren. Eight of their missionaries had died in Kamerun. During World War I most of their stations were handed over to the Paris Mission Society.[64]

American Presbyterian Mission

There were other Protestant missionary groups working in the Kamerun colony prior to World War I. American Presbyterians, sponsored by the Board of the Presbyterian Church in the United States, had a mission at Benita in the Spanish colony of Rio Muni. From Benita they opened an outstation across the border at Batanga in the extreme south of Kamerun. The Presbyterian Church began its first mission in Liberia in 1833. In June 1850 their missionaries went to Corisco near the Rio Muni coast. The "presbytery" of Corisco was established in 1860 as part of the Synod of New Jersey, USA. They opened a station among the Batanga in Kamerun and then in French Gabon. Because of problems with French authorities over the use of the French language, they searched for a place in German Kamerun from the Batanga outstation they had opened in 1875. In 1889 the Presbyterians accepted working conditions demanded by the German government especially that the German language be used in their schools. After seventeen years of work in Spanish territory the missionaries moved to Kamerun.

Progress was very slow at first, and at one low point the American board suggested that the mission withdraw. It then decided to have a ten-year trial period. It was during these years, 1904–1913, that the mission was successful. Just before World War I there were 63 missionaries, 15,257 catechumens and 4,144 communicants. In addition 9,564 children attended their 125 boarding schools.

The Gossner Society

The Gossner Society was a German Lutheran missionary organization that worked briefly in Kamerun. It was named after Johannes Gossner, the pastor of Bethlehem Church in Berlin. Johannes Gossner was sixty-three years old when he founded a missionary training institution in Berlin in 1836. It was during the time of religious revival and led to the establishment of missionary societies in Germany and elsewhere. He had been a Catholic priest in Bavaria who had been influenced by an evangelical movement within Catholicism. His interpretation of the Bible brought him into conflict with his church, and finally he left to become a Lutheran in July 1826. Three years later he was pastor of Bethlehem church.

Gossner started a training college with six young men who had been turned away by other Protestant mission societies. They came to him in December 1836 asking to become lay missionaries. He trained them himself, mostly in Bible and hymn singing. His first missionaries were assigned to Australia to work among the Aborigines and in 1845 to work among the Dalits of North India. Johannes Gossner died in 1858, but the society he founded continued. The Gossner Mission to Kamerun began in 1914 with four workers. However, a few months later, with the beginning of World War I and the occupation of Kamerun by the Allies, all German nationals, including the Gossner missionaries, were forced to leave.

Roman Catholic Missions in the Kamerun

Roman Catholic chaplains accompanied Portuguese sailors exploring the coast of West Africa from the end of the fifteenth century. "It may be presumed that at least sporadic efforts at evangelization were made along the coast," said one report. But "little was done for the African people even at the coast. . . ." So it is unlikely there were any Catholic missionaries in Kamerun before the arrival of Pallottine missionaries in 1890. The Pallottines were met by five Catholics at Kribi. The five had been taught and baptized on Spanish Fernando Po.[65] Prior to World War I there were two Catholic missionary groups in Kamerun.

Pallottine Missionaries

In June 1885, Fr. Weik, a German-born member of the French congregation of the Holy Spirit, tried to approach Chancellor Bismarck about opening a Catholic Mission in Kamerun. Instead of seeing Bismarck he was interviewed at the Foreign Office. At the time almost all things French were mistrusted, and so his request was denied. French priests from Gabon visited Cameroon before the annexation, but those visits were stopped. Between 1885 and 1890 French Trappists and Jesuits asked for permission to work in Kamerun, but they too were denied. Then in 1889 the Pallottines applied to Berlin.

The Society of the Catholic Apostolate, known as the Pallottines, was founded in Italy by Vincent Pallotti in 1835. On 9 January 1835 Pallotti, while celebrating the Eucharist, had a religious experience in which he understood he was called to dedicate his life to the church. One of his hopes was to help spread the Christian faith throughout the whole world. To accomplish this he formed a group for men who came to be called the Pallottines. The Society was approved by Rome in April 1835. In 1838 the men were followed by a group of women who became Pallottine Sisters.

The mission office of the Roman Catholic Church, Propaganda Fidei, appointed the Pallottines to German Kamerun. One reason for their success with the government was the presence of a Catholic minority in the Reichstag. The minority accused the government of anti-Catholicism, and the Catholic-dominated Centrist Party demanded that Catholics be allowed to send missionaries to the German colonies. On 18 March 1890, the Pallottines of Limburg were allowed to begin missions in Kamerun. The government had three conditions: they must stay out of Protestant mission territory; only German nationals were allowed to be missionaries; and mission control must be in the colony itself, to avoid foreign interference. In his 1956 dissertation Norman Aste Horner thought that these conditions did not necessarily represent the will of either Catholics or Protestants. "It was clear that the Germans were wary of political interference by the Roman Church," especially by French missionaries. Such conditions were imposed due to the culture wars in Germany. The government had confiscated church property, closed convents and abbeys, and prevented the establishment of new foundations. Young men who wanted to join the Pallottines were trained in a missionary college in Masio, Italy, and not in Germany. Later women were trained at their own missionary college, Regina Apostolorum, in Trastevere, Rome.[66]

The new mission territory of Kamerun was made a "prefecture apostolic" by Rome on 22 July 1890. Gerhard Heinrich Vieter was named the prefect and leader of the first group of missionaries. The pioneer group sailed from Hamburg on 1 October 1890. On board the ship were Vieter, Fr. Georg Walter, Fr. Klosternecht, and five lay brothers.[67] Vieter was born on 13 February 1853 in Selm Cappenberg, Germany. He joined the Pallottines and became part of the Herz-Jesu Province of the North Rhine, Friedberg, and Westphalia. He did his studies in Rome, where he was ordained on 8 May 1887. After two years on a mission in Brazil, he returned to Europe, where he was appointed to the Kamerun. He would die there on 7 November 1914 in Yaoundé.

Heinrich Vieter, Prefect Apostolic of Kamerun

The Pallottine missionaries were offered reduced fares on a Woermann Co. ship to Africa. The company also gave them free transportation up the Sanaga River and the use of Woermann buildings for temporary housing in Edea.[68] This

Heinrich Vieter, Prefect Apostolic of Kamerun. Wiki Commons.

may not have been a good idea because it put the missionaries in the debt of business interests. The governor suggested that the Catholic missionaries work in Kribi or at a place north of Bibundi, both far removed from Protestant missionary activity. Vieter preferred to work in central Kamerun at Edea.

In 1891 Roman Catholic stations were opened at Marienberg[69] and Edea on the Sanaga River among the Bakokos. In 1891 a mission was opened at Kribi on the coast south of Douala. In May 1891 Marienberg started a school with twelve students. At Edea the first Catholic Church was built, a simple frame building. But it was at Kribi that Vieter established his main station. He bought a hill-top site overlooking the beach from some African Catholics who had been trained on Fernando Po. Kribi became the seat of the first "episcopal see," the headquarters of the church, when Kamerun was officially designated by Rome as an apostolic prefecture and Vieter named to the office of apostolic prefect on 15 January 1894.[70] By 1894 the three stations were staffed and included Pallottine sisters who had arrived a year earlier. In 1894 a mission was opened near Buea on the slopes of Mt. Cameroon.

Sister Mary Monica, one of the first missionary sisters, described the arrival of her group in an article published in the *Catholic Mirror* of Baltimore in the United States. After a voyage of thirty-three days they reached Kamerun, "where a scene of surpassing beauty met our gaze. On a cliff about 30 feet high the pretty white houses of the Europeans peeped out between groves of bananas and palms, while at the foot of the rock lay the Agencies. To the left stretch away thick forests of palms . . . and behind these in the distance rise the majestic Cameroon Mountains . . . at last we have reached our final destination, the scene of our future labours." Three of the sisters were to go to Marienberg and the other three by steamer to Kribi. Because there was some trouble among

Early Pallottine Missionaries for Kamerun. Pallottine archive. Limburg. Reprinted with permission.

the Limba people, orders came for all of the sisters to go to Kribi. They were joyful and grateful that they had reached the place where, "with the grace of God," they "might labor and toil, live and suffer—perhaps die—for the salvation" of the poor Africans. After a short time the sisters were instructing the people, especially the young, and had a school, using the shed that was serving as a church. "We now have 43 boys," she wrote. "All are good tempered, obedient and devoted to the mission." The sisters hoped one day they would become good Christian men. Already they were wondering how to provide for a boarding school for girls. They questioned how they were going to feed so many students. "Still we do not permit ourselves to yield to anxiety or trouble, for we have entrusted our household cares to St. Joseph and are confident that he will provide."[71]

In September 1899, during the Bulu Wars, the sisters at Kribi were robbed. Work at Edea had already slowed and so Vieter decided to move his residence to Douala. He also opened a school at Yaoundé in 1900, and sisters arrived in 1901. Vieter had befriended Ntamata Atangana at the mission school in Kribi. Atangana was to later give land to the Catholic Mission at Yaoundé. He will be prominent in the story of the retreat to Spanish territory in 1916 and internment on Fernando Po as Charles Atangana.

Vieter was consecrated bishop in the cathedral of Limburg in Hesse, Germany, by Bishop Dominicus Willi. His official title was "Apostolic Vicar of

Kamerun" and "titular Bishop of Paratonium." His motto was "I am your servant." Vieter returned to Kamerun on a steamer in February 1905 with Fr. P. Bernard Wiengold and three lay brothers: Joseph Stadlin, Johann Spork, and Robert Ulrich. He celebrated his first Mass in Douala on 5 March 1905. The port city was growing in importance but had a much smaller Catholic membership than the other stations. According to Horner, Vieter's decision to make Douala the headquarters of the Catholic Church before it seemed justified was "an early example of the insight and skillful management which promoted the rapid growth of Roman Catholicism in the important centers of this African territory." This was true at the port town of Douala, and at Yaoundé, where in 1907 there were more baptisms than in all the stations combined. In that year the Catholics had a total baptized membership of 4,967. New stations were opened at Ikassa, 1906, Einsiedeln, 1907, Victoria, 1908, Ngovayang, 1909, Dschang, 1910, Ossing and Minlaba, 1912.

Vieter received help in 1913 with the appointment of Franziscus Hennemann as his co-adjutor, his assistant with a right to succeed him. On 7 December 1914 Bishop Vieter died. After twenty-five years of service he joined forty other Pallottiners who died in Kamerun.

In a 1913 report, the Roman Catholics had 15 stations, 34 priests, 36 brothers, 29 sisters, 223 African teachers, a total of 37,592 baptized Christians and 17,650 catechumens. There were also 19,578 schoolchildren. During 15 years of work in Kamerun by the Pallottines, 8 priests, 14 brothers, and 2 sisters were to die.

A collage of thirty Pallottine Sisters who were in Kamerun at the outbreak of W W I. With permission of the Provincial Archives of the Pallottine Missionary Sisters in Limburg.

A hero among the Pallottines was Karl Hoegn. Nol Vehoeven calls him "a voice of the voiceless." Hoegn complained about the exploitation of Cameroonians to supply a labor force of 200,000 plantation workers and even worse the demand for porters, or carriers. In 1913 he estimated there were 80,000 on the road between Yaoundé and Kribi. The suffering and degradation he saw became too much to bear for Fr. Hoegn. Even women and children were used. He took 1st Class Lt. Scheuemann to court, but the governor sided with his officer and demanded that Hoegn be sent back to Germany. But Vieter managed to forward all the details to Berlin. The officer was disciplined, and the protest contributed to a case against the governor, who was removed from office. Hoegn remained in Kamerun and proved to be a dependable friend to the local people and an effective missionary.[72]

Sacred Heart Missionaries of Sittard

The appeal of the Pallottine missionaries "for more workers in this vineyard blessed by God" was answered when the Sacred Heart of Jesus Missionary Society offered to help.[73]

In 1903–1904 the Catholic Mission in Kamerun asked the government for permission to work in Adamaua in the north of Kamerun, an area dominated by rulers who followed Islam. The German government left the decision to Governor Puttkamer. Puttkamer had recently traveled through the region, and it was his opinion that Christian missionary work in the area was impossible. This decision was due to the government's political relationship with Islam. More appeals followed, but each time they failed. In 1911 two Catholic missionary societies asked for permission to work in Adamaua. The government again refused, saying there was no real colonial administration in Adamaua and so no protection possible for missionaries. One of the societies was the Sacred Heart Fathers of Sittard in the Netherlands. They then decided to withdraw their request and offered to cooperate with the Pallottine Mission.[74]

The government refused a request of Bishop Geyer, apostolic vicar for Central Africa, for permission to travel through the area in 1913. He wanted to learn if there was any possibility of a missionary presence. Finally, in June 1914, the Colonial Ministry relented and allowed him to travel through Adamaua in German Kamerun, provided he keep the purpose a secret and he follow a route chosen by the government. Bishop Vieter had earlier written to Europe in September 1906 stressing the importance of dividing the area of the Pallottine mission in Kamerun and opening a new station at Ossidinge on the Cross River. In 1909 the government station was moved 30 km up-river to what is present-day Mamfe. Before Vieter's death, the Kamerun was divided and the Cross River station opened.[75]

The Congregation of the Priests of the Sacred Heart of Jesus was founded by Leo Dehon. Dehon was born in La Capelle, France, on 14 March 1843. On 19 December 1868 he was ordained priest and appointed to a parish in St. Quentin. Ten years later, on 28 June 1878, he professed his religious vows and founded the Congregation of the Priests of the Sacred Heart of Jesus. The group first worked in St. Quentin and then, in 1883, opened their first seminary for missionaries in Sittard, The Netherlands. The society expanded. "Dehonians," as they were called, went to other areas of Europe and America. In 1897 Fr. Dehon accepted a mission in the Congo and briefly in Tunisia. In 1910 they accepted the call to the Kamerun.

Fr. Gortz   P. Emonts   Fr. Lennartz
P. Mannersdorfer, Mgr Lennartz P. Procureur   P. Aug. Mannersdorfer
Robert   1er départ - 10-11-1912

Fr. Weber   Fr Rommerskirchen   - Fr Kupper   - Fr Schreiber Lag
P. Zicke   P. Procureur   P. Schuster   P. Bintener
2e départ - 10-5-1913

Sacred Heart Missionaries. From *75 ans de l'Eglise dans l'Ouest du Cameroun*. Used with permission.

The Imperial German Colony of Kamerun 37

Sacred Heart Missionaries were already working in Gabon and Ubangi. One reason they wanted to go to the Muslim north of Kamerun, especially in the eastern part, was because it was connected with their other missions. They also proposed to work in Neu- Kamerun, an area recently conceded by France to Germany.

In a Rome decree of 27 June 1912 Missionaries of the Sacred Heart of Jesus of Sittard were assigned a mission in Kamerun. The first missionaries left Hamburg on the ship *Henry Woermann* on 9 November 1912 and arrived at Victoria on 28 November 1912. The new missionaries included Fr. Joseph Lennartz, who had worked in Congo for five years. He was the leader. The group included Frs. James Emonts and blood brothers, August and Robert Mannersdorfer, and two lay brothers, Krispinus and Felix. In Victoria they were welcomed by the Pallottine missionary Fr. Albing at the Bota mission. The next day they travelled to Douala and went ashore on the feast of St. Andrew. It was in Douala that they met Bishop Vieter.

In December 1912 the missionaries trekked to Kumbo in the grassfields, and on 1 January 1913 they opened Shisong mission nearby, dedicating it to the Sacred Heart. New missionaries arrived in June, and outstations and schools were started. They took over Ossing Mission at Mamfe from the Pallottines and opened a mission at Fujua, Kom, in July 1913. A third group of missionaries, including sisters, arrived in June 1914. By the time the Prefecture Apostolic of Adamaua was declared in 1914, there were nine priests, eight brothers, and five sisters already at work in three mission stations at Shisong, Kom, and Ossing.[76]

On 28 April 1914 Propaganda Fidei established the Apostolic Prefecture of Adamaua. It included the entire northern part of Kamerun, with Lennartz as the first prefect. The plan to go to the Muslim north was supported by traders, especially the Woermann Company. The German Colonial Office hoped the missionaries would at least reach Ngaoundere, where there was a government school staffed by a Muslim teacher, a fact that was criticized in Germany because Germany considered itself a Christian country. But in Kamerun the governors had called it "utopian" for any Christian mission to work against Islam. The Kamerun government relied on Muslim Fulbe princes to rule the territory to Germany's advantage.

The new prefecture extended to the southern boundaries of the civil districts of Ngaoundere, Banyo, Bamum, Bamenda, and Ossing. The prefecture covered, in reality, only a small portion of Adamaua. It would be the North West Region of today's Cameroon, to which Ossing was added.

Ossing in the district of Ossidinge on the Cross River had already been visited by the Pallottines in 1906, and it was the hope of Bishop Vieter to extend their work into the area. But the Pallottines were already overcommitted in other parts of Kamerun. It was not until 1911 that Fr. Karl Hoegn was sent to Ossidinge to find a site for a mission station. Work on a new station began

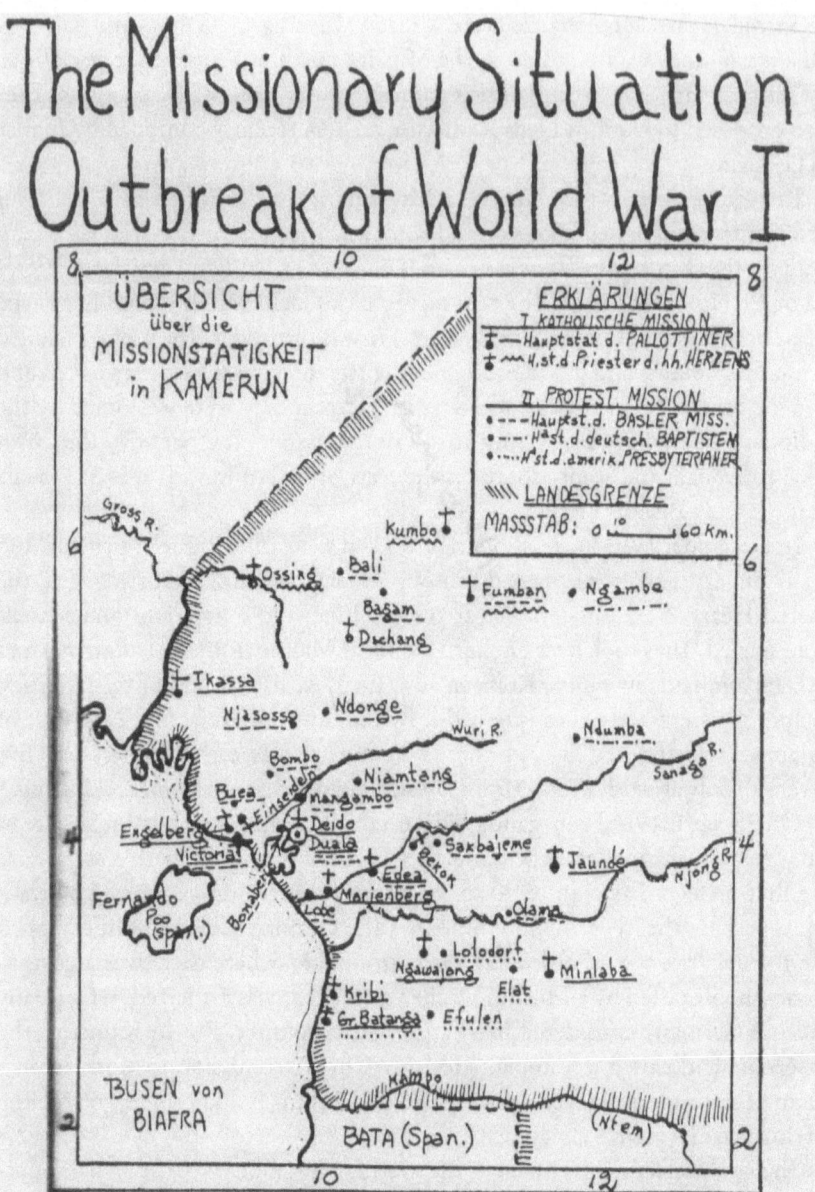

Map adapted from "Das Vikariat Kamerun im Jahr 1913," *Stern von Afrika* (April 1914): 204. See Norman Aste Horner, "Protestant and Roman Catholic Missions among the Bantu of Cameroon" (Ph.D. thesis, Hartford Seminary, 1956).

on 22 January 1912 near Ossing, about 20 km from the government station at Ossidinge. Basel missionaries were also active in the district. And so a Catholic Mission school opened with only thirty children. By the beginning of 1913 new schools had been started, and there were 430 school children. "It was a difficult beginning. But what had been achieved in this short period was a welcome gift to the new missionaries when they took over the station in July 1913."[77]

August 1914 and World War I meant the beginning of the end for German Kamerun and much of the work of missionaries, Protestant and Catholic.

Christian Missions at the End of German Kamerun

The Christian missions in practice, until the very end of the German period, almost never separated preaching the gospel from economic and social development in response to the needs of the people. Saker, for example, was criticized because of his emphasis on economic development. It was Saker who founded a technical school in Douala before the colonial era. It was this technical school that provided the Gulf of Guinea with the most skilled artisans.

In similar ways the Catholic Mission preached the gospel but also helped to develop the areas where they worked. For example, it could be said that in 1915 "the whole town of Yaoundé had been built by the missionaries."[78]

At the beginning of August 1914 news of the outbreak of World War I reached Kamerun. It was the beginning of what Werner Keller, in his history of the Presbyterian missions, called the "Time of Trial."[79] Carl Bender, an American missionary with the German Baptists, wrote that the war was a "terrible witness to the natives and an object of their scorn." It destroyed the beginnings of Christian culture in the colonies.[80] Yet the forced removal of all German missionaries and the hardships experienced locally were also an opportunity for growth in local autonomy, especially for Christians. Even in the grassfields of today's North West Region, the First World War became, according to Jaqueline de Vries, an important episode in the history of one group, the Kom, because of the participation of Christian soldiers in the war effort.[81] The next chapters will return again to that time of trial for all Cameroonians, Christians and non-Christians alike.

Chapter Two

World War I in Kamerun

The First World War ranks alongside the slave trade in terms of its impact on Africa. Its impact was felt across the entire continent. . . . (It) removed men—and women and children—from their homes; it undermined traditional patterns of authority; it destroyed many of the economic and especially agricultural benefits which colonisation had brought; and in some rare cases it triggered the first demands for African independence.

—Hew Strachan[1]

Using the opportunity provided by the war, the Allies took over German-held territory and secured it for their own colonial ambitions. . . . The war, sparked in Europe, enabled the colonial powers to once again redraw the map of Africa.

—Mahon Murphy[2]

We learned a few days ago the sad news of the outbreak of war. . . . What will become of our new Missions? One hopes the colonies will be spared from the war, but I can hardly believe that they will. All the Brothers, Pater Foxius and Pater August Baumeister have been ordered to report to Bamenda without delay and will be on the way already. . . . Pray for our poor mission.

—Fr. Lennartz, Baba Rest House, 9 August 1914[3]

War in Kamerun

World War I, the Great War, also known as the War to End All Wars, began on 28 July 1914 and ended on 11 November 1918.[4]

In Kamerun at the outbreak of World War I it is estimated there were 1,650 Germans.[5]

Britain declared war on Germany on 4 August 1914. In Africa, German Kamerun was surrounded by British and French colonies, with British Nigeria to the west and French Equatorial Africa to the south and east. British cal-

World War I in Kamerun

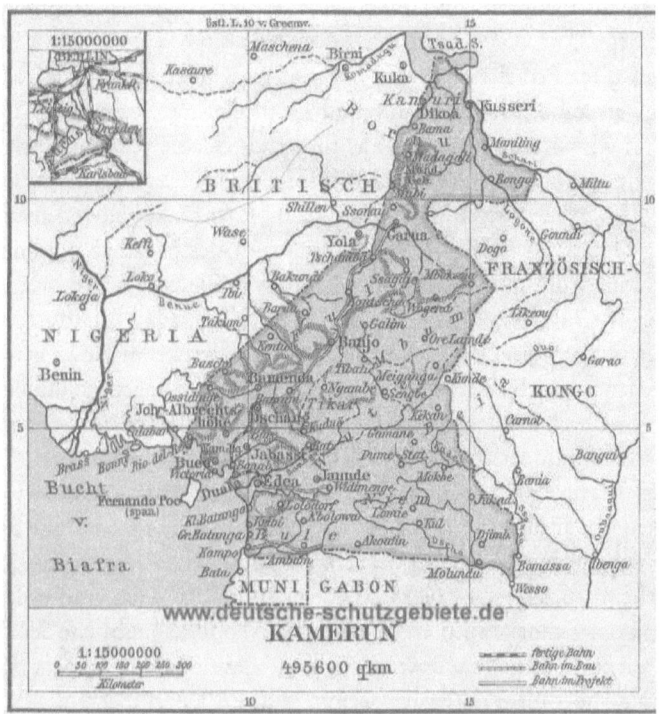

Map of Kamerun 1912.
© www.Deutsche-schutzgebeite.de, free use.

vary of the West Africa Frontier Force moved toward the border from Kano on 8 August. They crossed the border and attacked Tepe on the Benue River. After inconclusive fighting, the outnumbered Germans withdrew toward Garua. This was how the war came to Cameroon. No one predicted the effect it would have on German administration, the work of missionaries, and the local population.

In the appendix of this book are stories of Kamerun from the local population. For example, there is Mathias Anong of Widekum, a village on the main road from Mamfe where it begins the climb up the escarpment that separates the great West African forests from the grassfields of Bamenda. There is also the testimony of Peter Vewesse of Babanki Tungo and others. Their legacy continues in the Christianity of their villages and in the memory of their families.

World War I in Kamerun brought to a close the partition of Africa that began in Berlin in 1885. Germany was to lose all of her colonies. Hew Strachan believes that "relatively the impact of the war on the dark continent was as great as that on Europe, that few black families were unaffected, and that at the end the transfer of territory completed the partition of Africa commenced four decades earlier."[6]

While we read of the course of the war in Kamerun and the years in the camps of Fernando Po, Strachan's analysis of German intentions is useful to understand why events played out as they did. Germany had planned for the defense of its colony relying on her own forces, the *Schutztruppe*, to defend the territory. However, it was only when a decision was taken not to spend money fortifying Douala in 1913 that the local authorities began to plan on defending the colony from the interior of the country. The plan was drawn up on 24 November 1913 and was followed until the middle of 1915. It chose to focus not on Douala but Ngaoundere in the center of the northern highlands.

The Germans in Kamerun intended to conduct a defense sufficiently protracted to ensure that when hostilities in Europe came to an end Germany's claim to the colony would, at the peace talks, be supported by possession. "Thus, the stubborn resistance of the Cameroons was motivated not by any German desire to draw Entente troops from Europe, not by a wish to use a sideshow for a wider strategic purpose, but by the fact that colonization mattered as an end in itself."[7]

Even the 1916 retreat of German forces into Rio Muni, and eventually to Fernando Po, was not prompted by the fall of Yaoundé but by the decision, as at Douala, not to "sacrifice the investments and developments of peacetime colonialism in a short-term defensive action." On 28 December, four days before the British arrived in Yaoundé, Commander Karl Zimmermann ordered a retreat to the southwest. The gap at the frontier of Spanish Muni collapsed from 200 km to 50 km. By 15 February a great exodus took place. The *Schutztruppe* retained its integrity because of the German policy to integrate wives and children of the troops. This too was evidence that many Cameroonians saw the German defeat as temporary. After the war ended in Europe and peace talks took place they expected to return to Kamerun relatively intact.[8]

Zimmermann carried on a defense far longer and far more successful against superior forces than had been anticipated. Why he retreated to Spanish territory lay less in his lack of munitions than in the leadership of Governor Ebermaier. His objective was "to maintain Germany as a colonial power in the Cameroons."

The retreat and later the internment of the *Schutztruppe* on Fernando Po fit German political purposes. The Allies' General Joseph Aymerich had information that ammunition was reaching Ebermaiers's troops on the island. It was claimed that he had 500,000 rounds, "and his troops were drilling and training, awaiting the day of German victory in Europe before re-establishing themselves as a major West African power." Rather than a threat to the mainland during the war the German forces prepared for the day when they might return to Kamerun. If Germany had won the war or the terms of the peace treaty had been less harsh, this might have happened.[9]

But the tactics and objectives of the war do not help us to appreciate the effect the war had on people in Kamerun. For that we have the testimony of missionaries and the stories of Cameroonians and other informants.

At the beginning of the war, two German Sacred Heart missionaries in the Bamenda grassfields wondered what the future would be for their work. Father Lennartz wrote to Fr. Emonts from the Baba Rest House in Ndop Plain on 9 August 1914:

> Dear Father Emonts, We learned, a few days ago the sad news of the outbreak of war.... What will become of our new Missions? One hopes the colonies will be spared from the war, but I can hardly believe that they will. All the Brothers, Pater Foxius and Pater August Baumeister have been ordered to report to Bamenda without delay and will be on the way already. Pater August Mannesdorfer is on a trip to Bandam and should be back in 8–10 days, so there are no Fathers or Brothers to speak with the Captain (Adametz) about the Fathers and Brothers who have gone there, and to see, also, to the purchase of stores for the hard times to come. Do return at once to Kumbo. Pray for our poor mission.[10]

Emonts turned back and returned to Kumbo. "War! War!" he wrote, "the words rang continuously in my head. What would become of our Mission?" On the way back he met three Brothers and Fr. Foxius trekking to the military station at Bamenda.

> So I was all alone at the Mission. Father Mannersdorfer could not be reached and would only hear the terrible news on his return. Father Lennartz returned briefly from Bamenda where he had made large purchases of stores. He was lucky enough to find a few sacks of rice, some sacks of flour, tinned goods, peas, beans and suchlike supplies. Now we were cut off from any imports from Europe for the duration of the war. The establishment of new stations was now out of the question. How would it go? Who would win the War? How would the German Mission survive, cut off from the rest of the world?[11]

There were many unanswered questions for missionaries about the war and its effect on the new missions that had been opened and about their own position as German nationals. News from Europe reached them only through the telegraph station in Togo. It was relayed to Douala where it was carried by messengers to the interior. When the telegraph tower in Togo fell into the hands of the Allies, news only came infrequently through Spanish territory. In August 1914 the missionaries were far from the war but would soon be overtaken by the conflict.

The Great War

In August 1914 Germany had two colonies in West Africa, Togoland and Kamerun.

On 23 August the German under-secretary of foreign affairs contacted the American ambassador in Berlin, Mr. Gerard, to relay a message to Britain and France to learn their intentions about honoring the neutrality of the colonies. The answer was that the colonies were not to be considered neutral during the war.[12]

Togoland was invaded, and the Germans surrendered on 26 August 1914. The fall of Togoland eliminated the wireless station at Kamina. It had been completed in June 1914 and linked Nauen in Germany with its other African colonies. Togo had a police force of 673 and raised 1,000 troops, but they were unable to resist an invasion from Gold Coast. On the night of 24/25 August the Germans destroyed their wireless station at Kamina, "smashing its nine huge masts and burning its switchboard and batteries with oil."[13] On the following day Maj. von Doering surrendered. The whole of German Africa lost an important link with Berlin. Because it was difficult to learn the whereabouts of British prisoners of the Germans, the British War Office allowed Berlin to use British telegraph cables to communicate with its colonies.

Kamerun was unlike tiny Togoland. Kamerun covered about 300,000 sq. miles and had a military garrison that consisted of 200 German and 3,200

Troopers of the Kamerun *Schutztruppe*. Buea Archive.

African soldiers. These numbers were doubled by the mobilization of others in the colony. The force was organized into 12 companies with 12 field guns and many more machine guns than the British. The Royal Navy secured the coast for the Allies. The Germans had no fighting ships in the area, and this blockade cut off the Germans from supplies. The only lifeline was through Spanish territory. At the beginning of the war the Germans in Kamerun had 3,861 carbines and 2,250,000 million cartridges among other weapons and supplies.[14]

On 6 August 1914 French troops under Joseph Aymerich, the military commander of French Equatorial Africa, attacked. No instructions had come from France. The decision was a local initiative. There was little resistance from the Germans in the marshlands of this region. The French sent a column down the Congo and Ubangi Rivers and captured Singa, just over the frontier where one of the German telegraph lines passed. Another column came from the south and took Bonga. Aymerich then formed four columns to take the attack deeper into German Kamerun. One of the columns included 600 Belgian troops.

On 25 August British forces attacked from Nigeria at three points: at Mora in the far north, at Garua in the center, and Nsanakang in the south. At Mora the attack failed at first. At Nsanakang the British were almost destroyed by a counterattack. Near Garua, after the skirmish at Tepe, the first of the war, the Germans withdrew and then beat back a British attack on Garua by Col. MacLear on 31 August.

The British in Nigeria were confident that they would be received in Kamerun as liberators and the war might be over in six weeks. When a Nigerian column crossed the frontier from Ikom on 25 August, followed by two more columns the following week, they were confronted by a German force of fast moving colonial troops that drove them back. At the coast the Germans withdrew after the fall of Douala and the loss of 40,000 tons of shipping. But this was not the case in the interior and the north. Over the course of coming months the Germans held positions as long as they could, forcing the Allies to use up large amounts of ammunition, and then destroyed buildings (but it was not the policy to destroy colonial structure) and supplies that could not be moved. "Never once were their enemies able to surround them." The African soldiers and white officers completely baffled the efforts of Maj. Gen. Dobell's superior numbers of British, French, and Belgian soldiers, and finally were to maneuver their retreat in order to cross with thousands of Cameroonians into Spanish Rio Muni.[15]

The columns of West African Frontier Force troops from Nigeria were beaten back. Then an Allied expeditionary army was formed of French, British, and Belgian local infantry units under Gen. Aymerich. They attacked from three sides. In the north, French troops under Cols. Brisset and Ferrandi came from Tchad and were joined by a British force from Northern Nigeria

From Rémy Porte, *La conquête des colonies allemandes: naissance et mort d'un rêve impérial*, 2006 (Saint Cloud [Hauts de Seine], ed. 14–18).

under Gen. Cunliffe. In the south, there were two fronts. One attack was from Gabon, Moyen-Congo, and Oubangui led by Aymerich. It was joined by 761 troops from the Belgian Congo. The other front was an Allied expeditionary force under the command of Gen. C. M. Dobell, whose aim was to capture Douala and then the two railway lines to the interior; the southern railway from Douala and the northern from Bonaberi. In this attack from the sea there were 3,000 men from Freetown, Sierra Leone, and also troops from Nigeria, the Gold Coast, and Gambia, and 2,000 French Tirailleurs from Dakar, Senegal, under Col. Mayer.

Meanwhile, the paramount chief of the Duala, Manga Rudolf Bell, had been charged with treason by the Germans in May 1914. Anger was aroused among the Duala over suspicions that there was a plan to develop the town as a white settlement by forcibly removing the black population. The Germans intercepted a letter from Martin-Paul Samba of Ebolowa to the French that he was ready to lead a revolt against the Germans. Manga Bell was executed on 8 August. Strachan writes that the "Germans in Duala expended as much military effort in controlling the local population as in preparing to meet the British landing."[16]

Soon after news reached Cameroon about the outbreak of the First World War, one of the Basel missionaries, Rev. Hecklinger, heard that Manga Rudolf Bell, paramount chief of the Duala, and his secretary, Ngoso Din, had been sentenced to death for high treason. He went at once to the German governor to plead for the two prisoners. But the government wanted to execute them before the arrival of the Allies. That night Hecklinger visited the two prisoners, whose hands and feet were tied. The chief was "calmly dictating his last will and testament to an assessor." The missionary gave him Holy Communion, and Bell responded that he was "convinced that God will receive me. I die for my country." On the evening of 8 August the two men were hanged while the "Duala began an endless wailing" for their dead leaders.[17]

The Germans in Douala were expecting an attack in September 1914.[18] They had mined the estuary and scuttled some ships to protect the town, but the estuary itself was cleared. On 9 September a British warship entered the Wouri River, followed on 11 September by the British gunboat *Dwarf*, piloted up the river by Duala men. The Wouri is formed where the River Nkam and Makombe come together 32 km (20 mi.) northeast of Yabassi. It then flows 160 km (99 mi.) to the estuary at Douala. It is navigable for 64 km (40 mi.) upstream. Douala is on the southeast shore of the estuary.

The Allies attacked the town's canon. On 23 September a British cruiser sailed past the town, and two French ships arrived the next day. The harbor police reported that there were now six enemy ships anchored offshore.

Four of the ships were British and two were French, along with two gunboats. Finally converted passenger ships arrived from Northwest Africa carrying troops.

At first the Germans refused to surrender, and Douala was bombarded on 26 September. It was clearly useless to defend the unfortified town with two companies of African troops led by German officers, and four cannons. And so, on 27 September, the Germans surrendered Douala and Bonaberi. Two African companies, about 300 men and their officers, abandoned Douala. They withdrew into the interior leaving behind only 65 Europeans with rifles, two machine guns and four mortars.

According to the diary of a German officer, Lt. Nothnagel, at 7:30 am instructions were given ordering Captain Haedicke to withdraw from Douala with all of the African troops. Two officers of the reserve, Nothnagel and Bottcher, were to surrender to the commander of the British and French force. The Germans were probably unwilling to face both the British and a hostile local population, especially after the execution of King Manga Bell.

One of the Protestant missionaries later wrote that the "Native population of Duala . . . had proved itself before and during the war uncertain, traitorous and hostile to Germany."[19]

German troops withdrew from Douala in three directions. One group went north on the railway line to Kaka and Nkongsamba. Another went up the Wouri to Yabassi, while a third took the midland railway line to Edea and Yaoundé. The war in Kamerun was to last about eighteen months. The allies lost about 3,500 killed and wounded while the Germans lost much less, ending the war with almost as many men as they had started with.[20] After the fall of Douala, Yaoundé became the provisional capital for the next fifteen months.[21] The German strategy was to gradually retreat to the interior, while ambushing and harassing the Allied forces in the forest. They had the advantage of knowing the land, had loyal troops, and controlled the areas of fighting.

Missionaries in the colony continued to work whenever there was the slightest hope that they might be allowed to remain at their stations or they could avoid arrest. The hope was that if the war in Europe ended soon they would still be at their stations. This was especially true in the interior, where they thought that the German troops in the forest could hold out till the end of the war in Europe.

The Presbyterian Church in the United States published a report written by one of their missionaries in Kamerun, Dr. H. L. Weber. It was about the journey of a party of missionaries that was due for home leave when the war began. It was titled "From Africa to America in Time of War."[22] The missionaries were to leave Kamerun in early August but were unable to get any money because of the war. They went to Governor Ebermaier, and he arranged for them to take a small steamship to Fernando Po on 20 August. At Fernando Po the Spanish governor could not cash the postal order they had for expenses. The postal order was sent to the German consul, but he too was unable to cash it. Finally the governor of Kamerun asked the Spanish government to advance the money for their passage. While they waited, a Christian man on Fernando Po with the support of the Primitive Methodist Mission planned to raise the funds if needed. One missionary wrote that "words would fail to express our gratitude for his hospitality."

There was only one way off the island, and that was by a Spanish ship that stopped on trips up and down the coast of Africa. Due to the war it was delayed on its way down the coast when it was stopped and had to turn over all its coal to a Spanish warship. Only on 16 September did it finally arrive at Fernando

Po and the missionaries taken on board. The party was not far at sea when they were stopped by a French warship and searched looking for Germans. Fifteen German nationals were found on board but allowed to continue. The ship stopped at Dakar, and again French officials allowed them to go on. When they reached Tenerife in the Canary Islands all but four of the Germans left the ship. But once the ship was underway again and outside the three-mile limit a British cruiser that was following them stopped the ship and took off the four remaining Germans.

Mr. and Mrs. Love and Mr. and Mrs. Patterson found passage to England. There was no room for more, so the others went on to Cadiz and then Gibraltar, where they found two ships sailing to the United States. (One was the *Carpathia*, the ship that had rescued survivors of the *Titanic*. In July 1918 it was sunk by a German U-boat in the Irish Sea.) The missionaries finally landed in New York on 21 and 29 October 1914.

At the end of the report the editor gave the latest news of life in Kamerun at the beginning of the war. It was a very tense time for missionaries and local people, he wrote, but at that point the missionaries felt little anxiety. At each meeting with local people they were assured that if they stayed "we will protect you in every way." The Kamerun government took all their stores and trading centers but the governor had assured Mr. Adams that they would be allowed supplies via the Spanish colony if they were clearly for the mission. The missions needed supplies, but money was the more serious problem since the Kamerun government was unable to cash post office or bank checks.

After the capture of Douala, the Allies' policy was to evacuate the white civilian population of Kamerun. It was badly organized. General Charles Dobell ordered German nationals to the courtyard of the Douala hospital supposedly for a roll call. The Germans had been told that they were to register with the new authority. "It came as a shock when it was announced that they had only three-quarters of an hour to gather their belongings before returning to the hospital, where they would then be marched off to the docks, without the aid of porters, and put aboard the SS *Obuasi*, a 4,416-ton merchant ship, for transportation via Accra, the Gold Coast, to Britain."

When all Europeans were instructed to assemble in the garden of the general hospital several hundred, including women and children, turned up. The day after the town was occupied the first unmarried missionaries were transported to Dahomey as prisoners of war. One by one all the German missionaries were interned. Among the Basel missionaries there were some Swiss, but they were sent home as well.[23]

Germans who were part of the Catholic Mission were also among those brought to the government hospital. We know some of the details from Hermann Skolaster. The next day Fr. Heinrich and four brothers were taken by a French steamer to Fernando Po. Father Mekes stayed behind as a prisoner.

Gen. Charles Macpherson Dobell (1869–1954), by John Singer Sargent. Wiki Commons.

Other brothers had been drafted into the German army. One of them, Alfons Herrmann, had been caught in a failed attack on the British warship HMS *Dwarf*. Brother Alfons, a Basel missionary, on 15 September 1914 used a mission boat, the *Max Broch*, filled it with TNT and planned to ram the *Dwarf* in order to block the river. It failed to catch fire. According to the account, Br. Alfons became a hero among Kamerun Germans.[24]

Another, Jakob Eberwein, had been dismissed from the army but was still considered a soldier by the Allies. He was among the Germans first shipped to Cotonou, Dahomey. As prisoners of war they worked at building roads until August 1915 when they were taken to Morocco and in June 1916 to a prisoner-of-war camp near LeMans, France.

In the meantime, the British forces reached Deido on 29 September. Father Paul Franke and three sisters from the mission left for Douala. Brother Jakob Meuer, who was in the bush, immediately left for Dschang when he heard that Douala had fallen.

The British quickly rounded up Christian missionaries. They were suspicious of Basel missionaries, who were mostly German nationals. To the Allies they were very much enemy aliens, and there was no possibility of allowing them to remain in Cameroon. The commander of the British forces in West Africa, Gen. Charles M. Dobell, reported that although not all were on active service, "171 of the Basel Missionaries were reservists." Basel Mission buildings in Gold Coast were seized and turned into internment camps for missionaries on their way back to Germany.[25]

On the night of 28 September, the town of Douala was plundered by local people. Missionary Charlotte Schuler was made prisoner on Tuesday, 29 September, and taken to the hospital in Douala. She was one of the prisoners who were taken to the "small English steamer Bathurst," which sailed on 30 September. Schuler wrote that the women went to cabins and the men stayed on deck. For two days they had no food because all their money had been taken, and so they were unable to buy anything. The *Bathurst* sailed to Accra (one report says Lagos), where they were rowed ashore through the surf. On the way to a barrack the women and children were spat upon and pelted with stones by local people. On Monday, 7 December, they boarded the steamer *Appam*. The passengers were all whites and considered prisoners of war. On

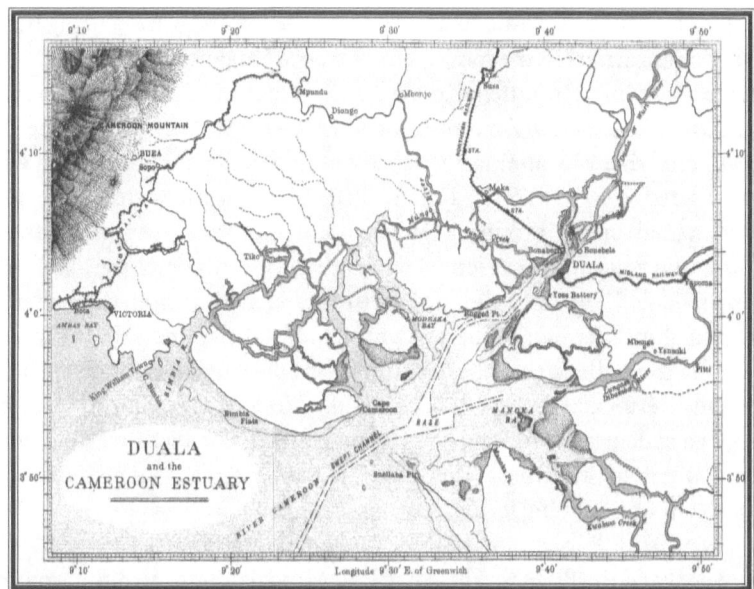

Douala and the Cameroon estuary, from *History of the Great War, Naval Operations*, October 1–6, 1914, by Julian Corbert and Henry Newbolt, 1920.

28 December they arrived in Liverpool, where the nearly 250 prisoners were taken off by guards in groups of 40. The United States consulate arranged for them to travel to London, where the German Benevolent Association helped the women and children to reach Rotterdam and from there to the border with Germany.[26]

On 30 September 1914 all of the Germans who were confined in Douala were shipped out. The missionaries were put on a British ship, the *Bathurst*. When they arrived in Lagos on 7 October the Catholics were allowed to stay in the Catholic Mission. The French vicar apostolic wanted them to stay till the end of the war, but it was not allowed. The missionaries were put on a British freighter with 700 Germans and Austrians, and on 23 November they landed in Southampton. The men were considered prisoners of war and kept in England while the women, children, and missionaries were given papers to Rotterdam. They finally arrived in Limburg, "the first of the missionaries expelled from Cameroon."[27] "Two days after it was taken Douala was emptied of Europeans."

For the Baptist Mission and for the whole colony the war was to have a devastating effect. Education was interrupted and school buildings, furniture, equipment, and invaluable records were destroyed. Those buildings not wrecked were to fall into near ruin after two years of neglect.[28]

Near the coast there was widespread suffering by the local population. It was reported that the Germans were executing local chiefs as they withdrew, suspecting their loyalty, while "many fled into the forests to avoid being pressed into service as carriers in the movement of troops" of both sides.[29]

The local population suffered at the hands of both Germans and the Allies. In the *Cameroon Diary of Lt. Arthur Lees, 1914–1915*, Lees writes of the "brutal treatment" that was summarily meted out to them by the British and which he was ordered to carry out. On 16 January 1915, in the Mora area of the north, he participated in the execution of two local men, non-Christians or non-Muslims. The editor of Lees's letters writes that the position of the local people was "unenviable." "Not only did they have to suffer a fluid war in their own land where British or German soldiers might appear at any time without warning demanding their allegiance, but they were also subjected to raids on their food stores and livestock by besieged Germans on Mora Mountain. . . ." And once there was a stalemate at the end of November 1914 "the British were prepared to shoot any domestic animal they came across on sight . . . denying it to the Germans but also robbing its local owner."[30]

The New York Public Library presented an exhibition in 2014 titled "Over Here: WWI and the Fight for the American Mind." It illustrated the "vigorous- and at times, vicious public debate" over the relationship of the United States to the war. Pamphlets were used by both sides, Germany and the Allies, "to win the hearts and minds of the nation."[31] Therefore while the war continued, the deportation and treatment of all Germans from Kamerun became an issue in the United States; the United States maintained its neutrality until 1917 when it joined the Allies.

Governor Karl Ebermaier wrote a protest letter to Gen. Dobell from Yaoundé on 24 November 1914. It passed through Spanish Governor Barrera in Santa Isabel on Fernando Po. The German governor complained that the removal of all Germans from Douala and manner in which it was done were contrary to international law. The treatment of German subjects and their property was at the center of the complaint. The Allies refused to accept the decision of the Congress of Berlin that the colonial territories be considered neutral in time of war. On 18 June 1915 the American ambassador in London wrote to the secretary of state for foreign affairs concerning Ebermaier's complaint about the treatment of German subjects and their property in Kamerun. General Dobell responded, explaining that the Germans had left Douala in "a state of chaos," after blowing up the wireless station, smashing the interior of the telegraph office and telephone exchange, stopping the water supply, setting fire to buildings." Papers followed listing "German atrocities" in Africa with examples of the "cruelty to natives by Germans."[32]

In turn, Germany accused the British of offering a bounty of 50 shillings for the head of every German, and also a bounty on any soldier. Erich Student, an employee of a German company at Edea and also a member of the colonial troops, alleged that English troops called upon Sanaga natives to deliver or "put out of the way" Germans employed by the government on the lower Sanaga. He claimed to have witnessed the murder of Seaman Nickstadt and Quartermaster Schlichting of the steamer *Kamerun* in Douala harbor. Student writes that he himself was attacked, beaten, and brought to the steamer *Remos*. An American missionary, Valentin Wolff, and two Basel missionaries, Schwarz and Gehr, reported this. Later they met Student while in detention in Douala.

Pauline Kessler, a German Baptist missionary in Ndongeri, claimed to have seen German workmen attacked, robbed, and murdered, and their hands brought to the British authorities at Douala to be exchanged for money. She described the bodies of the mutilated left near her station.[33]

The German Baptists alone had 150 missionaries before the war, and all but four were forced to leave. There were only four recently ordained African pastors able to take on leadership. The only Baptist missions that were not greatly affected were at Soppo and Victoria. Carl J. Bender was at Soppo with his wife, Hedwig. He was an American of German descent who had been in Kamerun since 1899. They had married in 1904 and were pioneer missionaries in Cameroon until the 1930s.[34]

On Sunday 15 November 1914, while Bender was at church, people started shouting that "the English are coming." One hundred African soldiers arrived with fixed bayonets under Maj. Rose. After asking for food for his officers they moved on with their troops toward Buea. The mission had "a faded red white and blue old glory" flag flying, but they were included on a list with 170 Germans, including 68 women and children who were ordered to Douala. Bender put his books away and visited his faithful assistant, Mwafisa, in his hut. He then began the 22-mile trek with porters to Victoria. His wife, who was expecting, went by plantation train. At Victoria they were put on board a freighter with others. The Benders were dropped at Douala while the others were taken as prisoners to the ship *Appam* in the estuary. Bender and his wife were taken to a prison in Douala.

Although he and his wife, Hedwig, were forced to leave Soppo under military escort, when he was questioned in Douala he insisted that he was a citizen of the United States. One of the officers told him he should go home. Instead they were allowed to return to Soppo.

He continued to work in Soppo until 1919. All during the war he flew a homemade United States flag over the Soppo mission station.

Bender criticized the British and the French for treating the missionaries in a "humiliating way" as "criminals" by interning them and confiscating their property and halting mission work. His view was that "missionaries should be serving Christ above their homeland." He also saw the war as "a terrible witness to the natives and an object of their scorn."

Pastor Stark's pamphlet of alleged eyewitness accounts was published in German in 1915. It accused England of ruining the flourishing mission stations of German, Swiss, and American mission societies in Kamerun for years to come.[35]

One report was by Baptist missionary A. Orthner, an American citizen. He alleged that he was near Nyamtang on 6 November when it was attacked. The missionaries were taken prisoner and allowed to take seven packs of fifty pounds each of their possessions. On the way to the coast all the packs disappeared. At Douala they were confined to the second floor of a house surrounded by a high fence and guarded by six soldiers. On 22 November they, with wives and children, prepared to board the ship *Appam*.

Meanwhile, the German troops had withdrawn to Edea. By 25 October a gunboat appeared before Marienburg Mission. Two priests, one brother, and three sisters were ordered to Douala. On the way they stayed for three days at the Protestant Mission in Lobetal before reaching the town. They were kept for four weeks in detention. During their detention Fr. Paul and one Basel missionary were allowed to return to their missions to collect what things they needed. The people of the mission thought the missionaries were to return soon, so they had not touched horses, cattle, and sheep running about Marienburg.

Father Gippert was at Edea, but the two brothers were away with the German army. On 26 October, about 9 am, the first French troops arrived. On Tuesday, 10 November, a colonel came to the mission "and told us we were all prisoners of war." At 6 am on 11 November they were taken by car to Douala. They arrived at 5 pm and were put up in a big building of the Basel Mission store. On the 25th, with the rest of the German prisoners and the Protestant missionaries, they were put on the steamer *Appam* for England. The Catholic missionaries, including the sisters, were offered a chance to go to Fernando Po. Since they thought the war would be soon over, they agreed and arrived in Fernando Po the last week of November.

Germany sponsored a weekly pamphlet in neutral United States called *The Fatherland*. It was produced in New York City and sold for ten cents. It proposed to devote itself to "fair play for Germany and Austria."

It has already been noted that the British government responded by publishing many of the complaints and the official response to the allegations. Based on the reports of Gen. Dobell, the British stressed the need to remove all civilians from what was a war zone. Dobell said that all captives were treated respectfully, and he insisted that because of the "passive resistance" of the German population it was necessary to trick them to assemble at the Douala Hospital. In a dispatch to the War Office in London in 1916 Dobell stated that by early 1915 one thousand male Europeans, of whom only thirty-two were incapable of bearing arms, had been deported for internment in Europe. For the British any German male was considered a potential combatant.[36]

After the fall of Douala the Allies aimed to encircle Yaoundé. A large British column came from the southeast, while a French unit from Edea and Eseka and another French column attacked from the Congo. Other allied forces came from Mt. Cameroon. Two companies of the Gold Coast Regiment, West Africa

Frontier Force, landed as part of the British force that captured Douala. These two companies joined two others of the Sierra Leone Battalion and formed a battalion that was commanded by Lt. Col R. A. de Burgh, the commandant of the Gold Coast Regiment.

Dobell ordered two columns to move north and attack Susa and Yabassi. Yabassi was about 80 km up the Wouri River. Brevet Col. E. H. Gorges of the West African Regiment commanded the Yabassi column. The movement up the Wouri River began on 7 October. The long line of ships led by the *Mole* was met along the way by a local chief, who came aboard for a visit. "He had been hiding in the bush for three days as the withdrawing Germans were hanging anyone in authority who was thought to favour the Allies." When the ships reached a fort at Nsake it came under fire, but when a company seized the fort they found it had been abandoned and the Germans had withdrawn further up the river to Jabassi.[37] The German defenders at Jabassi were the 1st Company of the *Schutztruppe* supported by local police and Europeans. On 7 October, at 8 am, the ships came within sight of Jabassi. What followed was a defeat for the Allies, with the loss of British officers and men killed and wounded. At dusk, a retreat was ordered, and the flotilla sailed first to Nsake and then back to Douala.

A second attack was ordered on 13 October. The columns were formed by Nigerian and Gold Coast troops. By 3 pm Jabassi was surrounded, and an hour later all the trenches were captured. Some prisoners were taken, while the Germans continued to withdraw toward Nyamtam. The 1st Battalion Nigeria Regiment was left to control the fort, while the rest of the column returned to Douala.

On 6 November, troops landed from the *Cumberland* at Victoria. The British told the local Germans that they were prisoners of war, but it was not clear what they were to do with them. As a result Victoria was left in peace for weeks. Before the attack on Buea they were brought to Douala and then back again to the mission. Finally, on 29 November all Germans were ordered out of Victoria. Fathers Rieder and Maurer packed their things but "hoped from week to week for peace which would put everything right again. But it was not to be." While the guns thundered in Victoria and Douala the missionaries in Einsiedeln and Engelsberg were able to observe "the spectacle of war."[38]

After taking part in action near Douala, Allied troops came together for an attack on Buea, the German administrative center on the slopes of Mt. Cameroon. The aim was to capture a German force of about four hundred troops.[39] The attack split into two columns. One, the Tiko column, was made up of Nigerian and French Senegalese infantry supported by Royal Navy and Nigerian gun detachments. The second, the Mbonjo column, was a mixed battalion supported by Gold Coast artillery. It was commanded by Lt. Col. Rose. Each column had half a company of Gold Coast Pioneers, who did light engineering work, cable laying, and medical detachments, and several hundred porters. While the columns moved on Buea a detachment of Royal Marine light infantry under Capt. C. L. Hall was to capture Victoria from the sea. Another group, the 2nd Nigerian Regiment, was to advance up the Northern Railway line and capture Muyuka. Colonel E. H. Gorges, commander of the Tiko column, went by water from Douala to Tiko on 12 November 1914 and two days later advanced on foot toward Buea. At Dibanda, the defenders, four Germans and fifty soldiers, were driven out. "The defenders, 4 Germans and 50 soldiers fled in haste...." The Germans were captured. Just before the column reached Molyko, after nine hours climbing through thick forest, they stopped for the night. The next day they continued to Buea, where the German district commissioner surrendered to Col. Georges at 1:45 pm.

In the meantime, Col. Rose led his column from Mbonjo on 11 November and on the 13th advanced westward on both banks of the Mungo River. They were supported by some shallow draught vessels. After a brief fight the Germans withdrew from Mpundu. Rose pushed on for three miles but found the terrain difficult as they were moving through cocoa and rubber plantations crossed with roads and light railway tracks. Advancing on Ekona on the 14th they were harassed by a small group of two Germans and thirty soldiers. The Germans kept withdrawing to well-prepared positions. The *Schutztruppe* was not the only hazard. In the forest one British patrol was attacked by bees and another was routed by an elephant. Likona was taken, and a detachment was sent to hold Lisoka.

The next day Col. Rose sent out patrols. One made contact with troops of Col. Georges. Another captured the local German commandant, Capt. Gaiseer. Another patrol returned with the official German mail bag from Yaoundé. On 16 November, Rose marched into Buea but left Lt. J. F. P. Butler of the Gold Coast Regiment with thirty men and a machine gun near Lisoka. His mission was to attempt to capture German forces hiding in the nearby forest.

According to Skolaster's account of the final days, after Soppo and Buea were taken, on 17 November, the first British troops, two officers and ten black soldiers, arrived in Einsiedeln. "They had orders," wrote Fr. Lettenbauer, the rector of the catechist school, "to check all European settlements along the Buea–Victoria road and to bring all suspicious Europeans to Buea." On 21 November an Irish Catholic captain visited the mission. He and his superior, Maj. de Rose (*sic*), "thought there was nothing against the missionaries remaining in the mission." But on the 25th they were called to Buea and told they were to be transported to Douala. A problem arose when the missionaries from Engelsberg arrived. The mission was caring for forty orphans at Engelsberg. An English doctor went to the orphanage, and it was decided that the missionaries could remain but those from Einsiedeln had to leave. And so on 29 November 1914, the first Sunday of Advent, Fr. Lettenbauer gave his final sermon, and the next day he and others were marched off as prisoners of the British. They went by plantation railway to Victoria, where they met other prisoners of war. All of them were taken by boat to the *Appam*, a big passenger ship anchored off Cape Suelaba.[40] On board they met Germans who had been taken from their homes on the slopes of Cameroon Mountain between the 15th and 30th of November. The *Appam* stopped in Ghana and took on fifth to sixty more German prisoners before finally arriving in Liverpool on 29 December 1914. The women and children were sent back to Germany, while the men, including missionaries, were brought to a prisoner-of-war camp at Queensferry. The three priests, Rieder, Lettenbauer, and Mauer, were prisoners for only eight days. On 15 January 1915 they traveled to Tilbury Docks via London and from there by a Dutch ship to Rotterdam. Brother Mauer was freed in November 1915 in an exchange of prisoners. Brother Bauer returned to Germany only after the war, on 15 March 1919.

Skolaster's account continues: At Engelberg the missionaries carried on until Sunday, 6 December, when orders came that the whole mission staff had to be on board a ship the next evening and carried to Fernando Po. Brother Britz wrote a description of the last hours of the missionaries at Engelberg.

> It is Sunday 6th December 1914, 8 o'clock in the evening, the last evening in our beloved mission. Deep peace lies over Engelberg on this moon and starlit night. And yet there is no peace here . . . the English have made themselves at home like sparrows in a swallows' nest. With sorry hearts we sit here on the veranda after a hard day's work. It was a really hot day. Now the cool of the evening breeze passes. Tomorrow we have to leave; what is going to happen? We gaze across the beautiful landscape, across the wide silvery sea. . . . The bright beam of a searchlight plays across from down in the harbor where the English are. From time to time we too are bathed in its light. In the early morning the church is packed as a priest offers Mass and gives a farewell sermon. There are even six couples waiting to be married, along with a lone bride whose partner has not arrived.

The time comes for the prisoners to leave. "Soon we see guns flashing and we hear somebody shouting orders. Now the soldiers line up. They load their guns and are divided into sections and we are ordered between those sections. It is a hard thing to be deported." The path they follow is narrow and so the march is disorderly. There is a commotion and the bridegroom who had been late arrives to meet his bride who has been following the missionaries. The groom is a Catholic teacher by the name of Vincent Lionge. His bride is Maria Imbale. When the march stops for a moment a priest hears them exchange consent and then gives their marriage the blessing of the church. "The last work, the last missionary deed, a war wedding! Now the bride is happy. But our own road still goes on. . . ."

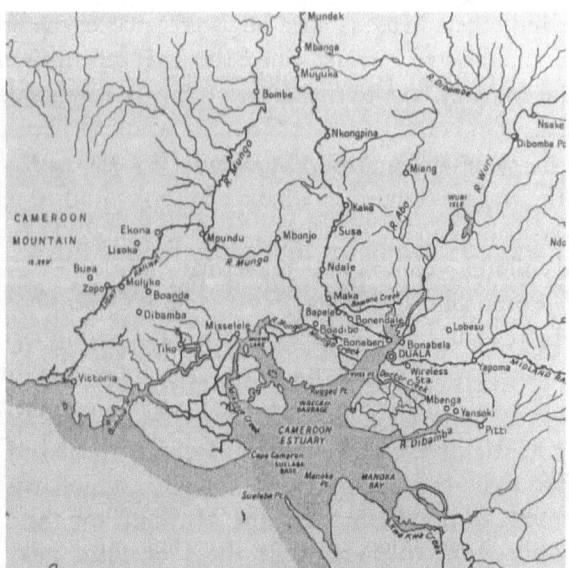

The Cameroon Estuary, Douala, and the surrounding area. Wiki Commons.

While the missionaries of Engelberg were being taken away, the end came for the missionaries at Kribi and Big Batanga. Already at the end of August, to prepare for an attack from the sea, the Kribi hospital patients and medical supplies had been transferred to the mission. The hospital was in the line of fire if the town was shelled from the sea. The mission church and carpentry workshop were used, and the school was changed into an operating theater and dispensary.

> A Red Cross flag was hoisted on the church tower. Finally, on 13 October, a day after they had shelled Kampo, two French warships appeared, the cruiser *Bruix* and the gunship *Surprise*. An envoy came ashore and demanded surrender (and) when this was refused the French shelled the town for six hours and the next afternoon did the same. No troops were landed and on 15 October the two ships left.

The purpose was to keep some German troops occupied so they would not go to the defense of Douala.

Skolaster thought that if the Allies had attacked in the south it would have been easy to cut off an escape route to Spanish territory for the German army. The captain of the French cruiser, *Boissarie*, later told him that this was the plan of the French, but the English Gen. Dobell insisted that the main attack on Yaoundé needed to come from Edea. "He did not want to push the Germans into a war of despair. He presumed no doubt that they had enough ammunition for their rifles. But this time the French were right. There was too little ammunition in Cameroon for the Germans and when it was finished there would have remained only an honourable surrender."[41]

Meanwhile the Allies continued their push to the interior. One engagement in late 1914 was an example of the action the Allies faced as the Germans withdrew into the interior. Lieutenant Butler and thirteen soldiers surprised a German rearguard of about one hundred troops with a machine gun. At first the Germans retreated but once into the forest they made a stand. Butler had followed so quickly that about half of his soldiers were left behind, and now they faced a machine gun at 27 meters. Butler began shouting orders to imaginary rifle companies to fix bayonets and attack. The bluff succeeded, and the German force retreated again.[42]

Colonel Hayward's 2nd Nigerian Regiment seized Muyuka on 13 November. The commander of the Allies in the Cameroons, Maj. Gen. C. M. Dobell, ordered Col. Gorges to clear the Northern Railway. He joined a force at Muyuka on 2 December that included two Nigerian Regiments, a 12-pound gun, and two machine gun teams from the Royal Navy, along with artillery batteries, a section of Royal Engineers, and others. The 1st Nigerians moved along the railway to Loum, supported by troops on either side. On 5 December, a Nigerian reconnaissance party found that the Germans had destroyed the Nlohe railway bridge over the Dibamba River. There was an ambush, and Lt. H. H. Schneider was killed.

Over the next four days the British built a temporary footbridge at Nlohe and reached Manengole. They were under constant fire from German snipers. But on 10 December the Germans sent an officer under a white flag to see Col. Gorges with a message from Lt. von Engelbrechten, the local German commander. The railhead at Nkongsamba and all the surrounding countryside up to Bare surrendered.

On 1 March 1916 Maj. Gen. Dobell sent a report on the campaign in Cameroons.

> Early in 1915 the situation was as follows: British troops holding Duala, the Northern Railway with Bare, Victoria and Dibombe... French troops on the line of the Midland Railway up to and including Edea, which place was partially isolated as one span of the first of the two bridges had been destroyed. A detachment at Kribi was protecting that seaport from land attack. Ships and armed craft of the Allied Navies had visited the whole of the Cameroons sea-board and had established bases for small craft to patrol the rivers where navigable.... Towards the end of 1914 the French, under Gen. Aymerich, and Belgian troops based in French Equatorial Africa, commenced to make their presence felt in the South and South-East, but my force was separated from them by a distance of

approximately 400 miles. In the North an Allied force was fully occupied in observing Mora and Garua. At and near Ossidinge a small British force from Nigeria and German forces were in contact.[43]

At the beginning of 1915 the Germans continued to evade pursuing Allied forces by withdrawing to the interior of Kamerun. As the Allies moved forward missionaries continued to be taken up as prisoners of war and transported back to Europe or to Fernando Po.

Once the railhead at Nkongsamba and all the surrounding countryside up to Bare surrendered, Bare was occupied. The Allies found in the stores two uncrated German airplanes. On Christmas Day 1914, the British advanced on Dschang with two columns. One went directly up the Nkam valley while the other smaller force advanced from Mbo under Col. Haywood. The day after Christmas Haywood faced serious opposition but drove the Germans back, losing twelve men.

Now both columns had to force out German detachments in steep and heavily wooded terrain. On 2 January 1915 at a road junction southwest of Dschang both columns met and pushed on at once. By 5 pm Dschang Fort and the town were in British hands. The Germans had withdrawn without a fight.

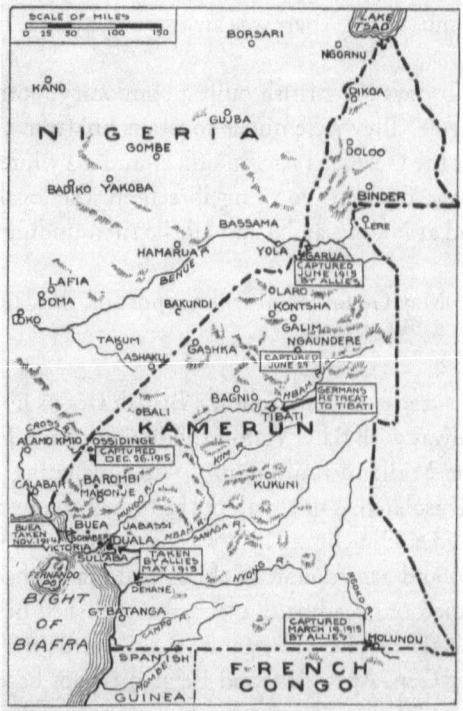

Kamerun Campaign, WW I, 1915. *New York Times*, August 1915. Wiki Commons.

General Dobell did not want the army to remain in an exposed position for too long, and so he ordered the fort destroyed and the troops to withdraw to the railhead at Nkongsamba. While the Nigerians pursued the Germans down the Bamenda road the Pioneer troops demolished the fort.[44]

Catholic missionary Skolaster gives us an account from the German side. The 4th Company of the German *Schutztruppe* under Capt. von Engelbrechten was not able to resist the attack of the British in December 1914 at the foot of the Dschang plateau and so he withdrew. The missionaries had come to Dschang for a meeting before the British army attacked. Father Huf, two brothers, and the sisters decided to stay. The others decided to leave. Father Hoegen left on 30 December for Yaoundé with two carriers. Brother Meurer and Br. Pohlman went north to Kumbo, where there were Sacred Heart Missionaries. One brother, Thomas Rothkegel, was a low-ranking officer with the 4th Company, German army, and he stayed with the troops. The missionaries who remained at Dschang flew a Red Cross flag over the mission. There was a German lieutenant who was seriously ill, along with three white women and six children in the mission. On the afternoon of 2 January 1915 the British were outside Dschang. They fired their three big guns and then took over the government station as well as the mission. On 6 January it was announced that all Germans had to leave Dschang. Everyone was ready to leave. Since the British did not plan to remain they destroyed the government buildings but spared the mission. The destruction was an attempt to keep the Germans from returning in the rainy season. The prisoners traveled for four days on foot and arrived in Douala on 10 January. On the 12th they boarded a British ship for Fernando Po.

On another front the British had reached Ikassa on 2 December 1914. The Europeans at the factory in Ndian were arrested, but the missionaries were not bothered. On two occasions British officers visited and advised them to go to Fernando Po. But the missionaries thought the war would soon be over and so stayed on. On 1 February 1915 a lieutenant arrived with soldiers and politely advised them to accompany him. He had to abandon the border post at Ikang and could not leave them behind. On the 2nd they arrived in Nigeria at Calabar, where they thought they might be allowed to stay at the Catholic Mission. Instead they were confined in a school at the American mission. They remained there until the end of the month, and then on 1 March they were put on board the steamer *Salaga* bound for Douala. Imprisoned in Douala they met other Germans and missionaries from the mission at Ossing, including Fr. Zick and two brothers. Finally on 9 March they sailed for Fernando Po.

Some of the British forces had come from the Gold Coast (Ghana), a British colony approximately 690 mi. (1,110 km) west of Kamerun. An infantry battalion of the Gold Coast Regiment had its own artillery support; two 2.95-inch mountain guns. After taking part in the campaign to defeat the Germans in

Togoland they were sent to Cameroons. They pursued the retreating German army between 8 August 1915 and February 1916 as they withdrew across the border into Spanish Muni. In thick bush north of the border, the regiment suffered twenty-nine casualties.

At the beginning of the war Dobell reported that he had 4,300 West African soldiers. On 21 November 1915 an additional 9,700 arrived, including Indian troops. He wrote that there was an equal number of French troops as well.[45] On All Souls Day a British gunship landed at Big Batanga. The telephone was damaged, but the two missionaries, Frs. Gustav Schwab and Anton Weller, were not bothered. At Kribi, the town was shelled again but no troops landed. The missionaries heard that in Douala their colleagues had been deported and the missions looted. They decided to leave Kribi. "We had no intention to give ourselves freely into captivity from which nobody benefitted." On 27 November 1915 the British landed a force at Longji and on 1 December they moved overland to Kribi. Father Vogel hid in the forest with some Christians and then escaped south to Big Batanga where he met Fr. Schwab. After a short discussion they decided to escape to Spanish territory. On reaching Bata on 10 December, they asked for political asylum. By the end of February they were on Fernando Po.

Late in 1915 all the missions along the coast were empty of German missionaries. It was only in Dschang that missionary work began again when the British withdrew. By then ten Catholic priests, thirteen brothers, and sixteen sisters had been given asylum on Fernando Po and stayed there with Spanish missionaries. Some of them decided to return to Germany as soon as possible. Three priests, five brothers, and all the sisters asked for passports from the British consul on Fernando Po, and they were granted. They traveled to Barcelona and then to Genoa before reaching Germany. On 9 April, five more priests followed and left Santa Isabel for Spain aboard *Ciudad de Cadiz*.[46] In September the German ambassador in Madrid, with the help of the vicar apostolic of Fernando Po who had been traveling with the priests, received a safe conduct guarantee. It enabled the missionaries to pass to Germany via England. They were to reach Limburg on 2 December 1915.

In the interior of Kamerun the missionaries had continued to work. They believed that the German troops who had a strong ally in the forest would be able to hold their positions until the war was over in Europe. Meanwhile, after the capture of Edea, French troops pushed on into the forest. The *Schutztruppe*, with only forty men, had to withdraw. On 2 January Skolaster left Yaoundé for Andreasberg. He found that the French had established themselves near Edea and the Germans on the Ngwe River, 46 km away. Skolaster celebrated Mass several times with these groups. Two German battalions under Capt. Dickmann were stationed in South Dibanga. On 23 February the

French advanced toward the German position on the Ngwe and pushed the Germans back. But when the 2nd reserve battalion attacked from the flank they withdrew to Edea.

In the second week after Easter the French advanced again. This time they came in great numbers from two directions. The German positions on the Ngwe and Kele were lost. Andreasberg was abandoned and Skolaster went back to Yaoundé. He returned briefly in June when the Germans had pushed the French back to the Ngwe after they had advanced about 100 km. This reversal lasted for only eight days.

Meanwhile at Dschang, where the British had unexpectedly withdrawn on 10 January 1915, the Germans had returned. By Easter the mission staff came back as well and continued to work as before. Finally, at the end of the rainy season, on All Saints Day 1915, the British moved against Dschang again. This time it was decided that the brothers and sisters would remain. It was thought "wiser to let the English bring them to Fernando Po than to suffer the hardships and troubles of another escape which would have benefitted nobody." Father Hoegn, the leader of the missionaries after the death of Bishop Vieter on 7 November 1914, decided to remain in the country as long as possible. He left Dschang on 5 November, and the British arrived on the 6th. The other priest, Kramer, had already been appointed to Minlaba. The missionary sisters and brothers were escorted to the coast and arrived on 24 November. They were taken by a British gunboat to Fernando Po.

On 1 May 1915 Gen. Dobell ordered an advance on Yaoundé, the German center of administration. The attack was to be along the main road and railway. Two days later they came against well-prepared German positions at the Mbili River crossing west of Wum Biagas. The German commander, Maj. Haedicke of Number 1 Depot Company, had destroyed the bridge and placed stakes and tree obstacles in the waist-deep water. Haedicke commanded over 300 riflemen and three machine guns. On the east bank the Germans were well concealed in trenches 1,600 yards long that controlled a field of fire of about 300 yards. The trench was anchored on the right by a steep forest slope about 800 ft. high, and on the left by the unfordable Kele River.

Although the offensive was delayed by the rainy season, by June 1915 the British column was only fifty miles from Yaoundé. They were driven back at first with 25 percent casualties by Maj. Haedicke's action. The French were 140 miles east of Yaoundé by June, but their offensive was also brought to a standstill by the rains. But it was to begin again in earnest when the dry season arrived in November 1915.

In another area, in the northwest of Kamerun, it was not until October 1915 that a column of four companies under Maj. Crookendon advanced from the Cross River on the Nigeria border toward Bamenda. The force met with only token rearguard resistance. The Germans withdrew first from Bakumba, then Numba, passed through Widekum, all on the Ossidinge–Bamenda Road. Informants at Widekum remembered the district officer of Mamfe, Dr. Alfred Mansfeld, telling the local people to remove all the goods from the German trading post and hide the salt and other things in the village. Otherwise, "the English would take everything for themselves."[47]

The British set up their field guns, light howitzers, and machine guns in pits dug above Widekum, facing Tiben village and German defenses. There was a brief engagement, and the Germans withdrew through farms toward Bali-Nyonga. The local people supplied plantains and palm kernels to the porters who carried arms and ammunition for the British force. A market was set up where the British troops traded salt for foodstuffs.

The Germans were being routed. A German officer, von Summerfield, advised the Fon of Bali-Nyonga that "the war was between white-men and not for natives." He relieved the Bali of their rifles and instructed them to give food and carriers to the British when they arrived. "White is white and the war does not concern black-men." Summerfield warned the Fon that the British would destroy his town if they resisted. Fon Nyonga took his advice.

The British took Bali-Nyonga on 21 October 1915. They immediately moved to attack the Bamenda station, 16 miles away. In the meantime Capt. Adametz, the German commander at Bamenda, abandoned the fort and began a retreat toward Yaoundé with many carriers (levies) recruited in the grassfields.

A Time of Trial for the Christian Missions

The fall of Bali-Nyonga in today's North West Region, began a time of trial for the grassfield Christians of Bali-Nyonga, and especially the Basel Mission. As soon as the German missionaries left Bali, at the end of October 1915, Fon Nyonga, the Bali chief, gave orders that the mission church was to be locked and the keys kept at the government station in Bamenda. Whoever dared to preach was to be beaten and imprisoned. "The enemies of Christ claimed that with the departure of the missionaries the religion of the whites had also to disappear from the country."[48]

We have four sources among the missionaries that describe this "Time of Trial," as the Basel Mission puts it: Werner Keller's *The History of the Presbyterian Church in West Cameroon* and books by Catholic missionaries Emonts, Skolaster, and Huppertz.[49]

With the arrival of the dry season in November 1915 the encirclement of the *Schutztruppe* by the Allies came rapidly. On 23 November 1915 Sacred Heart Catholic missionaries at Kumbo were made prisoners and taken away. "The two fathers from Bekom and the four sisters were our companions in misery. After a few days Father Lennartz, the Apostolic Prefect, was also in English hands and joined us as a prisoner of war on the way to Banyo. That was a terrible blow.... We were taken from Banyo to Gashaka and Karabi, then to English Nigeria, where from Ibi on the Benue we reached Lokodja and from Lokodja on the Niger to Bara and Zinguru. Our journey then took us to the prisoner-of-war camp at Lagos. These sad journeys as prisoners lasted three months."[50] While the British soldiers were entering Yaoundé on 1 January 1916 the missionaries left Kamerun, crossing the frontier to Nigeria at Karabi.[51]

One of the Sacred Heart missionaries reflected on events of 1914 and 1915. He thought that since there had been no preparation of defenses the colony could hold out at most till December 1914. "Yet it took almost another year and a half before the last bit of the finest of our colonies fell into the hands of the enemy. The missionaries taken to Bamenda served as medical auxiliaries of the *Schutztruppe*. Father Schuster became a practicing doctor and at the battle of Nssanakang had complete charge of medical matters."[52]

Their missionary work was crippled by the removal of the missionaries to be medical auxiliaries, but "we held on as best we could. The *Schutztruppe* held out longer than they thought possible. They praised Station Head Adametz, "but the five- to tenfold superiority of the enemy brought resistance to an end. Douala, Kribi, and Victoria fell to the enemy, who could now penetrate inland. Most of the Pallottines in the south of the colony were soon taken prisoner and their mission stations plundered...."[53]

On 15 January 1915, the southernmost of their mission stations, Ossing, was captured. Emonts continues his story. Father Zicke and the two brothers fell into English hands and were taken to Nigeria. A few months later the two Fathers, Robert Mannesdorfer and Bintner, also had to leave their station at Fujua in Bekom and go to Kumbo.

> The danger from the English frontier was too great (at Kom). Kumbo remained unscathed until 23 November 1915. Until then work had gone on as usual.... Indeed a few new outposts at Tabesob... Mbot and in Ndum (Ndu) were taken over as it then seemed the war would soon end. I found myself with Fr. Bintner in the Nsungli area to complete the schools at Mbot and Ndu and set them in motion when I received a message to return home by shortcuts as soon as possible, since the English were in the neighborhood. I informed Fr. Bintner, who was a few days' journey ahead seeing to the school foundation. We escaped capture by the skin of our teeth and arrived back in Kumbo.

Aloys Huppertz gave an account of what happened to many German missionaries in the grassfields after their arrest and forced trek to Nigeria. From there most were taken back to Europe and only a few to Fernando Po. On 23 November 1915 the Sacred Heart priests at Kumbo were told to start the trek to Banyo at once. They protested that the sisters could not leave so abruptly. "This couldn't be helped," the officer said. In the end, the officer lost his patience and decided as follows: "Orders are orders. Everybody march! Otherwise I shoot." This is the way we left Kumbo. After fourteen stopovers, Huppertz described the reception of this army of prisoners and company at Banyo on 8 December 1915.[54]

Near the town's entrance they saw a British soldier on guard. "Everyone was courteously welcomed." But it was at Banyo they were formally declared prisoners of war. Up to this moment their status had been undecided. The sisters were given a stone house with four rooms, one of which was immediately declared their chapel. "The priests were put up in a grass house, with openings at either end, where a door would easily fit. Inside one could see nothing.... Here we were given 3 days to recover our breath. Nurses looked after the sick well. Water and firewood were plentiful. Some of the British invited the sisters to come over for tea."

From Kamerun they made a long and complicated trek through Nigeria. The missionaries could not understand why such a route was taken through Nigeria. "Why not have left Kumbo and go South-West by Mamfe and on to the Cross River," they asked? They first trekked northwest to enter northeast Nigeria and then for hundreds of kilometers before being shipped in boats—first nine days down the Benue River, then eight days on the Niger River—finally completing the journey by train. At one place the locomotives halted on a "very long and shaky bridge." The train was taken apart, carried across on large ferries, and reassembled on the other side. They continued toward Lagos. There were incidents between missionaries and guards. Father Bintner from Luxembourg, a neutral country, complained that an angry officer accused him of hiding a gun under his cassock.

After more than two months of traveling, the prisoners reached Lagos on 26 January 1916. Arrangements were made for certain civilians, sisters, and other missionaries to be shipped to Europe. Meanwhile, Spain had agreed to the French and British military's request to accommodate some of the prisoners and refugees in large camps, just outside Santa Isabel on Fernando Po. Only three religious brothers were allowed to cross the sea to the island, as were the chaplains Zeus and Foxius of the Pallottine missionaries and from the Sacred Heart mission the priests Baumeister and Schuster.[55]

Basel Mission missionaries, like those of the Catholic Mission, were part of the great exodus of Germans from the colony. Along with others on 29 September 1914, the first of their unmarried missionaries were taken as prisoners from Douala to Dahomey. In time they were interned one by one. The Swiss were sent home.

As we have seen, in November 1914 the Allies took Victoria and soon after Buea. By the middle of 1915 they controlled the whole coastal area, with the exception of Ndogbea. Reverend Timothy Wittwer and his wife carried on at Ndogbea for another year, until November 1915. After that the only Basel missionary left in the colony was the Australian Reinhold Rohde. He was asked to live at Soppo with the American Baptist missionary Carl J. Bender.

One of the largest of Basel missions was in the grassfields, at Bali-Nyonga. The Germans held the grassfields until October 1915. When British troops reached Bali they were met by a messenger sent by Dr. Vielhauer of the Basel Mission and carrying a white flag. The next day the missionaries were taken prisoner and the German army abandoned Bamenda. Missionaries from many stations were gathered as prisoners in Fumbam. By 2 December the capital of the Bamum area was captured. Three days later, the missionaries at Fumbam were ordered to be taken out of Cameroon. By January 1916 the only remaining Basel missionary was Rev. Rohde at Soppo. In October 1917 he too was forced to leave Cameroon.

After heavy fighting, the British in the west were in sight of Yaoundé by 15 December. Although trenches were prepared, the Germans thought there was no point defending the town. It was possible that twenty years of work would be destroyed, with many casualties and no prospect that their position would improve. The British entered Yaoundé on 1 January 1916. The Germans had withdrawn. The first significant encounter on Beti land was a rearguard action on the Nyong River on 8 January 1916. The British commander wrote that "the retreating Germans returned all our prisoners of war, amongst them some British and French officers and civilians, native soldiers and a few non-combatants who had been taken by the Germans at various stages of the campaign. All had received fair and humane treatment during their capture."[56]

Governor Ebermaier and the Germans fled from Yaoundé over 125 miles to the border, and asylum. There was a fierce battle with Allied troops on the banks of the Nyong River in early 1916—and then they crossed to neutral territory.[57]

From the day that British and French forces took Douala and Bonaberi without a fight in September 1914 five companies of German troops had retreated into the interior. These German forces fought small engagements in Yaoundé and other areas and managed to hold out until the end of 1915. When Yaoundé fell they moved southwest into Spanish territory between 6 and 15 February 1916. In the northeast Maroua had been taken on 14 September 1914, and Garoua and Ngaoundere in June 1915. Other German troops had retreated to Mora Mountain and held out until February 1916. Finally all German forces either surrendered or retreated toward the border of Spanish Rio Muni.

Skolaster remembered those final weeks: "Towards the end of 1915 Cameroon's fate was sealed." The German troops had run out of ammunition. There was nothing left to do but withdraw into the neutral territory of Spanish Muni. The paramount chief of Yaoundé, Atangana, and 72 chiefs joined the retreating

With Major Friedrich Wilhelm Dominik and troops leaving Yaoundé. Possibly "for the last time, 4 February 1916." Permission Goethe-Institut, Frankfurt.

Germans. On 1 January 1916 Yaoundé was occupied by the Allies. Frs Traub and Baumann who had remained in the mission celebrated Mass on Sunday 2 January. Only a few Christians turned up. They were kept under guard in the club house until 25 January when they began their journey to the coast via Edea to Douala and finally to Fernando Po. The other missionaries who had withdrawn to Minlaba were taken prisoner on 19 January. They too were taken to Fernando Po. "When the war is over we'll come again," they told the people. Four missionaries accompanied the German troops across the border into Spanish territory: Fr. Skolaster was an army chaplain, Br. Rothkgel was a junior officer with the *Schutztruppe*, and Brothers Wohrmann and Junger were also in the army.

On 2 February 1916 the British arrived in Ngowayang and arrested the missionaries. There were five priests, two brothers, and three sisters. They were brought to Douala, arriving on 16 February. It first seemed that the British would agree to them remaining in Douala to work. But when Cameroon was reorganized on 1 April, Douala became a French territory and the missionaries, as French prisoners of war, were ordered to be transported to France. Two left with three sisters on 28 April aboard the *Europa* for Bordeaux and then to Saintes in France. Fathers Hoegn, Wachter, and Mayer, along with Brothers Eisner and Lumpp, left Douala on 5 May, stayed two months in Dahomey, and reached the camp at Saintes near the end of June 1916. The sisters were released in July and returned to Germany via Switzerland. The men remained prisoners of war until October 1918.[58] The last northern stronghold of the Germans surrendered on 18 February 1916, ending World War I in Cameroon.

In the next chapters we will learn that many of those who fled to Spanish territory with the German army were allowed to go from there to the island of Fernando Po. They joined others who had arrived earlier. Most would live out the war "interned" as guests of the Spanish government.

The island of Fernando Po had always interested the Germans. They had developed economic ties over the years, and the Spanish authorities were their supporters during the war. The Germans were using Fernando Po as a transmitting station for their warships scattered in the South Atlantic. The British also claimed to have evidence that the Spaniards were engaged in gun running for the Germans during the fighting in Kamerun.[59]

From the outset of the war, German forces in Kamerun were heavily outnumbered by the British, French, and Belgian troops attacking the colony—even after police units and German officials, farmers, employers, sailors, and traders were called up for military service with the protective troops. They were outnumbered by the Allies. In addition, the British naval blockade, begun immediately after the outbreak of the war, cut off almost all of Kamerun's supply lines.[60]

The Germans had economic ties with the island of Fernando Po before the war, and trade was largely in their hands. The Spanish authorities were also solidly pro-German. Even after the war in Kamerun was over, in 1916, the Spanish authorities continued to give assistance to the defeated Germans and their African soldiers who were on Fernando Po but who were allegedly training to reoccupy the Cameroon.

Although the fears of the Allied powers about subversion through Fernando Po did not happen, Fernando Po in the hands of a hostile power was a problem for the British authorities in Nigeria. Even a neutral Fernando Po during the World War I caused considerable anxiety in Nigeria.

The *Schutztruppe*, German nationals, and Cameroonians retreated into Spanish Rio Muni. Thousands of the refugees were sent back to Kamerun, but many joined the troops, and Germans and were eventually brought to Fernando Po. All Germans who did not have to stay with the troops to keep discipline were sent to Spain. On Palm Sunday, 16 April 1916, two transport ships, the *Isla de Paney* with 297 passengers and the *Cataluna* with 500 Germans on board, departed from Fernando Po. There was only room for four priests, four brothers, and two sisters on the first ships to Spain. A month later others followed. Father Zeus, Fr. Ruf, and three brothers were among those who remained on Fernando Po till the end of the war to look after the Christian refugees and the soldiers.[61]

The rapid expulsion of all German nationals at the very beginning of the war was to ensure that Germany was completely out of Africa. The presence of any missionaries and the thousands on Fernando Po was a threat to that plan. An organized force was ready to return when the war was over to reclaim their colony. The injustice and destruction caused by the expulsions were among the postwar grievances in Germany against the Allied powers.

Spanish territory, Rio Muni on the mainland, and the island of Fernando Po off the coast of Cameroon were mentioned already in connection with the beginning of the Baptist mission in Cameroon and the place where people escaping the war would pass through on the way to Europe or America.

The next chapter will tell how Spain came to colonial West Africa and the asylum Spain offered to retreating Germans and their retinue in the colony.

Chapter Three

Retreat to Spanish Territory and Transportation to Fernando Po

Notwithstanding the number of troops, British, French and Belgian, in the country it was impossible at this period to co-ordinate their movements, owing to the vastness of the area over which they were scattered and the impossibility of establishing any means of intercommunication between the various Commanders. Furthermore, it was difficult for me to pursue a very active policy, as it was necessary to maintain comparatively strong garrisons in the places already occupied.

—General Charles Dobell, 1916 [1]

With the last bullets in their pockets and pursued by a force six times their number, the Germans withdrew into Spanish territory. There they laid down their arms. Thousands of natives, most of them from Yaoundé country, under their paramount chief Atangana, with their women and children opted for the hard lot of exile. They accompanied their soldiers because they expected a German victory and the return of the Germans to the colony. Among the Cameroonians were leaders ranging from Fulani chief Adjia Lifida to the Christianized Ewondo leader Charles Atangana.

—Ibrahim Sundiata[2]

Retreat to Spanish Territory

German forces first began to cross into Spanish Rio Muni on 23 December 1915. The commander Karl Zimmermann ordered the remainder of the Germans in Kamerun to escape.

After occupying Yaoundé on 1 January 1916 Col. Georges ordered columns to pursue the Germans and cut off their retreat. They reached Koimaka on the Nyong River. On 8 January the Germans released prisoners, and on the 18th they evacuated Ebolowa and Okono-Linga. Governor Ebermaier and Commander Zimmermann crossed to Spanish Muni. Major Rammstadt held the

Governor Karl Ebermaier

Colonel Karl Zimmermann, commander of the *Schutztruppe*.

last parade in Kamerun on the birthday of Kaiser Wilhelm II on 27 January 1916. As a rearguard he left Kamerun on 7 February.

There were also two small French columns in the south trying to prevent their escape. One was moving from the coast and the other from French Congo. Ebolowa was taken by the French and Mafub by the British on 24 January. By the 28th, Belgian troops were in Yaoundé, the coast was in the hands of the Allies, and the last of the Germans continued to fall back to the frontier. On 19 February, the British made an official announcement that the conquest of Kamerun was complete. The governor general of Nigeria sent a telegram on the 18th to report that the German garrison at Mora in north Kamerun had finally surrendered.[3]

The Germans, outnumbered, almost out of ammunition, and pursued by Allied columns withdrew into Spanish territory. There they laid down their arms. There were thousands of Africans with their women and children, most of them from Yaoundé area and under the Ewondo paramount chief Charles Atangana. They accompanied the *Schutztruppe* because they expected a German victory in the war and the return of the Germans to the colony.[4]

Spain, the Island of Fernando Po, and Mainland Rio Muni.

Even before the annexation of Cameroon the Germans had an interest in the island of Fernando Po. The head of the Woermann Company wrote from Hamburg to one of their agents in early 1884.

> I am quite in agreement for you to establish more stations. As a result of the present situation the establishment of a German factory on Fer-

nando Po is wanted by the Government. The steamers would also have to call regularly at Fernando Po, and the connexion arranged through there with Cameroon. If you see any chance of doing business, I have nothing against establishing yourself there....[5]

European Presence in the Gulf of Guinea.

During voyages to the Gulf of Guinea in the early 1470s the Portuguese explorer Fernan Gomez da Minha discovered four volcanic islands. The farthest south was one later named Annoban. It became a foothold for the Portuguese in Africa even though it was uninhabited and only 17 sq km in area. To the northeast were two other uninhabited islands, São Tomé and Principe. And to the northeast of these was a larger island that was known to its inhabitants as Hedepette. A Portuguese navigator Fernao de Po called it Formosa Flora, that is, the "Beautiful Flower." In 1494 it was renamed Fernando Po. It was green with forests and populated by a small tribe later called the Bubi. These four islands along with Cameroon Mountain and the Adamawa Range on the nearby African mainland "form a chain of volcanos which stick like a dagger into the continent."[6]

A year after the voyage of Columbus in 1492 Pope Alexander VI decreed that all territories west of the Cape Verde Islands were to belong to Spain while all to the east were under Portugal. The following year, 1494, Spain and Portugal negotiated a treaty at Tordesillas in Spain extending the line 370 degrees west of the Cape Verde Islands. This allowed Portugal to claim all of the west coast of Africa and the Indian Ocean!

The island of Fernando Po, now called Bioko, is made up of three extinct volcanos. It has a coastline of 250 km and an area of 2,017 sq km. The highest point is Pico de Santa Isabel, rising to 3,007 m, where on a clear day one can see the Nigerian and Cameroon coasts. The second volcano is Moka Mountain. It was the home of the Bubi kings. There is a crater lake at 1,800 m. A broken-down crater rim is what remains of the third volcano, and it provides a deep water harbor on the northern end of the island.

Archaeological evidence suggests that the first inhabitants of the island began arriving from what is now Cameroon about 1,300 years ago. The Bubi are likely descendants of groups of Bantu who arrived at different times. Until well into the twentieth century the Bubi remained hostile and isolated, and this allowed others to take political and economic power over the island.

The Portuguese recognized the value of Fernando Po, especially of its strategic location, fertile soil, and sloping mountains. Almost any crop would grow. Oil palms, sugar cane, and cinchona grew wild. But the climate increased the dangers of sickness. Along with the eastern half on the coast of the Gulf of Guinea, the island has heavy rainfall, penetrating mists, and oppressive humidity.

Exploitation of Fernando Po by the Portuguese did not begin at once because of the climate, disease, the opposition of the local people, the Bubi, and the lack of technology to clear the dense forests. One persistent but unsuccessful colonizer was Luis Ramos de Esquival, who tried to settle colonists. He established a warehouse and a sugar cane plantation near what later became the town of Concepcion. It failed due to the irregularity of supplies reaching the settlement and the hostility of the Bubi. Settlers either died of hunger or were killed by the Bubi. Some went to the interior to live with the local people in order to survive. What did survive was the cultivation of coffee and the slave trade introduced by the Portuguese.

In 1642 the Dutch East India Company, without the consent of Portugal, established trading posts for their slaving along the West African coast. Six years later the Portuguese reappeared and replaced the Dutch with their own centers for the slave trade on Fernando Po, and another on the island of Corisco. Meanwhile, the Bubi protected themselves from slave traders by moving away from the coast and settling in the interior. This was especially under Chief Molambo, 1700–1760. Among the Bubi there was a succession of prominent chiefs: Chief Molambo was succeeded by Lorite, 1760–1810; Lopoa, 1810–1842; Mandabita, 1842–1860; Sepoko 1860–1875.

In October 1777 Spain and Portugal signed the Treaty of Ildefonso which gave Spain a list of territories and rights. Fernando Po was one of the territories. Six months later the Treaty of El Pardo of 1 March 1778 reaffirmed Spanish sovereignty over Fernando Po. It was followed by a Spanish expedition under Brigadier Felipe José, Count of Argelejos de Santos y Freire. Felipe José was sent from Montevideo in South America to take possession of Spain's new possessions and establish a base for slave trading. He arrived at Fernando Po on 21 October 1778 to claim the island for Spain. Three days later, the expedition sailed for Annobon. On the way Argelejos died and the crew mutinied. When the expedition was forced to stop at São Tomé, the Portuguese imprisoned the mutineers. What was left of the expedition finally returned to Montevideo on 12 February 1783. After five years, the loss of 124 of its 150 men, and the sight of the rest in irons, Spain took almost no interest in West Africa for half a century.

The demands of the Spanish possessions in the Western Hemisphere claimed most of Madrid's attention. Although the market for slaves was great in Spanish America, Spain's search for slaves was small when compared to other European nations. However, two trends were rapidly bringing the Spanish Empire to an end, the age of revolutionary ideas and a change in the very nature of imperialism.

The time for ships to sail the seas in search of slaves, gold, and silver had ended. The industrial revolution in England demanded raw materials to produce goods for a consumer society, not slave labor and luxury goods. The production of plantations and mines was becoming more important than the acquisition of slaves. The slave trade was ended by Britain in 1807 and by Spain north of the equator ten years later. The Spanish government decided that the real value of Fernando Po had disappeared.

Early in the nineteenth century, Spain had almost abandoned Fernando Po. The African population of Annobon and Fernando Po were so completely unaware of the Spanish claims that when representatives finally visited Annobon in 1836 they found that the Africans thought they were still subjects of Portugal.[7]

The British attempted to extend their influence to Fernando Po. In 1817 an agreement with Spain leased the island to Britain. The Royal Navy wanted to use its crater harbor as a base for the West African squadron, whose task it was to intercept slave ships attempting to run the British naval blockade. In 1821 a Capt. Kelly explored the eastern shore of the island. Kelly was the first to use the term "Bubi" for the local inhabitants. He started a settlement at Concepcion and chose the crater harbor at the northern end of the island as the site for the future naval base.

In the summer of 1825 some British merchants sent a petition to the Colonial Office in London asking permission to settle on the island. Portugal and Spain complained about the unhealthy climate of Sierra Leone as the seat of a commission to oversee the punishment of those who were caught trafficking in slaves. Britain suggested it be moved to Fernando Po. Discussions took place, but Spain soon understood that Britain was not interested in buying the island as they hoped. Although negotiations were still underway with Spain, in 1827 a Royal Navy officer, Capt. William Fitz-William Owen, started a settlement at Port Clarence, now Malabo, nicknamed "death's waiting room," because of the unhealthy climate. Owen had mapped most of the African coast and was known to be zealously against slavery. Within a few months, three-quarters of the members of the expedition had died. By July 1828, buildings were ready to accommodate the commission. But negotiations failed between Britain and Spain, and the commission did not move to the island as planned.

By 1835, 818 Africans who had been freed from slavery had landed on Fernando Po. After the British officially withdrew from the island in 1834, some of the liberated slaves remained behind rather than transfer to Freetown, Cape Coast, or Bathurst. Others continued to be brought by the Royal Navy after 1834. A commissioner was sent in 1838 to look into the condition of the liberated Africans who were under British protection and found that there were over a thousand.

Although the settlement was abandoned by the British, its Navy continued to visit. By 1836, the political vacuum on Fernando Po was filled by a company of British merchants. The group included the John Holt Co. and its representative James Lynslager. There was also Messrs. Dillon, Tennant and Co.

whose famous partner was John Beecroft. Beecroft was a mulatto civil servant. He had been superintendent of the Owen expedition and stayed on after the naval base was closed at Port Clarence. In 1839, the British government offered Spain 50,000 pounds for the two islands, Annobon and Fernando Po. Spain wanted 60,000. Negotiations failed over the price. Public opinion in Spain then changed in favor of keeping, not selling, their claims in Africa.

And then in March 1843, Juan José Lerena y Barry raised the Spanish flag at Port Clarence. Lerena appointed Beecroft as governor without pay. He then ordered that all the place names be changed from English to Spanish, set up the colony's first court, and ordered the recently arrived missionaries of the Jamaican branch of the British Baptist Missionary Society to leave. Lerena left Beecroft in charge and sailed to the mainland where he concluded treaties with several hundred chiefs. He then went on to Annobon to reaffirm Spanish control before returning to Spain.

In his years as governor of Fernando Po, Beecroft also served as consul of the Bight of Biafra and Benin for the British government. "His 21 years on the island are recorded in both London and Madrid with praise."[8] Between 1846 and 1857 the British continued to have influence over Fernando Po. This was due to a lack of support from Spain as no help was given to the governor and no Spanish warships visited.

The most lasting effects of British influence on Fernando Po are connected with the arrival of the freed slaves. The British navy settled them around Santa Isabel, San Carlos, and Concepcion. They were joined later by freed Angolan slaves who had been settled by the Portuguese on São Tomé and Annobon. Portuguese-African mulattos followed. And finally migrants started to arrive from Liberia, Sierra Leone, and Nigeria. Together all these people became known as *Fernandinos*.[9] They spoke Pidgin English and became a close-knit community of middlemen between Europeans and the Bubi and other African groups along the mainland coast. When Beecroft died in 1854 he was replaced by his assistant James Lynslager, a British trader of Dutch descent. He retired in 1858 to run his own trading company.

In 1856, Britain declared that the freed slaves taken by the Royal Navy and living on Fernando Po were not entitled to be considered British subjects. Rather, because Fernando Po was not a British possession, they were subjects of Spain. The freed slaves wanted to set up their own government to protect themselves against the unpredictable Governor James Lynslager. The news of this threatened rebellion forced Spain to send a governor from Spain. In May 1858 Madrid appointed the first truly Spanish governor of Fernando Po, Don Carlos Chacon. During his eight months as governor he proclaimed Catholicism the official religion and expelled the Baptist missionaries who had not obeyed the order to leave in 1844. He also improved access to the harbor, built some new roads, and took a census of the 858 inhabitants of Santa Isabel.

Chacon's proclamation that the Roman Catholic Church was the religion of the colony and that other denominations "would have to confine their worship within their own private houses or families" was unenforceable at first. It was only when the Baptists were asked to leave by the Madrid government that they did so. They had hoped that the presence of the British navy would enable them to remain. Support from Britain never came.

In a proclamation of 27 May 1858, Chacon wrote as "Commander, Her Catholic Majesty's Spanish Navy Squadron": "The religion of this colony . . . is that of the Roman Catholic Church, as the only one in the Kingdom of Spain. . . . Those who profess any other religion which be not the Catholic, shall confine their worship within their own private houses or families. . . ." Saker appealed the order, but his requests were denied. On 2 August the BMS in London issued a statement that the main object of Spain was the destruction of the Baptist mission on Fernando Po. One "can scarcely desire that the people should remain in a place where conscience is denied its rights, and freedom to worship God is refused. It may be perfectly practical to find on the opposite coast (Cameroon) some safe refuge, favorable alike to commerce and to freedom, from whence the word of life may extend to the interior of Africa. . . ."[10]

The Primitive Methodist Missionary Society also began to work on the island. They had missions and schools where until 1885 English was the only medium of instruction. They were forced to use Spanish by 1887 or close down.

Chacon was replaced by José de la Gandar. The new governor arrived with 166 soldiers and 128 Spanish settlers. After ten months, due to deaths and returnees to Spain, only 3 settlers and 60 soldiers remained. He himself left in 1862. Over the coming years Spain tried to populate the island with an assortment of people, including Cuban political prisoners, Spanish colonists from Morocco and Algeria, and Catalan traders. Most died or moved on to escape "the nightmare of disease which Santa Isabel had become."[11]

Cocoa became a major crop when a West Indian freeman named William Pratt sent for cacao seeds from the West Indies. Within a short time cocoa became the main economic crop of Fernando Po. Another version is that cocoa was introduced from Brazil to São Tomé in 1822 and in 1854 to Fernando Po. The Sierra Leonean settlers invested their profits from the palm oil trade into cocoa plantations. By the 1880s, one of them, William Allen Vivour, was Fernando Po's largest land owner.[12]

Sir Richard Burton was appointed consul to the Bight of Biafra in 1861. He avoided Santa Isabel as much as possible and is said to have had "no sympathy whatsoever" toward Africans. His writings about the inferiority of Africans have led one historian to call him "the man who saw everything and understood nothing."[13] He left in 1864.

Santa Isabel was expanding during this time, and there was a great demand for labor. Many Kru tribesmen from the mainland were recruited and worked under dishonest circumstances. They were hired as dockers, carriers, and sailors and also as plantation and construction workers. Their working conditions were very poor and became a scandal that continued for many years to come.

Santa Isabel was changing under Spain. Houses, shops, and gardens multiplied, and the island became a resting place for explorers, traders, and missionaries.[14] In 1870, Governor General Zoilo Sanchez Ocana suggested that healthier elevated areas should be used for settlement. A year later, Governor General José Montes de Oca established his residence at Basile, 8 km south of Santa Isabel at a height of 450 meters. Disease, combined with the removal of whites to Basile, meant that fewer amenities were found in Santa Isabel as it continued to expand. There was to be little improvement in the standards of health and sanitation in Santa Isabel.

The last two decades of the nineteenth century were years of great competition on the eastern shores of the Gulf of Guinea. The British, French, and Spanish were all involved in a race for territory, but the one who was ahead of the rest was Germany. In 1849 the Hamburg-based firm of Adolf Woermann sent agents to the Cameroon coast. The British were already in the Niger Delta so they moved along the coast from Mt. Cameroon to Gabon opening warehouses and expanding to the Portuguese and Spanish islands and inland rivers by the 1880s. Other firms followed, including Moritz, Kuderling and Jantzen and Thormalem. They sponsored missions and explorers such as Gustave Nachtigal in surveying and later claimed a territory for Germany that was to become Kamerun.

The Spanish were the least successful imperial power in equatorial Africa. If not for a few dedicated explorers and traders, they might have been excluded from the mainland entirely. Between 1862 and 1865 Governor General Pantaleon de la Torre Ayllon advised Madrid to occupy a section of the African coast. About the same time Madrid commissioned José Pellon y Rodriguez to inspect Fernando Po. Over fifteen years Pellon also explored the coasts of Nigeria, Cameroon, Gabon, and Rio Muni. He also urged Spain to pursue her claims, but no action took place. During these years there were great changes taking place in Spain, and there were problems with Latin America, especially Cuba. Some were also concerned about Spain's very presence in Africa.

In the early 1880s a society was formed, the *Sociedad de Africanistas y Colonialistas*, to exploit Spanish claims along the coast of Africa. A Basque adventurer, Manuel Iradier y Bulfy, had organized an expedition in 1875 that landed on Corisco Island in the Muni River estuary. The best organized of the Ndowe people living in the Muni estuary were the Benga. Under a nineteenth-century dynasty of three kings, each named Bonkoro, Christianity and a money economy were introduced.

Corisco Island is 29 km southwest of the Rio Muni estuary. Although only 14 sq km in area, it has been important since the fifteenth century. Slave traders from Portugal used it as a "slaving yard." In the late 1800s, the area of the estuary was overrun with trading companies. Riverbanks were dotted with the warehouses of British, French, German, and Catalan firms.

Iradier returned to Africa for a second expedition sponsored by the Africa Society. He was joined by José Montes de Oca and Dr. Amadeo Ossorio Zabala; they reached Santa Isabel in September 1884. From there they set out for the coast and signed hundreds of treaties, annexing 13,300 sq km in less than two months. Iradier fell sick and returned to Spain, but the others carried on until Montes de Oca also became ill. When Ossorio completed the trip, 50,000 sq km were claimed for Spain. Unfortunately, while they were traveling the coast, the representatives of fourteen nations were meeting in Berlin from 15 November 1884 to 20 February 1885. In the bargaining the Spanish delegation ended up with a large area, but had no access to the coast. It was not until 1901 that Spain and France discussed the issue. Finally 26,000 sq km were allotted to Spain. Borders were drawn up, with Spain's territory confined by the Rio Campo to the north and the Rio Utamboni to the south. The status of Rio Muni, as the enclave was now called, was changed in 1911 when Germany obtained 107,000 sq km of French Equatorial Africa in return for recognition of French dominance in Morocco. As a result, Rio Muni was surrounded by German Kamerun.[15] The German retreat of 1916 aimed to reach this Spanish territory.

While thousands of German soldiers and civilians crossed into Spanish territory seeking asylum, the Allies were negotiating with Spanish authorities on what was to become of their guests.

Governor D. Angel Barrera

An agreement was finally reached locally between the Allies and the governor general of the Spanish territory, Angel Barrera, on 3 February 1916. It addressed the future of the Germans who had retreated into Spanish territory. No mention was made of Cameroonians. The Allies understood that the Germans would be interned on Fernando Po and from there transported back to Europe. The agreement proposed:

- That all German male Europeans passing from the Cameroons into Spanish territory other than members of the religious bodies and medical profession should be interned by the Spanish authorities.
- All Spanish ships leaving Bata were to carry as many interned persons as their capacity would allow.
- As many Spanish ships as could be made available were to be utilized to expedite the evacuation of the interned Germans from Muni to Fernando Po and thence to Europe.
- The governor general of Fernando Po was to supply every Spanish ship pro-

ceeding from Fernando Po with a written guarantee signed by him to the effect that the vessel was carrying no contraband.

For their part the Allies agreed that they would not interfere with Spanish vessels between Rio Muni and Fernando Po. They would only stop them on their southward journey.[16]

Angel Barrera y Luyando was governor of Fernando Po on two occasions. His first tour was brief, from 20 September 1906 to 8 February 1907. He was again governor between 10 September 1910 and 8 February 1924. Under his administration colonization brought an increase in medical care and the development of infrastructure and some stability. But stability in colonial empires, and in Spanish Muni, was dependent on force. Repression and stability become interconnected.

D. Angel Barrera y Luyando, governor of Spanish Guinea.

Rio Muni was a territory of dense forests. It rose gradually from a narrow plain at the coast to hills rising from 1,000 meters to 1,200 meters in the east. The Fang people of the area were Bantu speakers from the Sanaga-Ntem area of Cameroon. They had probably moved toward the coast partly to eliminate middlemen in the trade with Europeans. They resisted the expansion of Spain into the interior.

Miquel Vilaroy Guell, in an article "Rio Muni en el contexto de la I Guerra Mundial," describes the problems Barrera faced along the border with Kamerun during World War I. They were most serious at the time the Germans were in retreat.[17] Barrera had to show a firm hand when trying to maintain Spanish neutrality during the war. He did this by the use of the Colonial Civil Guard to put down all resistance among the Fang people. Guell argues that the local people were unfairly and disproportionately punished. This contradicted the myth that Spain was the only colonial power in Black Africa that took control of their colony without the use of military force.

An example he uses concerns the village of Ayameken, north of Bata, where two Germans and five of their carriers were murdered and mutilated. In court on 2 July 1915, it was charged that five of the men who were accused were dressed in British army uniforms. One of them, Asam, was tried *in absentia*. He was accused of cutting off the hand and ear of the victims and wrapping them in banana leaves. Five of the carriers for the Germans were caught in the forest and shot. The judge ordered the execution of six of the accused, including N'Saban, the village head of Ayameken. The sentence was carried out before more than a thousand local people and the bodies hung in a tree for a few days as a warning.

The incident threatened the neutrality of Spain. The German consul charged that the British had paid the accused murderers while the British consul accused the Germans of smuggling weapons and ammunition across the Campo River into Kamerun. Nowhere in the trial is the issue clarified about the uniforms. Nor was the motive for cutting off and keeping the hands and ears of the Germans explained. The question about why some of the carriers were killed is not followed up either. Barrera admitted to the minister of state in Santa Isabel that he had a dual purpose in making a swift example of the accused. He wanted to prevent the colony from becoming involved in the European war and to ensure that such acts would not be repeated.

Mahon Murphy discusses this incident in his PhD dissertation. In January 1916, the British Foreign Office received a report from the Spanish Embassy in London about the discovery of the bodies of two Germans in Ayameken close to the Kamerun border. The German businessmen, Arms and Lehing, were first reported killed on 13 March 1915.[18] "When the grave was completely reopened, we found the bodies of two Europeans already considerably decomposed, with bush ropes around their necks . . . we could positively recognize Arms and Lehning, who were both known to us." Both ears and left hands were missing.

Governor Barrera investigated. According to a letter written by Governor Ebermaier to Berlin on 29 August 1914, Governor Barrera should have been rewarded for his help to Germany in Kamerun and then suggested that Spanish Guinea be absorbed into a larger German Kamerun. Ebermaier still hoped for a "Prussian decoration." The investigation cast doubts on whether the Ayameken people would kill in this manner. The report accused a party of five natives under the command of a British officer, Lt. Law. Law was in charge of a vessel harbored at Dipikar Island at the mouth of the Campo River. His task was to monitor Germans crossing from Kamerun into Rio Muni.

The two leaders of the accused were British levies by the names Undomingo and Makamendo. They were accused of having received orders from Law to follow the Germans into Spanish territory and seize documents they were supposed to be carrying. Lieutenant Law argued that he had not offered a reward to the five but had asked them to bring in any weapons, ammunition, and books and diaries they could capture. Law said that Undomingo had ambushed and shot the Germans and looted their possessions. A large amount of money was taken and divided. The money was recovered by Law and with the arms and ammunition sent to Fernando Po. Undomingo and Makamendo fled, and the others returned to Law with evidence—some ears—to prove they had killed the German and four carriers. The Arms and Lehning murders "fulfilled European preconceptions of colonial brutality."

But the punishment did not prevent a rebellion of the northern Fang groups between 16 August and 20 September 1916 along the border with Kamerun.

A leader of the rebellion was captured and questioned in Bata on why they rebelled. They were also attacking German caravans entering from Kamerun, no doubt part of the retreat as resistance in Kamerun collapsed. He claimed that others had instigated the rebellion and that they had been handed gunpowder by the British in order to attack the German internees in Rio Muni.

Barrera recovered a box in which stolen goods were stored and handed it over to the German consul in Santa Isabel. Among the loot were forty silver coins and three silver goblets. The governor was intent on maintaining his authority over the tribes living along the frontier. The context for this action in 1916 was the increasing movement of German refugees escaping from the German colony into Spanish territory. The Germans were also laying a telephone line between M'Bonda and Mikomesen. Along with the Germans there were large numbers of carriers unwilling to return to the war in Kamerun. The British and French claimed that all this movement was accompanied by armed German soldiers. This was something Barrera was unwilling to accept.

During the war France and Britain accused Spain of allowing Rio Muni to become the umbilical cord by which German Kamerun was supplied with food and arms. They also considered all of the white population of Kamerun to be part of the enemy army. Therefore, all European food arriving at Spanish ports was considered contraband. The Allies had declared a blockade of the coast on 24 April 1915, with the exception of Douala. Traffic between Cadiz in Spain and Santa Isabel, and especially to Bata, was subject to search and seizure of goods by Allied ships.

We know from the reports that for every soldier there were many civilians, first in Rio Muni, and afterward three of every four interned on Fernando Po. Many were not German soldiers but carriers. Pa Paul Neaka of Ashong in the grassfields told the author in 1984 that "there were only three German soldiers from this area (of Ashong). Others were carriers. The three were Mba Kuro, Mba Ngongew and a Bundji man. They all ended up at Fernando Po."[19]

ABC Reports from Spanish Territory and the Island Camps

José Vincent was a journalist for the Madrid daily newspaper *ABC*. The paper published articles sent by Vincent from the island of Fernando Po over the years 1916, 1917, and 1919. They described, according to an introduction, the activities of African soldiers in the German army and other "natives" of Cameroon during their internment for those years. The pamphlet does not reproduce the articles in full but gives the main points of each story.[20] In the summer of 1916, on 9 August, Vincent began to send his copy from the camps to Spain. The publisher was the conservative newspaper *ABC*. The reports told of the "situation in the colony." They were part of the effort to portray Germany in the best possible light as a colonial power in Kamerun and in her relationship to

Cameroonians. It was aimed at the postwar peace agreement negotiations. It was hoped that Germany would have her colonies restored. For Germany, by the end of the war, "colonization mattered as an end in itself."[21]

For William Roger Louis "the doctrine of Germany's 'colonial guilt' began at the outbreak of the war and was linked with events in Belgium: Huns could not be trusted with the sacred task of civilizing other peoples."[22] At the Paris Peace Conference claims were to be made on Germany's colonies not only by right of conquest but also in the interest of the indigenous people in the colonies. Propaganda like the *ABC* articles aimed to present Germany in a positive light as colonizers, using the story of the camps of Fernando Po as supporting evidence.

At the Kamerun–Rio Muni border the German forces surrendered their weapons and equipment to the Spanish Colonial Guard, which at that time numbered only 180 troops. Thousands arrived: civilians, soldiers, servants. How they were to be received and cared for was a big problem for Spanish authorities. Bata was a village of only 1,000 inhabitants. The refugees were to stay in the Bata area, with limited resources. Thousand were reported to have been sent back across the frontier and the rest settled on the beaches of Asonga near Bata. "One corner of paradise became a hell." There was no food. Hundreds died of starvation. Bodies were just buried.[23] There is no record, as yet, of a cemetery for Africans or of the one German soldier reported to have died there.

The last of the Germans and their retinue crossed the frontier between Kamerun and Rio Muni in February 1916. According to the official report of the governor of Fernando Po, D. Angel Barrera, more than 60,000 Africans followed the Germans. Due to the large numbers and lack of provisions, the Spanish authorities were forced to send back to Kamerun as quickly as possible nearly 40,000 of them. The rest, nearly 6,000 African soldiers, 12,000 women and children, in addition to 3,000 other Africans, were to find a welcome on Fernando Po. There they were to build towns, estates, roads, bridges and many other projects, and supply workers for the labor-starved plantations of the island.

Before leaving for Fernando Po the soldiers with their families stayed on the coast of Rio Muni south of Bata. Along with them were more than 100 tribal leaders of Cameroon with 1,500 family members and retainers. The Spanish administration at Bata gave the refugees land and asked the local people to provide them with whatever was needed. Within two months of their arrival at the coast, a place covered with virgin forest, they were able to set up temporary shelter, using local materials and primitive tools, which included huts, houses for the Europeans, and a hospital. Their encampments were surrounded by plantations.

The Allies wanted the governor to repatriate all the Cameroonians because they feared the soldiers might be reorganized and return to combat. Barrera decided that all German citizens, soldiers, their families and tribal leaders allied with the Germans be allowed to stay. International law permitted the German army troops to remain. The French and British threatened to take action. Rumors spread that Fang rebels, with the help of the Germans, were going to attack Bata. Finally an agreement was reached that allowed Germans and Cameroonians to go to Fernando Po and be kept away from the mainland.[24] By April 1916 the Spanish government, under pressure from the Allies, decided to transport the Germans and Cameroonians to Fernando Po. This took place over four months. By July 1916, all were transferred to the island.

The *New York Times* reported: "Madrid, February 13: The Governor of the Island of Fernando Po, West Africa, in a dispatch announces that 140 German officers have arrived at Santa Isabel from German Kamerun. They will be sent to Spain for internment by the next steamer calling at the island."[25]

The presence of so many troops off the coast of Cameroon made the British concerned about future trouble. The camps they would set up "could hardly be considered wartime internment." The troops were supervised by German officers and conducted military drills. The research of Jacqueline de Vries into German records showed that several large shipments of weapons were smuggled into Fernando Po and that preparations were made in 1916 to remobilize the African troops. The British wanted the Africans repatriated to the mainland quickly but this did not happen. As we have already seen, the Spanish authorities on Fernando Po were accused of pro-German sympathies, and clearly had an interest in keeping the troops on the island, hoping that the influx of Cameroonians would relieve the problem of labor shortages on cocoa plantations and boost the island's economy. It was reported that there were only about 100 Spanish officers and colonial officials on Fernando Po.[26]

Vincent reported that the first maize crop sown on the refugees' new farms before leaving mainland Rio Muni for Fernando Po was not very promising. The land was very poor near the sea. The harvest was ripening when the last Cameroonians left for the island. Each time a group departed on a small steamship, "the event was cheered by the local people since there were hundreds less to support." Only when most had gone was there enough food. Some Cameroonians hesitated to leave for Fernando Po because of the prospect of starvation, which had already taken the lives of many.

One Cameroonian leader at the coast was given special attention by Vincent. He was chief of the tribe of the "Ekaba," a man called Nanga Eboko, who with "an iron hand dominated with an almost absolute independence his great native land over the last decade." Eboko, he said, used the same iron hand in the settlements suddenly created in the bush at the coast near Bata. Eboko died there and "found eternal rest under the shadow of the mango trees by the seashore." There was a promise to maintain his "lonely tomb at the seashore" as a reminder of the many Cameroonians who followed the Germans into Rio Muni.[27]

Pallottine Missionaries from Kamerun awaiting passage to Europe on Fernando Po during World War I. Pallottine Archive, Limburg. And Las Missiones Catolicas: 3, 423, 20 Marzo 1915.

Expelled Pallottine Sisters in transit to Europe. The twelve are in white habits and were staying with Spanish nuns at Basilé, Fernando Po, December 1914. Archives of the Pallottine Missionary Sisters, Limburg.[28]

The Cameroon town of Nanga Eboko takes its name from this man. Today it is a town of approximately 20,000 people on the railway between Yaoundé and Ngaoundere. One story says that he was a strong warrior who married a Yekaba girl and settled with his father-in-law at the site of the current town. When the Germans came he sent his son to negotiate with them. Another account says he was a precolonial outcast of the area who agreed to work for the German Lt. Dominik, especially to violently suppress the anticolonial uprisings of the Maka. He went into exile during the war and died at Bata.[29]

There were various estimates of the number of Cameroonians and Germans taken to the Fernando Po. Governor Barrera calculated the number of refugees. According to his report, he immediately evacuated 16,000 Cameroonians. 5,000 to 6,000 were soldiers, along with thousands of carriers and their families. The French commander, Gen. Aymerich, wrote to Lugard in Nigeria that there were 6,000 Cameroonians as well as 5,000 German African soldiers, 83 German officers and N.C.O.s, 6 government officials, 5 doctors, and some invalids who were later to sail for Spain.[30]

"Under the leadership of the former governor of Cameroon, Karl Ebermaier, they virtually took over the island and started plans to rearm and retake Cameroon. Britain and France threatened to invade the colony if the King of Spain did not act. The problem was solved by shipping the European captives to Spain where, much to the annoyance of the British, they were kept in relative luxury and were allowed to communicate freely with Germany."[31] But this was not true of all of them.

The next chapter will describe life in the internment camps of Fernando Po until 1919.

CHAPTER FOUR

The Internment Camps on Fernando Po, 1916–1919

> *When they made the first roll call for Christians from their Adamawa mission, that is, the grassfields, only four turned up, along with a few catechumens. "So, that meant that from now on we had to start work afresh, if we wanted to make the best use of the precious time of internment, which had brought together people from all the tribes of Cameroon for the good of their immortal souls."*
> — "In the Prison Camp on Fernando Po," by Fr. C. Schuster[1]

The camps to be set up on Fernando Po were to be supervised by the Spanish but effectively run by the Germans under the governor of Kamerun, Karl Ebermaier, and German officers. They began at once to prepare camp sites, often in the bush, complete with schools, hospitals, offices, and workshops. The internment was not imprisonment. The people were free to move about and even engage in trade. At the same time, there was illness and often food shortages, especially during the first months.

Temporarily the internees were sent to three sites. One was at the hospital of Santa Isabel and the other two were in the barrio de las Caracolas of Santa Isabel. At the first opportunity the Germans among the internees were to be sent to Spain, leaving behind enough officials to run the camps, which would soon be set up away from Santa Isabel.

The Military Camps near Santa Isabel[2]

After arriving on the island in early 1916 the Kamerun troops found it even more difficult to survive than they did at the Bata coast. Because of the sudden influx of thousands of people, it was almost impossible to find fresh food locally. The plantations of the local people could not supply them. One of the small Spanish steamships that occasionally brought provisions to the east coast of the island could scarcely provide a meal for half the soldiers. After the rich diet of Kamerun, now they were forced to live on rice and codfish. There was even a shortage of these two staples. Starvation and disease, according to Vincent,

Map of the island of Fernando Po

claimed many victims, especially among the women and children. They also found themselves settled on swampy, unhealthy land. Island life was at first very difficult, and the internees were exhausted, hungry, and disillusioned. There was also a possibility that the Africans might revolt. The change came when the German embassy in Madrid agreed to pay for the care of the internees. After that, Spanish ships began to bring supplies, and more discipline was imposed.

The Spanish government handed over some land on both sides of Santa Isabel for the soldiers. The majority of them found lodging on the Moritz farm to the west of the town while the rest settled in the Puerte farm and some smaller places to the east. Moritz, a German company, let the soldiers use their cocoa farm. The soldiers were split up into twelve companies of five hundred men each. Two of the camps were set up in the Moritz farm opposite each other. The third was set up on the Puerte farm. Each company of Cameroon soldiers also had a retinue of seven hundred to eight hundred women and children.

The camps were officially under a Spanish commander, the chief of the Expeditionary Force Marines, with the help of German officers. A Spanish officer,

Photographs of the camps, in D. José Vincent, *Una Obra de Colonizacion Alemana en Fernando Po*, 1919.

a captain, was placed in charge of each area, along with two lieutenants and six sergeants.[3]

While the Germans devoted their energy to setting up the camps and restoring order, tension arose between the African soldiers and the local inhabitants. Many of the interned soldiers were single, and the complaint was that they tried to seduce wives of the local men. Venereal disease became a very serious health problem. One answer was found in a "rigorous discipline" imposed by the Spanish and the German officers. Sometimes they whipped disobedient soldiers and "even women and children." Disagreements arose between the German officers and the Spanish soldiers because the Spaniards saw that Governor Barrera relied more on the Germans than on them. There were efforts to improve relations, for example, by the use of a military band. The band, composed and directed by

African NCOs, was from German Kamerun and gave concerts in Santa Isabel. After the war the musicians handed over their instruments to members of the Spanish colonial guard before leaving the island.

The militarized camps alarmed the Allies. They feared that a reorganized force might return to Cameroon to fight again. The Allies repeatedly protested in Madrid. French and British diplomats accused Governor Barrera of allowing the Germans to control the camps and, with no evidence, of assisting the rebel Fang people on the mainland.

The presence of so many prisoners on Fernando Po was seen not only as a threat to the Allied effort in the Cameroons but also to Nigeria's security. Despite the blockade, the Spanish had still passed ammunition to the Germans in the interior during the fighting. It was also suspected that a possible Hausa rebellion in Nigeria was supported by the Germans. There was a suspicion that the German firm of Moritz and Co. on Fernando Po was using Hausa traders to carry messages to the mainland in support of a general uprising against the Allies in West Africa. The Allies were forced to increase the number of patrols along the coast of Fernando Po and the mainland. Small outposts from which the patrols could operate were set up between the port of Kribi and the Jabassi River. In addition, small groups of German soldiers were appearing along the coast and had to be driven off by landing troops. Because of a lack of concerted effort on the mainland of Kamerun the work of the navy became more important. Already short of staff, in February 1915 the British withdrew the warship *Challenger* for service in Europe, despite the protest of Gen. Dobell.[4] It was replaced by a smaller ship because the war in West Africa was considered a "side show" by many during World War I.[5]

Once there was food and building material, transportation to the camps by road became a problem. One solution was to go by sea, and for this local people built large canoes. Some of them could carry up to sixteen tons. They chose a small bay at the entrance of the colony of Bakoko as a port. Nearby, the interned Cameroon chiefs were building their own camp. Along the shore, huts were prepared for the canoes, along with warehouses, workshops, and quarters for the crews. At the same time a public square was created from which a person could easily reach the chiefs' farms. One could also travel by canoe to San Carlos. Fishing was started on a small scale. Near the port were the principal farms and the houses of the Germans, buildings for the administration, workshops, stables, and other buildings. The house of the assistant was found some distance from the center of the camp. The veterinary was at the center of everything with some rooms for visitors. It was a simple house, long and built on pillars, with a wide roof of palm thatch which shaded a verandah.

A captain, his assistant, and two sergeants were in charge of each camp, while the whole place was inspected by a commander. Each encampment had a sanitation service and a hospital, one for Europeans and another for the Cam-

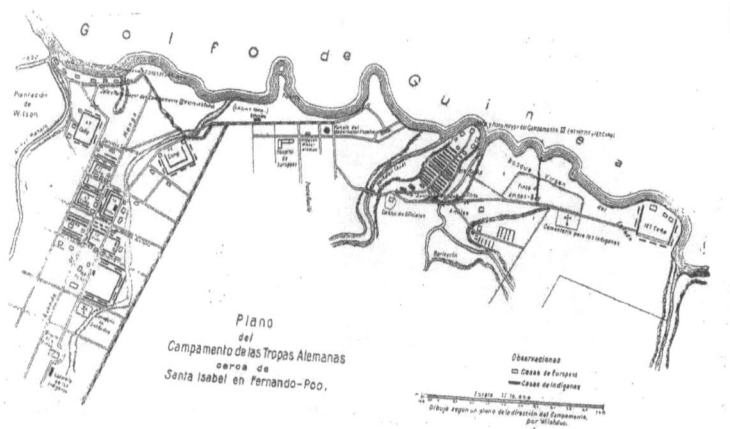

Plan of the camp near Santa Isabel. From Vincent, *Una Obra*.

eroonians. German civilians and some sergeants experienced in business were in charge of accounting, maintenance, and supplies.

Vincent's articles also described how, with the help of the Spanish governor general, people in the camps were able to cultivate the land. The soldiers remained in the camps, and most of the civilians not only cultivated the camp lands but "were sent to the interior of the island where they were put to work on labor-hungry plantations."[6]

The evacuation from Cameroon of so many Cameroonians along with the *Schutztruppe* in 1916 helped to solve the problem of labor on Fernando Po during the World War I. Ibrahim Sundiata writes: "Ironically the collapse of the Germans in World War I provided an unexpected benefit to the labor-starved planters of Spanish Guinea.... During the war the island was blockaded by the Allies, and plantation agriculture survived only through the fortuitous arrival of refugees from Cameroon."[7] But with the signing of the armistice at the end of the war the shortage of labor became acute again. Only later, after 1929, did workers come from the mainland, especially from French Cameroons and Gabon. After that source was blocked, they came from Liberia.

One cocoa plantation the soldiers were allotted "was in a neglected state ... uncultivated ... a wilderness. There was no road to the coast and paths in the rains were impassable. Much of the area was thick forest."

In the first six months the soldiers cleared more than one hundred hectares. After some time, there were "flourishing farms and a living area covering more than 500 hectares. In the center were the houses of 8 companies forming ordered towns. About 1 hectare was kept as a plaza for exercise. Next to it were the houses of the Europeans." Roads were constructed with a stone base. This enabled anyone to travel easily on foot or horseback. Long barracks were built for the soldiers

Overview of camp no. 3: From Hermann Harttmann, *Tribus*, Linden Museum, 2010. With permission.

in the first year, and in the second year they were reconstructed with larger rooms and terraces. Behind the barracks were open kitchens. The house of the camp director was built along the seashore along with a recreation hall of the officials. About 500 meters of shoreline were cleared and later turned into a garden.

To the east of the town of Santa Isabel was camp number 3. The land was mountainous and crossed by deep ravines. There were some farms, but they had been neglected. Further inland was a virgin forest. It was a much more difficult place than encampments 1 and 2. The soldiers began by bringing sand and stone from the seashore to build a usable path. Near the end of 1916 the soldiers' farms were extended in the west, almost to the city. After a year all the camps were connected by cultivated land where before there was forest.

All of this was done, according to Vincent, who aimed to portray the Germans in a very positive light, "because the soldiers had been trained well by the Germans and did everything in the 'German spirit.' Not only have they learned discipline and order, a sense of cleanliness and health," he wrote," but they are skilled in many kinds of manual work." There were carpenters, basket makers and carvers, masons and tailors, shoemakers and tanners. They were also able to eventually build the canoes that carried tons of goods to and from the port of Santa Isabel.

During the first weeks on the island some died as a result of wounds suffered during the fighting in Kamerun. Others died because of the unhealthy climate and poor accommodations on their arrival. Several soldiers along with women and children died. Vincent described the cemetery of the encampment being full of crosses.

The number who died in Muni and on the island is not clear. Another source says that due to poor hygiene, lack of food, and the worldwide flu epidemic of 1918 there were 1,031 deaths among the refugees.[8] The flu arrived on the island in May 1918 and killed many of them.

The shortage of food was acute in the first year because local farm production was inadequate. The camps also needed 45 tons of fish, 35 tons of oil, 15 tons of salt, 25,000 packets of tobacco, and 1,500 kilos of soap. It was very difficult to gather provisions because the steamship from Spain was not regular, and when it did come, at the beginning, it brought very little. The interned bought food at any price produced on the island or brought from the African coast and from small islands not far away. What could be gathered had to be carried by a small steamboat from the coast. Little by little supplies started to come by steamship from Spain with regularity. But one could never depend on this monthly delivery.

For this reason the encampments tried to build up a stock of provisions that would last for the months ahead. An office in Santa Isabel supervised the storage of supplies. It was under the direction of a German sergeant who had at his disposal each day hundreds of soldiers to carry the goods to the camps.

During the first year in Santa Isabel many soldiers could be seen moving about, four by four, carrying goods from the port to the provision office. Bags of rice and fish and boxes of other goods were carried on strong poles to storehouses. Provisions did not remain in storage very long. They were quickly distributed to the camps by the officers in charge generally twice a week. Sometimes there was even fresh food available at the office, including fish provided by a German fishing firm. Provisions were sold to the companies of soldiers in the encampments at cost. Like the Germans, many soldiers raised chickens, and some were breeding pigs. Next to the provision office near the exit from the city and in the direction of encampments 1 and 2 was the German hospital. It was built with wood and covered with tin plate. The hospital was supposed to be directed by a German military doctor.

In the same encampments there were several permanent buildings for health care. They formed small settlements and contained rooms for the sick men and others for those who came for treatment. There were also rooms for European and African personnel, kitchens, pantries, morgues, and toilets. With the exception of the main building in encampment number 3, which was an old cocoa store, all the others were constructed of the same materials and in the same style as the soldiers' encampments.

The chief doctor was assisted by white helpers and some twenty black nurses and sanitary workers. John Fomukong of Bali was one of the nurses. His story in the words of his son is in the Appendix. He was one of those who had been trained in Europe before the war.[9]

Each day the medical staff examined and treated all the troops who asked to be seen. All the seriously ill, like those who needed surgery, were transferred to the native hospital, which was near an exit of the encampment. The main hospital was built under the direction of a German carpenter and was covered with tin plate. It had a ward for internal sickness, another for external, and an operating room with a cement floor. A doctor, two European assistants, and twelve Africans helped to care for on average about one hundred sick people; there was at least one operation each day.

Military band on parade. Hermann Harttmann Collection. © Linden Museum, Stuttgart.

There was enough medicine with the German army when the internees arrived on the island. Sick people also received nutritious food for their illnesses, according to the doctor's orders, like fresh meat, fish, milk, sugar, and fresh vegetables. Good hygiene was strictly followed, as it was in Kamerun. The housing was clean, drinking water was brought in, and toilets were inspected constantly. Vincent insisted in his description of the camps that everything possible was done to control the mosquitoes and plague.

Many of the young men had received very little military training. Once the hard work of the first weeks was over they began to be drilled without guns. This was done with the agreement of the Spanish government. Some were also instructed in playing drums and flutes, and together with some other musicians they put together a band like the one they had in Cameroon. This band, under the direction of an old African soldier, was very popular.[10]

Along with Karl Atangana of the Beti, there were many other Cameroon leaders on Fernando Po. They were allotted a place to settle together.

The Colony of the Chiefs at Little Bokoko

The tribal leaders of Cameroon with their followers, after being transferred to Fernando Po, were assigned to an old cocoa farm on the west coast of the island and about two hours from the San Carlos seaport. It was called Little Bokoko.

Vincent boasts, "What has been done there illustrates more brilliantly the German genius for education than the work done in construction of the soldiers camps. The blacks here worked almost without direction."

Governor Barrera set up a military post, which he entrusted to the Cameroonians, at Little Bokoko. But because they did not speak Spanish, communication between the head of the Spanish post and the chiefs was very difficult. Two white Germans helped with the guard to keep away outsiders. They, of

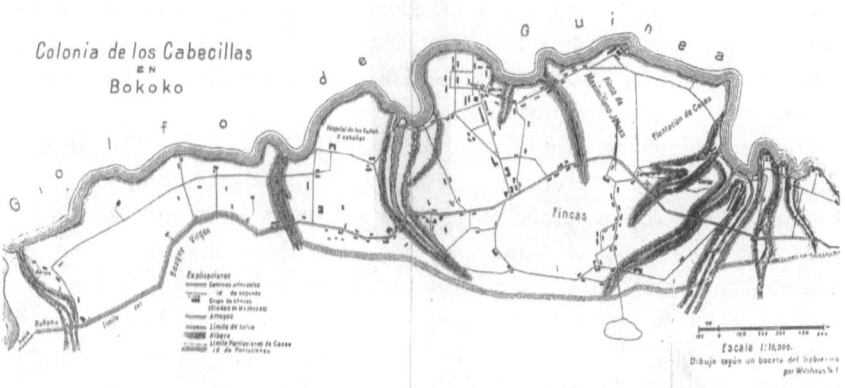

Camp of the chiefs from Kamerun: From Vincent, *Una Obra*.

course, could not be everywhere, and so the chiefs and their people were often left to themselves.

When the chiefs arrived in Little Bokoko there was only a hut of corrugated metal to show that people had once lived there. The farm was extended and two hectares cleared. A house and a road were built to the west of the town of Big Bokoko, a distance of two hours. The road ran along the coast about 500 meters from the sea for 16 km. The work was done in three months. It was "a testimony to the extraordinary zeal of the workers." The road had a width of 5 meters and was passable at all times by people on foot, on horseback, bicycles, and in light cars.

They crossed ravines with beech-tree bridges up to a height of 5 meters. The deeper ones were crossed with stairs and wooden dikes. Once the road was built the men began to settle on both sides of it to the west. The forests supplied the wood for construction. In the course of six months farms were extended from 200 to 600 hectares. "Small towns were built and inhabited by the different tribes and with different types of housing according to their customs." Vincent mentions the "Bane" and the "Bambellas." The farms were so productive that the "town of the chief of the Esum, called Evini Ngoa, almost disappeared inside fields of makako." The grain fields of the people were also impressive.

The best view of the colony was from the canoe of chief Atangana as it moved along the coast from Santa Isabel, a trip that took three hours. All along the main road there were paths in every direction for goods to be carried into the farms. In each town there was a sign that gave the name of the chief and the tribe.

The land was divided into three parts by two deep ravines that ran to the sea. The larger and closer part to San Carlos was occupied by the Jaundes, united under the paramount chief, Atangana. The big town had long houses made of bark on both sides of the main street leading to a meeting house. The small towns had farms that looked like gardens. And finally there were the farms of the tribal chiefs of lesser importance. Crossing over a ravine bridge, one came to another encampment that had a variety of houses. The houses of the chiefs were built on piles and had wooden roofs and ornaments that showed the influence of the northwest grassfields of Kamerun.

The third part of the camp was occupied by Muslims—Fulbes, Hausas, Konuris, and Lakas from the north of Kamerun. During their internment on the island they elected a common chief in the person of Adjia Lifida of Ngaundere. Of all the soldiers of Cameroon they were the last ones to find rest. For one month they had to live a poor existence near Big Bokoko. They worked hard to clear a virgin forest. The wide fields reminded them of their land to the north. At the far end of the camp, on the coast, was the Adjin farm, with its tall wooden houses and separate places for women and servants.

According to Vincent, almost everything was done by the Africans. There had only two Europeans to help them; a German veterinary officer and an agricultural assistant. They saw to the feeding, listened to complaints, and fixed everything that it was possible to repair. The two Germans lived in a house on the coast at the entrance of the colony. It was five minutes from there to the main road that ran from San Carlos along the coast and some hundreds of meters from the sea. Although there was a road to San Carlos, in the first months everything was brought by water.

There was a tower in the principal farm where drums called the chiefs to receive their assignments from the Spanish authorities. There was also a store where all the food and tools needed for working in the forest could be purchased at cost price and a monthly market that also had cobblers, tailors, carpenters and basket-makers.

The African clerks had a town of their own near the principal farm. There was a hospital of four buildings, with room for more than sixty sick patients. Everyone had to be vaccinated against smallpox, and the veterinary officer was at the same time the doctor of the colony.

Among all the Africans, the one who helped the most was Karl Atangana, the paramount chief of the Jaundes. He was very important in Kamerun and in postwar French Camerouns. Atangana was an educated Catholic who knew how to read and write, and he spoke several languages. He had his house in the middle of the colony, many farms, sheep, and a fishing business. Atangana's farm and other farms were at the center of the native camp, where a church and school had also been built.

The political organization of the Beti, a rainforest tribe of approximately 500,000 around Yaoundé, was made up of several thousand self-ruled lineage groups, each ruled by a headman, independent of other Beti groups. The Germans made contact in 1887 through two military explorers, Kund and Tappenveck, after a twenty-two-day march from the coast. The hilly area that would become the city of Yaoundé was from the word Ewondo, the name of the Beti of the region.[11]

According to Frederick Quinn, perhaps the most important event in local colonial history was the sending of a group of young men to the coast to be educated in mission schools. They returned as interpreters, clerks, and eventually soldiers, and were needed as agents to collect taxes and arrange for workers.[12] The most notable of these young men was Karl Atangana. Atangana's birth name was Ntsama. He was the eleventh of twelve sons of an Ewondo headman and therefore far removed in the line of succession. At Kribi, he studied at a school of the Pallottine Fathers and was a houseboy at the mission. There he met Bishop Heinrich Vieter, leader of the first Catholic missionaries who arrived, on 25 October 1890. Atangana studied German, history, geography, math, and took religious instruction. He was the first Ewondo to be baptized. When he returned to Yaoundé, he became an interpreter and eventually chief African auxiliary of the station commander, Maj. Hans Dominik. In 1911 he was sent to the *Kolonial Institute* in Hamburg, where he collaborated with Dr. Martin Heepe on an important two-volume collection of Beti folklore, history, and linguistics. In 1914 he returned to Kamerun and was named paramount chief of the Beti by the Germans.

After the fall of Douala, Yaoundé became the provisional capital of the colony. When it was taken by the Allies, Atangana, with seventy-two Beti chiefs and several thousand Beti people, accompanied Governor Ebermaier in the retreat across the frontier into Spanish Muni. The Beti leaders were among those who did not believe the Germans would lose the colony. They were convinced that they would return after the war ended. They were also reluctant to abandon the Germans in the exodus through the rainforest.

Atangana and his associates encouraged potential rivals to join them and left their own relatives in charge at home. This was to ensure that power would be returned to them when the war was over. In February 1916, along with Gov. Ebermaier and Col. Zimmermann, the commander of the German troops, they crossed the frontier into Spanish territory.

In 1918 Atangana left Fernando Po and traveled to Spain with six Beti chiefs. The trip was sponsored by the German government. Their purpose was to await the end of the war and a settlement, when it was hoped the Germans would return to Cameroon. It was also to collect one million to one and one-half-million German marks, which fifty Beti chiefs and notables had banked with the Basel Mission. While in Madrid they stayed at the Hotel Aurora and were given spending money. They were in Madrid for two years and one month in Barcelona. The German embassy arranged for them to be paid their savings in Spanish pesetas, which were later changed to French francs, as their home area was under a French mandate.

The group met four times with King Alfonso XIII and asked that he intercede on their behalf at the Versailles peace talks for a German Kamerun. Twice they were dinner guests of the royal family. They also met with the foreign minister. While in Europe they observed, studied, and discussed what they saw and heard, planning to bring new ideas back to Cameroon. Max Abe Foudda, an eyewitness, told Quinn during an interview that they had talked and talked about what they saw and asked how they could bring these things back to their country. In the meantime their people and families remained on Fernando Po.

In a report from the governor to the ministry of state in Spain, Governor Barrera included a census of the camps, dated 19 December 1916. There were 5,649 soldiers, 4,341 women, 967 young men, 292 boys, and 525 children. At that time, 1916, he lists 29 deaths and 124 births.[13]

Evangelization and Schooling in the Camps.

While on the island religious services and schooling continued for some internees. The primary sources are from first-hand reports in German Catholic Mission magazines. Father C. Schuster wrote in a German mission magazine about his experiences during the internment. He called the piece "In the Prison Camp on Fernando Po." His article, letters, and other information about the camps are found in Huppertz's book on the Sacred Heart Missionaries.[14]

Spanish and German missionaries looked after the spiritual welfare of the internees and also helped to treat the sick. One of the missionaries was Fr. Schuster, a Sacred Heart missionary. He wrote to his superiors that "14,000 indigenous people and 900 Germans" from Cameroon had accompanied the troops into Spanish Guinea. Many had followed Chief Atangana and taken wives and children with them, "believing in the German's ultimate victory, once their exile was over. Two thousand seven hundred settled a little way from Santa Isabel, in Little Bioko or San Carlos, where many perished because of the bad climate," he said.

As soon as all the people were settled on Fernando Po, the parish priests of Santa Isabel, Spanish Claretian missionaries, allowed the Sacred Heart missionaries to rent one of the parish houses for 107 pesetas a month. In that rented house the seven missionaries "lived an impoverished community life.... In addition to the daily masses and prayers most of their day was taken up by a strict routine of three visiting rounds to attend to the sick and dying."[15]

The Catholic bishop of the island was also a Claretian missionary. Pedro Armengol Coll was born in Catalonia, Spain, on 11 January 1859. When he died on 21 April 1918, at fifty-nine years of age, he had worked twenty-five years in the Spanish Guinea mission. The *Catholic Encyclopedia* noted that among the important events of his time in office two stood out. One was the dedication of the cathedral in Santa Isabel on 23 January 1916. The other event was the "internment of 20,000 people both Europeans and natives coming from German Kamerun."[16]

His successor in 1919 was Nicholas Gonzalez, the vicar apostolic of Santa Isabel. It was Gonzales who wrote to Propaganda Fide on 15 October 1919 praising the extraordinary courage of the four priests and the "harvest" of 3,516 baptisms, 5,064 registered catechumens, and, for 1919 alone, 54,786 communions.[17]

In 1920 a letter reached Europe that postwar missionaries met two hundred Christians at Kumbo and other places in the grassfields. The letter explained that these men and women had spent time on Fernando Po during the war. The missionaries interned on the island; Frs. Schuster, Foxius, and Baumeister, together with Pallottine missionaries, while doing their medical work, spent their free time evangelizing the Africans of the *Schutztruppe*. "Our own father undertook the Christian teaching of all the Africans from the grassfields and highlands of Inner Kamerun. They were able to baptize over 900, and over 1,500 grassfielders were, for a long time, exposed to their doctrinal teaching."[18]

If it had not been for the sudden repatriation of the internees in 1919 many more catechumens would have been baptized. Among them were the soldiers, the soldier's wives, porters, and messengers whose instruction was then suddenly interrupted. The baptized Cameroonians and catechumens who returned home were to be the guides for the new missionaries who came after the war. They showed their baptismal certificates to the missionaries and asked for a blessing. Banso had provided many military carriers, and of these over eight hundred were reported to have been baptized before they left the internment camps.

Like Vincent in his *ABC* article, Schuster estimates the number of internees, where they lived, and other details about their care. He writes that together with the native soldiers there might have been up to 20,000 people who went to the Spanish island, with most of them settled in three big camps near the capital, Santa Isabel. He thought that about 2,700 Yaoundés were allowed to settle in Small-Bokoko near San Carlos in the southwest of the island.

The pastoral care of the Cameroonians was in the hands of Frs. Zeus and Ruf and two Sacred Heart Fathers, Schuster and Baumeister. They remained in Fernando Po when the other Germans left for Spain. The two Sacred Heart Fathers taught their people in Pidgin English and the two Pallottine Fathers taught theirs in Ewondo. In this way everyone was cared for.

How interested were the Cameroonians in Christianity? It was significant that missionaries Zeus and Ruf were able to baptize 2,708 people within three years, and that over and above there were still about 3,000 baptisms in danger of death. When toward the middle and end of 1919 the Cameroonians returned to their country there were about 4,000 catechumens among them.

There is little information about the work of the other Christian communities. But one report, from Primitive Methodist missionary Rev. George E. Wiles to the Quarterly Missionary Committee, at the end of 1916, indicates that they had organized services each Sunday morning. They conducted an early morning service for the Cameroon soldiers and their wives. It was some-

School in the *Schutztruppe* headquarters. Harttmann Collection. © Linden Museum.

School of the 4th Company, Santa Isabel. Harttmann Collection. © Linden Museum.

times disrupted when Allied gunboats visited the island, Wiles wrote. At the service in mid-December 1916, there was an attendance of 236. "These people greatly appreciate these services and it is a joy to be able to help them in this state. On their own suggestion an offering was taken last Sunday which they handed over to me for our Church Funds."[19] Like their Protestant counterparts Spanish Claretian missionaries provided religious services for the interned Catholics. At the same time German missionaries continued to evangelize the Cameroonians in the camps.

For those who wanted an education there was a school with sixty students under the direction of an African teacher, a Cameroon native.[20] The school functioned just as the German schools in Kamerun had. Atangana himself organized a special course for the Cameroonians who already knew how to write. Some three hundred people took part in it.[21]

Kamerun refugees in Alcala de Henares, Spain, Spring 1916. In Sergio del Molino, *Soldados en el Jardin de La Paz,* 2009, p. 101. Standing: "Nsango," a servant of Paul Bieger, second from the left. From the personal archive of Pablo Bieger.

Father Lennartz also described how some missionaries had been captured by the British and were taken through Nigeria and then to Fernando Po where they found passage to Spain in the summer of 1916. Others, including Lennartz and Sisters of Divine Providence, returned to Europe via Nigeria and London. Some missionaries were listed as soldiers in the German army or as medics. They crossed into Rio Muni with the colonial troops and were then transported to Fernando Po, "Here we wanted to wait for an end to the fighting and then return with our good blacks to the mainland."[22]

In the early days of the war an order came from Madrid that all German Europeans who had come from the mainland were to be shipped back to Europe and interned in the Pyrenees. At first the missionaries among the prisoners managed to get a decision from the French government and Gen. Aymerich that "missionaries, priests as well as brothers, were not prisoners of war."

But then on 3 July 1916 a notice came from the Spanish government that all of them were to be shipped back to Europe. The missionaries complained to Governor General Barrera that they hoped to stay on Fernando Po. He finally gave permission for some of them to remain for the sake of the Catholics among the troops. Three missionaries of the Sacred Heart, Frs. Baumeister and Schuster and Br. Vincent, along with Frs. Zeus and Ruf and two brothers of the Pallottine Missionaries, were allowed to stay.

Although they had permission to remain on Fernando Po, the Sacred Heart Missionaries did not have enough money to take care of themselves. The Pallottines could manage with funds they took when leaving their missions in Kamerun, but the Sacred Heart Missionaries had only 4,500 marks left. The Mission Procure of the Spanish Claretians could not help because it was impossible to send money from Germany during the war. But a golden opportunity to provide for themselves was offered to the missionaries. Among the soldiers there was a lack of medical staff because most Europeans had been sent to Europe. Even the medical officer in charge, Dr. Schonigh, was forced to return to Europe because of a serious health problem. "The military doctor, Dr. Ekert, at that time chief medical officer of the interned troops, as well as Raumstedt, the acting commander, offered them work 'to fill the gaps' in health care."[23] And so they signed contracts with the government agreeing that in no way was their work to interfere with their missionary efforts. Father Baumeister and Br. Vincent became nurses in the sick bays of camps 2 and 3 while Schuster eventually replaced Dr. Schonigh as chief medical officer.

Once the three were assured of their livelihood they gave the money they had to the missionaries leaving for Europe. "With wishes that we would see each other again in Cameroon soon, they left hospitable Fernando Poo a few days later. They had no idea that they would remain on the island until Nov. 1919."

There had been serious discussions in Madrid about transporting the *internados alemanes* to Spain, where they promised to remain until the end of the war. In the spring of 1916 hundreds of Germans accompanied by African servants left Fernando Po for Cadiz. The ship *Cataluña e Isla Panay*, escorted by the cruiser *Extremadura*, reached Cadiz on 5 May. One report lists 856 refugees, including Gov. Ebermaier, Col. Zimmermann, and the ethnologist Gunter Tessmann. There were 244 active military, women and children, and other colonists. Another list had the names of many others, including Atangana of the Beti. (This conflicts with a report that Atangana left Fernando Po at a later date.) From Cadiz the first train arrived in Madrid on 6 May. It carried 124 in first, 209 in second, and 69 in third class, perhaps indicating the number of Cameroonians among them. A second train carried Col. Zimmermann and up to 800 others. Despite the neutrality of Spain, news reports described an enthusiastic welcome for the refugees on the railway station platforms and in the cities where they were settled. People sang the German national anthem, gave them gifts of flowers and food, and wore broches with the flags of Spain and Germany on them. The problem of what to do with Germans and some Cameroonians arriving in Spain was solved by sending most of them to cities like Zaragoza, Alcala de Henares, or Pamplona. Some of these German internees decided to remain in Spain after the war, and their descendants remain there today.[24]

Back on the island of Fernando Po the missionaries found a place to rent in Santa Isabel. The rents were very high, but the Spanish mission let them have a small private house for 107 pesetas. This enabled them to live together as a small community. If they lived in the camps, community life would not be possible because they were too far apart.

When they made the first roll call for Christians from their Adamawa mission, that is, the grassfields, only four turned up, along with a few catechumens. Most of the internees from the south of Kamerun and the coastal areas were cared for by the Pallottine Missionaries and taught in Duala and Yaoundé languages. The Sacred Heart Missionaries accepted all those who spoke neither language whether they were from their Kamerun mission area or not. So there were some who were from their mission and others from Nigeria, Liberia, and other places in West Africa.

They began their mission with about thirty catechumens who came to "doctrine" at least twice a week. "But the number of catechumens increased only slowly, very slowly, so much so that one would be tempted to believe that these people from the Grassland with their hard heads had no time, not the least time, for the Catholic religion." So they devoted much time to the dying and children. They thought they might have some helpers in heaven to bless their work, and this proved to be true.

In 1916 they baptized only 20 who were in danger of dying without baptism. This did not include the baptisms among the Yaoundé people. It was on 31 December 1916 that the first 5 catechumens who had started doctrine in Kamerun were baptized. They began 1917 with a community of 8 Christians and 53 male and 17 female catechumens. The 8 baptized received confirmation on 29 January 1917 from Mgr. Pedro Armengol Coll y Armengol, the vicar apostolic of Fernando Po.

The "hearts of the Grasslanders became warmer. God's grace was at work.... Over time the old stubborn fellows . . . bent their necks and came more and more to doctrine classes." At the end of June 1917 there were 43 Christians and 142 male and 33 female catechumens. A year and a half later, at the end of December 1918, there were 81 Christians and 786 male and 203 female catechumens.

At first the missionaries were using two local churches in Santa Isabel. Soon they became inadequate for the Sacred Heart Missionaries and the Pallottines, and so it was decided to build two "bush churches" in the camps. It also suited the army officers since they did not like to see their soldiers going into town.

There was also competition, a common experience at the time, with the Protestant church, represented by the Basel Mission and the American Baptists, and also with the Muslims. This is an important topic, but little information was found about the activity of other Christian missionaries other than the Catholics.

Sacred Heart missionaries were constantly busy not only with their hospital jobs but with helping the Pallottines to care for Yaoundé Christians "because the numbers of the Yaoundé Christians went into the thousands."

Schuster reproduced a timetable for a normal working day.

4:45	Rise, morning prayers, meditation
5:45	Holy Mass
6:20	Breakfast and going over to the camp
7:00	Visit to 70–80 patients, who stay in the sick-bays because they are confined to their beds; after that treatment of mobile patients, 250–300 daily; a second visit to those in bed; and lastly small surgeries as far as necessary
12:00, but often 1:00 or even 2:00 o'clock	Walk back to town; lunch
1:30	Doctrine for women and children
3:30	Third visit to the patients
6:00	Doctrine for the soldiers
7:30	Walk back to town. On the way still a short visit to serious patients if necessary; supper, rosary, breviary, written work

"All of the morning period was therefore dedicated to the care of the sick; the afternoon and the evening were for missionary work. Besides the regular doctrine we still had to give some special hours of instructions for baptism etc." Not every day was the same, and of course weekends were different. For example, Saturdays and Sundays, Schuster and the Pallottiner, Zeus, cared for camps 1 and 2, while Ruf looked after camp 3.

Father Zeus began on Friday afternoon with confessions, and that night he would sleep in a small bush house next to the church. At 4 am confessions continued. As soon as Schuster finished his hospital duties he would help with confessions until deep into the night. They both stayed in the camp Saturday night and started hearing confessions early Sunday until Mass at 6 am. There was a homily for the Grasslanders and then a Mass for the people from Yaoundé. Every Sunday, they had 800 to 1,000 communions. Because there was no tabernacle they devised a way to distribute communion between Masses and then consecrate enough hosts again at the second Mass.

Zeus spent the rest of the morning with the children while Schuster attended to his clinic. At 2 pm they taught doctrine, followed by singing practice till 4 pm, which was the time for "visits to patients, examinations for Baptism and settling quarrels." At 7 pm Schuster would go back to town.

The editor of the *Sacred Heart Mission Magazine* wrote in 1918 that Schuster, Baumeister, and Br. Vincent were still in exile on the island of Fernando Po. Very few of their letters reached Germany, but one did come from Fr. Baumeister. Writing on 17 September 1917, he explained that despite a bout of dysentery he and the others were well. The last letter was from Schuster on 21 January 1918. Their workload was increasing. Their first duty was to the colonial troops to which they had been posted as medics since the beginning of the war. "One should keep in mind that we are talking here of an army of 5,000 black soldiers with wives and children, of the numerous domestic servants and cooks of the Europeans, as well as several Yaoundé chiefs with their numerous families; altogether they would form a town of 14,000 to 15,000 inhabitants." Because of the bad climate there are always patients.

The article described again how the missionaries ministered to the Africans. By September 1917 they had more than 800 catechumens because all those who did not understand the Yaoundé language came to them. By 10 January 1918 they reported more than 1,000 catechumens. They had two bush churches and the Basel Mission and American Baptists each had one. The total number of catechumens for the Catholics, including the two Pallottine missionaries, was over 5,000. "We do not know where to find a roof for all those so keen on their salvation."

Since the island was under a sea blockade the missionaries received little help from home. They had a vegetable garden and kept a few animals; a young frutambu antelope, a few chickens, and young ducks. Both Baumeister and Schuster continued to hope that their work in the camps would bear fruit one day when their Christians and catechumens from the northern tribes became pioneer witnesses to the gospel in their home villages. The missionaries were all longing for the day when they could return to the Cameroon and make a fresh start.

Father Zicke reported at the end of 1917 that they were living well in the house they rented. It was at a pilgrimage shrine. He and the other priests were in demand to help with confessions, sermons, and liturgy on Sundays and feast days.

Cameroonians

We already met one Cameroonian, Peter Vewesse of Babanki Tungo, in the introduction and elsewhere. He was one of those who stayed on Fernando Po.[25] He remembered two German fathers at Fernando Po who used to look out for all the soldiers. "In May 1917 I was baptized and Cellilous was too." He remembered the doctor was a tall German whose name he had forgotten. "He had no wife."

> We were at Fernando Po with Chief Charles Atangana. At Fernando Po he was chief of a certain part of the people only. Four companies used to attend one church. There was a lot of food there. They used to bring rice in a ship. They used to bring food every Wednesday and Saturday. It was the government that bought the food. The country people were called "Bubi." They stayed in their cocoa farms and never came to the camps. There were Spanish priests and there was a big church. It was a Spanish bishop who gave me confirmation. There were many soldiers who took baptism including "boy-boys" [servants] who were there. We were taught doctrine in "Bush English." . . .

Matthew Fobang of Bali-Nyonga had been a soldier traveling to many places and rising to corporal. His son Daniel Ntah said that while they were at Fernando Po there were a lot of mosquitoes and a lot of food. At times there were so many people that there were no places even to stay. The people of Fernando Po used to supply them with food "and kept them well." They were told that "they shouldn't be afraid of war because it wouldn't go there."

What Became of Some of the Catholic Missionaries?

Father Franz Baumeister was born on 3 November 1885 in Oberhausen, Germany, and died in 1946 at Hales Corners, Wisconsin, United States. From Fernando Po he went to Spain at the end of 1919, where he remained until 1931. In 1932 he went to the United States.

Brother Vinzenz Groszinski remained on Fernando Po until 1917. He later went to Hales Corner, Wisconsin.

Father August Killian Mannersdorfer was born in Koblenz on 18 June 1892. After leaving Fernando Po in 1919 he went to South Africa in 1924 where he spent the rest of his life. He died at Allwal North, South Africa, on 28 January 1960.

Father Franz Xavier Schuster was born at Ulm a.d. Donau on 7 April 1883. After Fernando Po he returned to Germany and died at Ravensburg on 15 May 1945.

Cameroonians in Spain

Cameroonians among the refugees also continued religious instruction in Spain.

Along with many Cameroonians who were transported there in May 1916 were German soldiers, officials, colonists, and their families. Some ended up in Pamplona. There is a photograph of three young men standing behind the archbishop after their baptism in the cathedral. They had been catechumens taught by missionaries in Kamerun. The names of the young Cameroonians are Madan, Onama, and Achombo; they were baptized as Jesus, Peter, and Paul. They were baptized on the gospel side of the sanctuary with their godfathers and confirmation sponsors nearby. Afterward they went to the archbishop's residence, where he received them and the photograph was taken.

The war ended in Europe in 1918, and that meant the camps of Fernando Po were to close and repatriation was to begin.

Chapter V

Repatriation to the Mainland and a Divided Kamerun, 1919–1920

> *Father Ruf asked at the British Consulate if they could return to their missions in Cameroon now that the war was over. The British vice-consul answered in a letter sent to Fr. Schuster in Pamplona, Spain, on 18th December 1919: "Regarding your query as to whether German missionaries are to be allowed to return to their work in the Cameroons under British administration, I am directed to inform you that the answer is in the negative."*
> —Aloys Huppertz[1]

> *The indigenous peoples were never consulted and they never knew that Oliphant and Picot had partitioned their territory.*
> —Professor Victor Julius Ngoh[2]

> *My profound conviction is that in two and one-half years, real Christianity has made more progress in Cameroun, thanks to our four or five workers, than if the 110 German missionaries had stayed.*
> —Secretary General of the Paris Missionary Society, 1919[3]

Final Transfer to the Mainland

In early 1916, at the end of the fighting in Kamerun, the British and the French agreed to temporarily divide the former German territory into what has been called the *Condominium*. With the armistice in 1918 the Spanish began to dismantle the camps on Fernando Po and transport internees to the African coast.

On Fernando Po, virtually all were repatriated by mid-1919. Before returning to the mainland they were first kept in an improvised camp in Santa Isabel. The place is known today as the Parque de la Moncloa. The first group of 1,500 persons left aboard the ship *Ciudad de Cadiz*. The repatriation finally ended in 1920.

At another camp in Basile a company of Marines left by mail steamer by way of Santa Isabel.

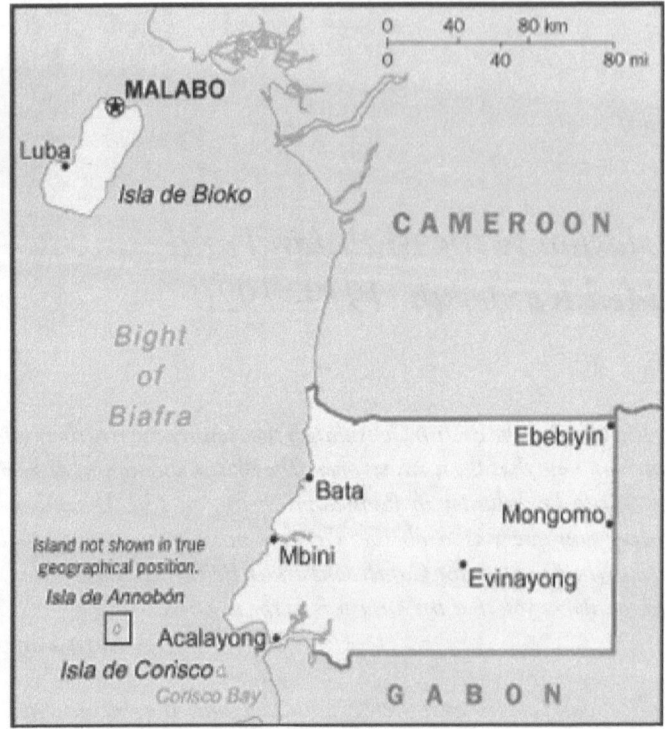

Map of Equatorial Guinea. Wiki Commons. UN Maps.

Five hundred decided not to return to the mainland. They were hired as laborers on the island, especially on cocoa plantations. Governor Barrera also continued to protect some of the traditional chiefs of the Ewondo and the Fulbe, who feared being accused as collaborators of the Germans. They had written to the Peace Conference pleading for the return of the colony to Germany. Finally, Atangana and 150 others sailed to Douala in 1920.

According to one report, from 7 February 1916, at the beginning of the internment, only two Germans had died; one by poison and the other from malaria. The number of internees reached 24,000 persons, and included military, natives, and relatives.[4]

Governor Barrera was considered a fair and humane administrator, who did not hesitate to welcome the thousands of refugees in 1916, despite limited resources and danger.

Along with the internees who did not wish to return to the mainland, others tried to escape, rowing across by canoe to Victoria. But thousands of Cameroonians remained for the three years in the camps where many learned to read and write and large numbers were either baptized as Christians or became catechumens. They had lived in a multi-cultural community under European leadership where social stratification and social mobility were based on criteria fundamentally different from the age-old structures pertaining at home. After their repatriation in 1919 the returned soldiers contested both traditional and British authority. Well into the 1930s the British feared that slumbering German loyalties were strong enough to pose a military threat to the British and French presence in Cameroon.[5]

Cameroonians Remember Repatriation

Sixty years later, some Cameroonians remembered the return to the mainland and their villages. Others had heard about it from family members. Most of the refugees on Fernando Po came back to their homes and village life in 1919 and 1920.[6]

When they arrived on the island they were told by the Germans not to fear because the war was behind them. The war would not reach Fernando Po. Family life continued. Some of the soldiers brought wives and children with them. Others married women from Fernando Po or from another part of Kamerun. At Bali-Nyonga one man said that he had been born on the island and given a name that recalled the war and internment for years to come.

Godfried Buma's parents, Mission Ngwesodong of Bali-Nyonga and his wife, Akemmesa, a native of Yaoundé, were among the Cameroonians on Fernando Po. When he was born people from the Bamenda area urged that a name be chosen to remind them all that during the war something had happened, the delivery of a child. Names were proposed, but one in the Bali language was finally chosen. It meant that the person had been born during the war.

While still in the island camps, some said that conditions were not bad after an initial shortage of housing. There were complaints about mosquitoes and fever, things Fernando Po was well known for. But they had enough food. There was also an opportunity for some to continue schooling or learn a skill. Many worked on the island, but others kept occupied taking care of their own lives in the camps. In addition, others found time to become Christians or prepare for the sacraments. Among the Catholics, there were so many preparing for baptism at one point that they could not be examined individually but only in groups.

When they were ready to return to the mainland they were divided into tribal groups and then into companies and taken by ships to Douala, where there was no one to meet them, except soldiers. Peter Vewesse was in company number 9 and was among the last to leave. Soldiers escorted them from the port to a train at Bonaberi where those leaving for the Bamenda area joined others traveling to Nkongsamba. From Nkongsamba they trekked for more than ten days to Bamenda, where they reported to the British district officer. After that they headed home. It took two more days for Peter to reach Babanki Tungo.

The ex-soldiers of the German *Schutztruppe* were in uniform, and one of them gave orders as they marched. A bugle was blown to announce their arrival. The group from Bali-Nyonga reached the border at the Naka stream, where a *chinda*, or servant, from the Fon's palace met them. When they were marching to the palace of the Fon at Bali-Nyonga, Godfred Buma was carried on his father's shoulders and shown to all the people who lined the road as the child born during the war on Fernando Po.

Babungo and Balikumbat soldiers were met at Ndop. Thomas Lambe was a child and grew afraid when he saw the ex-soldiers and heard the bugle, but his father called him over, gave him a bottle of water and a bag to hold as they marched from Ndop to Babungo.

The Kom returnees were greeted by people along the road at Baingo. One remembers his mother preparing fufu for a relative among the men.

As they marched, people lined the roads. At some places they reported to the palace. Many returned with only the "shirt on their backs." No one remembered any gifts being brought to the chief.

Once back in their own place they returned to farming and trading. A few had skills they had learned, like one who was a tailor and brought along two sewing machines: one a foot machine and the other a hand machine. He introduced sewn clothing to his people. Another, John Fomukong of Bali-Nyonga, had been trained as a nurse and continued his work under the British administration. John Kibo of Tabenken joined the British Army.

Of special interest were those who in many places introduced the Christian religion to their villages. One well-known figure was Michael Timneng of Wombong in Kom. His son remembered that when he returned with many others from Fernando Po he used to gather people for prayers in German in his house. At Mbonkesu there was a Bum man named Peter Njam, who, according to Bafmeng people, brought the Catholic religion from Fernando Po. And there were many others.

In some places the ex-soldiers had a regular meeting during which they came together to eat, drink, and contribute money to a Njange, a traditional savings association. A red feather identified their service in the German army. If they were Catholic ex-soldiers, prayers in German became part of their meeting. In Bali-Nyonga the meeting was remembered as being of men full of confidence, not ashamed of their service in the German army during the war.

When the boy who had been born on Fernando Po had grown, his father would bring him to the meeting of ex-German soldiers and show him to the people. They were happy to hear his name again and be reminded of the days on Fernando Po.

On the death of one of their number they came together. If the dead man had killed someone in war, a red feather was put on a cut bamboo, a sign that they hoped to make peace between the deceased and the person he had killed.

Map of the Northwestern grassfields in Nkwi and Warnier, *Elements for a History of the Western Grassfields*, 1982. The map shows the villages of many informants in this book. With permission of Dr. Paul Nkwi.

Kamerun Divided

On their repatriation the Cameroonians found the former German Kamerun divided between the Allies. This led to consequences for the people of Cameroon post–World War I and the Treaty of Versailles, which exist till the present day.

It was soon after the fall of Douala, on 26 September 1914, that the administration of the captured areas of German Kamerun began. The joint administration by Britain and France, what is called the "condominium" or "zones of influence," was agreed upon in September 1915 but was never implemented as it was planned. It provided for the joint administration of the territory. France was to administer its area under the Department of Colonies in France. Britain obtained two disconnected areas bordering Nigeria. General Dobell took charge of the British Cameroons.

Cameroon historian Victor Julius Ngoh described the process by which German Kamerun was partitioned between Britain and France. It began in February 1916 when the British foreign secretary, Sir Edward Grey, instructed Lancelot Oliphant to inform the French diplomat, Georges Picot, who was in London at the time, that Britain was prepared to give the former German Kamerun to France. Sitting in London, Oliphant and Picot divided Cameroon into British and French Cameroons. The Picot partition, which was meant to be provisional, gave France four-fifths of former German Cameroon while Britain took one-fifth.

> The indigenous peoples were never consulted and they never knew that Oliphant and Picot had partitioned their territory. . . . In early March 1916, British Maj.-Gen. Charles Dobell issued the Dobell Proclamation No. 10 which delimited the boundary between the British and French parts of former German Cameroon. The delimitation of the boundaries went into effect at midnight on 31 March 1916, and but for some minor modifications, it respected the London 4 March 1916 Agreenent relating to the division of the former German Cameroon which had formalized the Picot Partition.[7]

France also received back Neu-Kamerun, which had been ceded to Germany in 1911. On 28 June 1919, Germany signed the Versailles Treaty, and according to Article 119 of the treaty, it relinquished all its colonies, including Kamerun, to the Allies and the Associated Powers. On 10 July 1919, Britain and France signed the Milner-Simon Agreement, which, broadly speaking, respected and confirmed the provisional nature of the partition.

Finally, in July 1922, the Council of the League of Nations confirmed that the two territories, French and British Cameroons, should be held under a League of Nations mandate. Kamerun was divided into two unequal parts. Four-fifths of the territory went to the French, and the remainder, including the rich plantation area around Victoria, to the British.

Mandates were a result of President Woodrow Wilson's insistence that something other than annexation or colonization was needed for Germany's former colonies. Mandates were a form of trusteeship either under the League of Nations or colonial powers to be mandated by the League of Nations. But although one of Wilson's Fourteen Points talked about taking the interests of the indigenous populations into account, no one had bothered to consult the Africans, even though Blaise Diagne of Senegal and W. E. B. DuBois of the United States were busy organizing a Pan-African Congress. The congress passed resolutions calling for the League of Nations to take direct control of the former German colonies. But Britain and France worked out a deal in secret about their control of millions of Africans. On 7 May, just after Germany received its terms, the final terms for the distribution of mandates were agreed upon. When the League of Nations came into existence in 1920 it confirmed the agreements. But in the end the takeover of Kamerun looked like an annexation for Britain and France. Each year they sent reports to the League but otherwise did what they wanted to do. After World War II the United Nations took over the mandates and would grant independence to the former German territories.[8]

In the British sector, under the ad hoc agreement during the war, adminis-

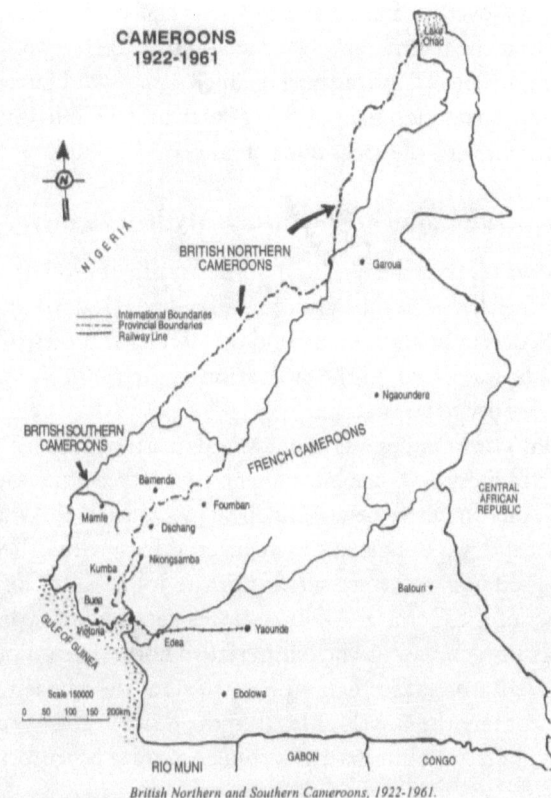

British and French Cameroons: in Anthony Ndi, *Mill Hill Missionaries in South Western Cameroon*, 2005.

trators faced problems resulting from lack of staff and information, contradictions over policy, all of which was compounded by the hardships resulting from the influenza epidemic of 1917–19, the disposal of German property, and the repatriation of soldiers and civilians from Fernando Po. It was only when Maj. V. Fitzherbert Ruxton became resident at Buea in 1921 that the problems were assessed and preparations made for the League of Nations mandate. With the mandate the provisional administration ended. For the British Cameroons this meant that the Nigerian legal system was introduced, a policy of indirect rule adapted, and local administration was integrated with southern Nigeria.

Legacy of the Germans

Victor LeVine notes that although the German protectorate over the Cameroons ended in 1916 with the "wholesale departure of all German nationals in the territory, from Governor Puttkamer to the fathers of the Pallottine Order, it did not mean that the German presence would soon be forgotten." Tangible evidence was everywhere reminding both Cameroonians and Europeans of the economic and physical development of the country under Germany. It was used to compare Kamerun with the areas under France and Britain.[9]

Kamerun Loyalty to Germany: Myth or Reality?

Mahon Murphy writes that the question of the loyalty of professional African soldiers is becoming clearer in the light of new research. The Askari, as African soldiers were called, fought and understood themselves as professionals "whose willingness to fight was based on the evaluation of their officers' mettle rather than an abstract loyalty to Germany."

One of Murphy's case studies was about Mbadamassi of Lagos. He was in the British West Africa Frontier Force but somehow was forced into German military service in Kamerun where he was involved in a mutiny of African soldiers in Banyo in 1909 and was deported to southwest Africa with others. Another was Chalgo, alias Mateo, a former servant of the John Holt Co. in Douala. He was a member of the German Askari and was deported to Spain, where he appealed to the British embassy to help him return home. Even though Chalgo was a soldier and still wore a German military tunic at the embassy, the British ambassador did not buy the "myth of loyal to the death" of Kamerun African soldiers. He thought letting him return would encourage other former soldiers in the Cameroons.[10]

According to Helmuth Stoecker it was an exaggeration if not a fiction that much of the population of Kamerun was attached to Germany. One needs only read of the pacification of the territory and the constant demand for porters and laborers to come to another conclusion. There was an admiration for German culture and education, a respect that lasted into the mandate and beyond. But Cameroonians at heart were never the "loyal native soldiers and faithful Africans" in the memory of some Europeans.[11]

During the fighting, as the Germans retreated, the population was either passively hostile or sometimes indifferent, or they assisted the Allies. The coastal peoples, notably the Duala and the Malimba, sided with the British and French forces after the outbreak of the war and served as pilots, guides, and scouts, enabling the Allies to gain control of the coastal area.

In the north the population preferred in all but a few cases to side with the Allies. In the grassfields most of the chiefs followed orders from the Germans as long as their troops were near. They continued to supply these troops with porters and provisions because refusal to do so would have entailed harsh penalties. But among hundreds of chiefs only a handful proved to be really reliable.

Nazi military experts analyzed the experience of the protective force, the *Schutztruppe*, in Cameroon twenty years later. They concluded that in areas where the fighting took place the natives often served the enemy as spies, porters or auxiliary troops who would ambush German patrols or at least report their presence to the enemy forces ... the protective force was left without native support in nearly all operations directed against the enemies rearward communication. In most cases the inhabitants of territory occupied by the enemy supported the latter, reporting all attempts by German detachments to come closer.[12]

There was also a mutiny of soldiers in June 1915 and a widespread rumor that Allied troops came as liberators.

The result of Cameroon being turned into a battlefield was that the local population lapsed into a state of extreme wretchedness and rot, as reflected in a staggering infant mortality rate, the spread of tuberculosis and venereal disease, and a growing incidence of sleeping sickness—a state of affairs against which very little could be done.

Expelled Missionaries and Seized Properties

According to a provision of the Berlin Act of 1885 it was implied that, if there was a European war, countries with territory from the Atlantic to the Indian Ocean across the center of Africa could declare their neutrality. The Germans expected this to take place in World War I. However, the Allies moved quickly not only to conquer German Africa but to forcibly remove all German nationals, including missionaries, as prisoners of war. In West Africa this took place in Togo and Kamerun, and for the Germans living in the British Gold Coast.

An important issue arose: What was to be done with the seized property of the missionaries? The Allies considered all mission assets as the property of aliens. At the peace conference after the war the Allies decided that all foreign seized property was to be sold to satisfy Germany's war debts. Due to pressure from groups in Britain and the United States, Article 438 was included in the Treaty of Versailles. Essentially it preserved German mission properties, allowing them to be handed over to other missionary societies.[13]

Evangelization Continues

Despite the "extreme wretchedness" of parts of the population and missions abandoned by European missionaries the Christian church did not collapse but often slowly flourished again. This led the secretary of the Protestant Paris Society to write in the society's annual report of 1919 that it was his "profound conviction" that in "two and one-half years real Christianity has made more progress in Cameroun, thanks to our four or five workers, than if the 110 German missionaries had stayed."[14]

For the Catholic Christians in the British Cameroons Bishop Joseph Shanahan of Nigeria made a four-month-long, one-thousand-mile tour in

1918–19. He wrote in his report, "The faith of these Christians is beyond praise. Few in numbers scattered over a wide area, bereft of their priests and all support, despised by their chiefs, their churches and schools closed or in ruins, they have remained faithful to God in the midst of these accumulated disasters." The people he met showed a "spiritual affinity with Christians of all ages. The holy fire of Faith, Hope and Charity never really ceased to burn in their souls."[15]

One of the Cameroonians of the Basel Mission who carried on when the missionaries left was Pastor Modi Din. Along with King Manga Bell of the Duala he had been accused of making anti-German propaganda. Modi Din was sentenced to four-years' imprisonment. While in prison, "his Christian witness became a blessing to many." He was finally set free at the border of Rio Muni by the retreating Germans in 1916. He was later to take over a district of the Basel Mission right up to Fumban.

Pastor Modi Din was the first African that Johannes Stöckle saw when Stöckle visited at the Protestant church in Korntal near Stuttgart in about 1927. "At the time I was an apprentice with an architect of landscaping. Modi Din, as it was winter, was well packed in a fur coat. He spoke very lively [sic] about the Church in Cameroon. He was translated from Douala into German by one of the missionaries. He told us that the Church and mission did not die when the missionaries were interned. He had traveled even to the grassfields, and in his report he said 'They are still singing.'"[16]

When the German troops retreated and it became clear that German nationals would not be allowed to remain in Cameroon, German priests of the Sacred Heart Missionaries handed over their work to Belgian and French members of their congregation. The Pallottines transferred their missions to the Holy Spirit missionaries, a society with a large French membership. Father Hoegn, who was a prisoner of war, handed his powers—subject to Rome's approval—to Père Douvry, a Frenchman who served as a chaplain in the British Army. During 1916–17 French priests came to Cameroon as *demolilisses provisoires* released from the Army by the government to help the work of the Roman Catholic Mission. In the meantime the missions were held together by the work of catechists such as Andreas Mbague and others.[17]

For the Protestant missions in the territory, including the American Presbyterians and all German missionaries, Chaplain Elie Allegret of the French Army was charged with keeping their work going. This meant Allegret was director of six missions during the war.[18]

The Basel Mission

Werner Keller asks what were the missionaries thinking when they were forced to leave Kamerun at the beginning of World War I. A major concern was what was going to happen to their congregations in the Cameroons. For the Basel Christians the Paris Mission took over their work in French Cameroons in February 1917 when Revs. Allegret, Ochsner, and Bergeret arrived in Douala. They were greeted by a church elder who said that in their coming God had heard their prayers. "In many places people said, the Mission is dead and God's work is destroyed. But God lives and his work shall live also."[19]

By the end of the war missionary activity in the French Cameroons was flourishing again, and the Paris Mission hoped Basel missionaries would return. But, because their personnel were German, they were not allowed back. Only those of Swiss nationality returned, working under the Paris Mission. This happened in 1924 when three Swiss missionaries returned to the British Cameroons. On 24 November 1925 the British Colonial Office allowed all German missionaries to return. They discovered "to their great joy that the number of Christians had not decreased at all but had on the contrary increased considerably." The growth of the church in the grassfields of the North West Region "was without compare. The number had multiplied twenty-three times. This was the Lord's doing." At Bali-Nyonga, for example, the congregation grew from 73 members in 1914 to 1,954 in 1925. While the church did suffer loss of membership in the forest area where it was opposed by "secret societies," with the help of the newly arrived missionaries they would concentrate on evangelism and education to combat the "paganism" of the area.[20]

Neither the Basel Mission nor the German Baptists returned to the French Cameroons after World War I.

The Paris Missionary Society—Société des Missions Evangeliques de Paris

From the time the Paris Mission began its work in French Cameroons during the war, there was uncertainty whether it would be a permanent undertaking. The president of the Basel Mission wrote at the end of 1918 thanking the Paris Society for taking on the Basel missions in Cameroon. The Basel Mission was hopeful that the peace treaties would allow them to return.

There was great admiration by the newcomers for the work German missionaries had done in developing "excellent African leadership" compared to the Paris Society's Gabon mission.[21]

The United Native Church

The United Native Church was the successor of both the indigenous branch of the German Baptist Mission and Alfred Saker's English Baptist Mission in Douala. When the German Baptist Mission withdrew it left its work in the hands of Lotin Same, head of the Native Baptist Church. During World War I Lotin Same succeeded in joining together the two Baptist organizations to form the United Native Church. When French missionaries returned after the war they reestablished some control over the United Native Church. In 1922 Lotin

Same was expelled because of his unorthodox attitude toward polygamy and politics. His supporters protested in the streets of Douala. A sailor from Marcus Garvey's *Black Star Line*[22] who was in the country promised to give support to the protestors. During 1922 and 1923 they paraded, singing anti-European hymns. One of them is translated as, "This is what our life is like here below; why bewail our lot? The Germans have left; the French have come in their place. They in turn will go ... liberty is on its way; in spite of all, sing Alleluia!"

However, the French administration forced the elders to resign, and the church lost its independence and returned to European control in May 1923. Lotin Same was allowed to preach only if he remained clear of "racial issues."[23]

The German Baptist Mission in British Cameroons

In 1919 Carl Bender and his wife left Cameroon. They had remained, as we have already seen, because they were U.S. citizens, and had not been deported with the German missionaries. On leaving Soppo Bender placed an ordained Cameroonian minister, Laban Moky, in charge of the German Baptist Mission. While the Benders were in the United States, Baptist work continued under Cameroonian leadership and in spite of, as Bender saw it, the looser control of the British administration. "Bender called this period when the missionaries were gone and the British were in charge 'a time of sifting the wheat from the chaff.'"[24]

Despite Bender's fears, Cameroonians expanded Baptist mission work in the 1920s, especially under Laban Moky at Soppo, Pastor Burnley of the Victoria Native Baptist Church, and men from the grassfields: Robert Jam, Joseph Mamdu, Robert Nteff, Daniel Nangu, Samuel Nji, Thomas Toh, and Johannes Tonto. They were among workers who had come to the coastal plantations where they were evangelized by the German Baptists and then returned home to found churches. In 1927 confiscated German property could be returned to former German missionary societies, and so German Baptist missionaries began to return. Bender himself returned with his daughter, a trained nurse, in 1929. He died of Blackwater fever in 1935.[25]

American Presbyterians

Because of the war the Presbyterian Board in the United States tried to replace missionaries only as they went on leave. In 1920, the French consul in New York continued restrictions on the number of American missionaries and held those with German names to be under suspicion. This resulted in a plan of cooperation between the Paris Society in French Cameroun and the French Mission directing the work of Protestant missionaries. After 1922 the American Presbyterians developed a good working relationship with the administration of the French-mandated territory.[26]

The Catholic Missions

After the war, on 10 December 1919, the last Cameroon Pallottine missionaries arrived in Limburg from West Africa. While the war in Europe continued, German priests of the Sacred Heart Missionaries had been able to turn over their work to Belgian and French missionaries of their order. However, because the Pallottines were all of German nationality they turned over their work to another missionary society. They were Holy Ghost Missionaries with a large number of French members. Today they are called Spiritans. When the fighting ended, Fr. Hoegn, who had replaced Bishop Vieter, handed over his jurisdiction to Père Douvry, a Frenchman and chaplain in the British Army. Hoegn is reported to have said to Douvry, "Save the Missions."

In 1916–17 French priests who were released from military service began to work in Cameroon. Finally in 1923 Rome assigned the vicariate to the Holy Ghost Missionaries who were priests, brothers, and sisters. The Office of Propaganda Fidei in Rome had hoped that the Pallottines might be allowed to return, but this did not happen.

After World War I, Cameroon came to be known as "the Pearl of African Missions." It grew more rapidly than any other mission not only in Africa but in the world. One Holy Ghost priest wrote that they were "besieged by such a wave of converts that they cannot properly supervise them."[27]

In the British Cameroon the Southern section was handed to the English Mill Hill Fathers in 1922. It was called the Prefecture of Buea and was only a small part of the former Pallottines' mission but included "the beautiful and strategic mission stations of Victoria, Engelberg, and Einsiedeln."[28]

The colonial government was anxious to have English-speaking missionaries in the British Cameroons. Rome decided to divide the whole of Cameroon between the Mill Hill Missionaries from London, the area under Britain, and French-speaking Sacred Heart Missionaries at Foumban and Holy Ghost Missionaries to the east and south. A small group of Christians welcomed John Campling and his party of Mill Hill Missionaries at Victoria (Limbe) on Sunday morning 26 March 1922.[29]

Christian Agents of Change in the British Cameroons: Catholic Experience

In today's North West Region, returnees from Fernando Po were agents of change in local traditional culture. According to historian Anthony Ndi, the returning soldiers, carriers, and others "emerge as the most zealous and intractable lot who fought the traditional and British administrators against all odds to promote the Catholic faith throughout the Grasslands."[30]

Mill Hill Missionaries with the Fon of Nso, NW Region, December 1923: l to r: William Scully, John Campling, The Fon, William Moran. Mill Hill Missionaries Archive.

Nkwen Village near Bamenda

In the grasslands of Cameroon near Bamenda in what is now the North West Region some villagers returned from Fernando Po in September 1919. We have a description of the event by Bernard Booth. It illustrates the growth of Christianity in villages of British Cameroons after World War I.

> In September 1919 four Nkwen Christians returned from Fernando Po after having been baptized there. They were Peter Ngomba, Peter Nbo, Henry Njum Cheo, and Peter Tamksong. There were not any Christians in the area at the time of their return. News of their arrival spread and many came to hear about Christianity. As the numbers increased, doctrine was held in the palace of Agefor, the Fon of Nkwen. But there was still no father or catechist in the area.

In early 1920 Fr. William Bintner visited Nkwen. Soon after, the people of Nkwen were given a catechist by the name of Andreas Ngwa. Ngwa organized the building of the first Catholic church in Nkwen. The first Mass in the new church was offered by Monsignor Plissonneau, who traveled from Foumban.[31]

The experience of Nkwen village was multiplied throughout the North West Region of Cameroon, as men and women returned from Fernnado Po.

"Severally and collectively," Ndi writes, returning Catholic Christians constituted a unique lot who tenaciously held to and strove to promote their Catholic faith against all odds. Every village with a Catholic community of any size had its own story of these repartees to recount... they tended to be overbearing, obstinate and even condescending to the Traditional Rulers, although they were not exactly submissive to their own catechists and priests either.... But the overall complaint was that these men, whose knowledge of the Christian faith was by no means profound, while proving recalcitrant both to Traditional and British Colonial Authorities, often did not accept the advice of their religious authorities especially if these were conciliatory toward the traditional religion and practice.[32]

When these people left the regimented life of German service and three years of internment on Fernando Po many had become, wrote Elizabeth Chilver in 1963, "enthusiasts uncompromisingly contemptuous of traditional mores." With the return of missionaries to Cameroon local sentiment was very often "polarized between the minority of new men looking to the Catholic missionaries and traditional authority looking to the divisional officer for support."[33]

Michael Timneng Returns to Kom

Jaqueline de Vries did much of her field work among the Kom people. She found that the adventures of the men returning from Fernando Po "conferred on them a great deal of stature and prestige."[34] In 1919 most of those who had been interned on Fernando Po returned home to Kom. There were 400 ex-soldiers, around 170 women, 50 children, and 95 servants. They were seen as a potential threat to the authority of traditional rulers. This was "not a welcome prospect to the British."

One such returnee was Michael Timneng, whom we have already met. Timneng was a former palace guard for the Fon of Kom who became a Christian when missionaries settled at the village of Fujua. More than five hundred men, mostly catechumens, were enlisted in the Kamerun colonial army as a "punishment imposed on them by the Fon for their acceptance of the 'Whiteman's religion.' The story of Timneng is unusual because he was remembered as a 'stubborn boy in the palace' who once 'stoned a Chinda.' For this offense he was 'sent to be killed by the Whiteman.'"[35] On Fernando Po he served as a servant to a German missionary priest, the same priest who instructed him to bring knowledge of the Christian religion back to his people.

About the "bewilderment and even fear" of the Fon on seeing so many Christian recruits returning to his country, de Vries writes that it was understandable for they came "bearing an infinitely mysterious and apparently threatening message, wearing whiteman's clothes, and claiming to carry a book of secrets about God that would no doubt engage in a power struggle with the Fon (as a direct representative of supernatural powers) himself."[36]

We are reminded again that the many of those Cameroonians who were recruited or enlisted by their leaders at home, like the Fon of Kom, "were not soldiers, or not primarily so. They were carriers," or porters, for the army. Pack animals were attacked by the tsetse fly in many areas. Railways were new. Roads and motorized transport were unavailable. "Therefore a human chain linked troops to their bases, and without it they could not move, feed, or fight." For example, the British and the Germans "reckoned that they needed between two and three porters for each soldier." Some units had their own "enlisted carriers." In Cameroon "the forces of Britain and Germany each employed a force of about 40,000 carriers." Such large numbers "could not be raised voluntarily. Most were impressed either directly or indirectly. Chiefs would undertake to provide quotas." Like Michael Timneng, "carriers chosen by headmen were frequently those who were locally dispensable, and probably the less fit."

Enlisted as porters in the army they were very often underfed and subject to health problems like "ulcerated feet, malaria, and chest infections." Strachan quotes F. J. Moberly's 1931 study "Military Operations: Togoland and the Cameroons 1914–16"; he reported that of the "20,000 porters sent to the Cameroons by the British, 574 died and 8,219 were invalided." In addition, on the German side, each German officer had four to six porters, a servant, and a cook.

One German doctor thought that Cameroonians were even more vulnerable to typhus, smallpox, meningitis, and sleeping sickness than Europeans. The German forces in Cameroon were fortunate compared to other areas because they "held up remarkably well through the eighteen months of campaigning." The Germans had taken delivery of a year's worth of medical supplies at the outbreak of the war. The Germans also had good doctors, with one assigned to each company. In a war of companies rather than battalions, the health of the soldiers and the porters who supplied them, was directly related to their efficiency in the field.[37]

Problems with British Administrators

Before the war was over, British administrators began to complain about German influence from Fernando Po. In a letter marked "Missions: Bamenda Division," Divisional Officer Crawford in Bamenda wrote to the Resident in September 1917 that the "German missionaries and their agents at Fernando Po are in constant communication with natives in the division." He singled out one letter he censored written by a German soldier to the Fon of Kom asking that the Fon "look after his women and repair the Governor's building [sic]." Since Crawford was placed in charge of the division, he had received "at least 200 letters and postcards from Fernando Po addressed to natives of this division."[38] He judged that the majority had been written by ex-mission boys and at the instigation of German missionaries. "Judging from the handwriting," he believed "that many were written by the missionaries themselves."[39]

Crawford recommended that no religious groups be allowed back into the division at that time because their hold on the population was uncertain. There was a consensus among the chiefs that the missionaries not be allowed to reestablish their missions because "the German missionaries undermined their authority and created many difficulties." The war was not over, and they were understaffed and facing an "overwhelming native population." The British administration had to "bluff" a great deal but that was being worn "threadbare in the division at present."

In 1919, after the war and repatriation, Crawford was writing again that he approved of Catholic Bishop Shanahan of Nigeria traveling through the division but "on no account should the German missionaries be allowed to return to the division."

In a report from Mamfe Division in 1923 the divisional officer explained what had happened to the Protestant Mission during the war and afterwards. The Basel Mission disappeared with the war, he wrote, and organization went with it. All able-bodied men were concerned with the effects of the war and little else. But in 1916,

> Christian communities began to appear in those villages that had formerly possessed Basle [sic] Mission schools. First the communities were under teachers chosen by the people. But after a visit by Pastor Ekeze of the Société des Mission Evangeliste at Douala they began to increase. He baptized about ten of the popular teachers. Then in 1921 the Society sent Pastor Modi Din so that by 1922 forty of those chosen by the people were confirmed.

In 1921, Fr. William Bintner (as a non-German he was allowed to return) of the Catholic Mission in Kumbo wrote to the district officer in Bamenda about the returned "German soldiers." They were allowed to build houses on the mission because they came morning and evening for instruction and their homes were far from the mission. Bintner had spoken to the chief and repeated that if the chief calls them for work they must go "it is their duty.... The chief is the authority... for pagans and for Christians."

The divisional officer in Bamenda, N. C. Duncan, wrote to Msgr. Plissonneau on 18 November 1921 about the Catholic missions. He had received information from Mr. Williams, the assistant district officer in Kom country, that the Catholic mission had been removed from its old site and reopened in the village of Njinikom. This led "to a disturbance of a very serious nature, which in my opinion may lead to open civil war between the animist natives and the Christian Political community... already native police (were) severely flogged by this Bolshevistic society and Mr. Williams after much careful enquiry reports as follows:

Under the Germans the mission was to the west of the Bamenda-Kentu Rd. and there was no trouble. When Fr. Bintner returned from Luxembourg, against the Fon's advice and without the Fon's consent or permission of the British Government, the mission was moved to the village of Njinikom. The community "aided by ex-German soldiery are continually seducing the women of the Fon and other chiefs and keeping them in the mission." The teachers he said refuse to acknowledge the Fon and defy native law and custom.

By 1923 Hawksworth, the assistant district officer, Bamenda, wrote to the divisional officer about the "German soldiers." "The question of the ex-German soldiers from Fernando Po was not easy to solve. Father Moran stated that throughout the Province these men are a constant thorn in the side of the mission." It was decided that they "would either obey the order of the chief and reside in their fathers' compounds or migrate to another country."[40]

Colonial Ambitions Realized

The war gave the Allies an opportunity to take over German-held territory and secure it for their own colonial ambitions. The war enabled the colonial powers to once again redraw the map of Africa.

Hew Strachan writes, "The Great War was the prelude to the final stage of the scramble for Africa, played out at Versailles. Despite all their misgivings at the outset, the European powers advanced rather than retarded the cause of colonialism between 1914 and 1918." By 1914, colonialism had begun to move from conquest to civilization with the withdrawal of white administrators and the Africanization of missions. "But the war reinvigorated territorial ambitions dormant since the turn of the century. Annexation or retention remained the dominant European motivation in the war in Africa." Governor Ebermaier's primary concern was for Germany to survive in Africa, not Germany in Europe. "In the last analysis German's African claims resided not in the preservation of land but in the unity of the Schutztruppen themselves."[41]

In this they succeeded in the encampments of Fernando Po. But with the Versailles treaty Kamerun was lost and its government and army disbanded.

John C. Barrett, in his article "World War I and the Decline of the First Wave of the American Protestant Missions Movement," points out the powerful impact World War I had on American religious life and mission work. "The sight of Christian nations engaged in brutal trench warfare contrasted with the secularized, postmillennial optimism that was infused into mainline Protestant beliefs." And the sight of so-called Christian nations at war challenged the supposed superiority of Western civilization. James Barton, foreign secretary of an American mission board, wondered in 1916 whether the war's impact on religion was greater than it was on politics. Had Christianity failed because it did not prevent the war? [42]

Not all who returned to the North West Region were agents of radical change. Many returned and quietly resumed life in their country while steadfastly holding to their trust and hope in the gospel message.

Our story returns to the North West Region of Cameroon.

Matthew Fobang of Bali-Nyonga[43]

In 1919 Matthew Fobang, Daniel Ntah's father, returned to Bali-Nyonga after three years on Fernando Po. The English government arranged the returnees in groups: those to Bali, to Nso, and so on. They sent messengers to all the chiefs: "here are your people." The Fon of Bali sent a chinda and received the group on the road. "There were many but I can't estimate the number." He thought as many as eighty might have left to become German soldiers.

He and others were baptized Catholics at Fernando Po. Back home in Bali-Nyonga they started the Catholic Mission near the small market around Forkwa's compound.

According to Daniel, those who returned from Fernando Po brought new ideas.

> Some of the new ideas the soldiers returned with were the wearing of cloth by their women; frying with oil and with onions (the seedlings of onions).... My father learned tailoring at Fernando Po and had a hand sewing machine. They were all very social and met regularly. They all had a meeting in Tita Fonkwa's compound. All the ex-German soldiers came. If one of their group died they all came eating, drinking and firing guns for 3 days.... When they buried a friend they would take a bamboo, cut one side and put red feathers. The feathers meant he had done something in war and was manly. If the person was not "manly" they put no feathers.

He named the ex-soldiers. They were Tita Fomukong, Tita Fonka, Tadoh Ndop, Kobe, Bikai, Fogam, who was a servant of the Germans, Caspar from Mantum, Kunchebe, Bambat Muyuka, Kerosene, Mbindanglu, Kansen, Peter Nukuna, Taka Benda, "Sergeant" Nkette.

"When they returned to Bali there was no trouble. They were carpenters and bricklayers. They brought many seedlings of onions, Irish potatoes, mangoes, bananas, varieties of corn; up to then we only had guinea corn."

Tailoring did not go well for his father, and so he turned to farming and hunting. "He used a Dane-gun and spear, usually hunting cutting-grass [a cane rat] and sometimes buffalo and elephants. On his farm he grew maize, cassava, beans, and plantains. His house was of bamboo, mud, and grass."

"Later he sold his sewing machine. He no longer had his soldier's uniform, but he praised the Germans very highly. He was never absent from prayer, morning or evening; always in German."

The Catholic Church was made stronger on their return. The Basel Mission had tried to catch everyone at Bali up to then. His father used to say that "life on Fernando Po was very tough and that the German people were good."

Conclusion

Even when he was dying he said that the "Germans will come back." He used to wear a red cap, a Fez, and he had a bugle which he was very good at playing.

—Daniel Ntah[1]

There is still much to learn about the West African campaigns of the war. The pattern for historians writing on the African campaigns has been to adopt a social-labor history approach that largely views African soldiers in the war as appendages of the colonial state. This approach is insufficient to understand the Cameroon West African campaign, in which over 90 percent of Cameroonians fighting for either the Germans or Allies were recruited during wartime and began fighting without any European training.

—George N. Njung[2]

The Catholic community in the remote village of Fonfuka in the North West Region of Cameroon has a distinguished pedigree. It was founded nearly one hundred years ago, in 1919 to be precise, by a returnee from the island of Fernando Po.

—Fons Eppink[3]

Matthew Fobang until his death told family members that the Germans would return. He held on to this hope from the days of German Kamerun and his life as an internee on Fernando Po. A study of the Bali-Nyonga in 1967 showed that there were others like him.[4] Such fond memories for German Kamerun place him among those who supported what has been called the Golden Age myth of German colonialism.[5]

German Kamerun never returned, but some missionaries, planters, and, much later, tourists did.

In 1932 Harry Rudin heard the local people praise the German administration that "they were very strict, at times harsh, but always just." He did not deny the existence of great evils in the German administration but thought there remained an impression "of a continuous administration that was manifesting a greater concern about native well-being."[6]

Edwin Ardener wrote in 1958 of the "Kamerun Idea," which was based on what he considered an exaggerated belief that thirty-two years of German rule had welded the diverse populations into a distinctive unity. The idea was that in the past a single Kamerun nation had existed under the Germans. At independence a federation of British and French mandates joining in a federation, it was proposed, would restore that unity.[7]

In 1964 Victor LeVine wrote about an intangible legacy that "the Germans did not try to conceal the fact that their primary purpose in the colony was to exploit it; yet in the process they brought intelligent, often enlightened, administration." "The German experience remains, for many Cameroonians, at once a political touchstone and a potent symbol of a half-mythical golden age when Cameroonians were one."[8]

But that legacy and the German imperial presence in Cameroon often appear to have been forgotten. A *New York Times* article concerning recent disturbances in the English-speaking regions of the country makes no mention of the country's German colonial past. "Before independence in the early 1960s, Cameroon was colonized by the French and British. The Constitution allows protections for both languages, but Francophones rule the government. Most official documents are offered in French and not translated, evidence that Anglophones cite as proof of their marginalization."[9]

A more recent article from Rome does recall a German colonial past when it refers to the root of a crisis in Cameroon of 2017 being the division of German Kamerun during World War I:

> English-speaking regions of Cameroon . . . have now been without the internet for 50 days, which is causing serious inconvenience to the local population and heavy economic losses. The measure was taken to try to block the protests which since mid-November disturb the only two English-speaking provinces (out of 10) of Cameroon and the rest is a French-speaking country. Demonstrators call for the full implementation of bilingualism established by the Constitution. . . . The root of the crisis stems from the division between France and Britain of the then-German colony after the First World War. The French-speaking part became independent in 1960 while the Anglophone in 1961. This latter with a referendum established to join the Francophone Cameroon. . . . Given its bilingualism, Cameroon is at the same time part of the British Commonwealth and the Organization Internationale de la Francophonie.[10]

A book of this size gives only an introduction to a period of Cameroon history. At the same time it suggests topics for further study.

The *Schutztruppe* was mentioned in an earlier piece in the *New York Times* about Namibia and its history as a German colony. The article speaks of a wound reopened when people protested about a statue, erected in 1908, that depicts a German marine holding a rifle in his hands and standing guard over a dying comrade. Unlike Kamerun, South West Africa attracted thousands of settlers, whose descendants remain to this day. The statue commemorates the soldiers of the *Schutztruppe* who helped crush a rebellion against German colonial rule by the Herero and Nama ethnic groups, between 1904 and 1908. The plaques read that with God's help the soldiers fought for Kaiser and Empire. No mention is made of the make-up of the *Schutztruppe*. It was usually African troops led by German officers. The article states that Germany is ready to formally acknowledge the action as genocide.

The experience in Kamerun was not that of South West Africa in its extremes of violence and charges of genocide. In Kamerun news of the Herero and Nama uprising and the Boxer Rebellion in China alerted the colonial administration that there might be a general uprising of the native population. But with a superiority of firepower, especially the use of the Maxim machine gun, the colonial *Schutztruppe* were able to put down any threat with light casualties on the German side and heavy losses by the Africans. For example, there was a rebellion near the Cross River in Anyang country. The civil administrator, Count Puckler-Limburg, was murdered while on tour in January 1904. The DO from Bamenda left the station with the second company of 5 officers and 120 troops to meet with another German force at the Cross River under Col. Muller. "The uprising was put down in six months, and the villages that had taken part were looted and destroyed with the inhabitants fleeing to the bush."[11]

The monument to the *Schutztruppe* of Kamerun on the cover of this book pictures an African, not a European, soldier. This is a reminder that most of the troops of the Germans and the Allies were Africans. Therefore Africans were killing Africans in Kamerun and elsewhere in Africa.

The composition and use of the Kamerun *Schutztruppe* are worthy questions. By 1914 only 13 percent of the soldiers were from outside Kamerun. Most were recruited from the Yaoundé area, but others came from the Bamenda grassfields.[12] The point has been made that not all who were labeled German soldiers from Fernando Po were actually ex-troopers but may have been among the thousands of porters that the Germans, and the Allies, needed. But it is more likely that those who came back as ex-soldiers were troopers who also carried supplies and equipment, did construction and clearing and other tasks when needed.

The topic of the *Schutztruppe* and the Allied troops during World War I in Kamerun is explored in a recent PhD dissertation by George Njung. Not only does he reflect on the conscription and mobilization of African troops but also on the wretchedness, resistance, and violence this action produced in the whole region.[13]

It is known that when the German army retreated into Spanish territory

Members of the Fonfuka Catholic Church, 2017. Photo by Fons Eppink, Mill Hill Missionaries.

they were accompanied by many porters or carriers. These were among the thousands that the Spanish governor sent back to Kamerun. Those who were transported to the island of Fernando Po were Germans, the troopers, their wives and children, the important local leaders of Kamerun, like Karl Atangana, and their retinue, and various servants and skilled workers of the Germans. Therefore not many carriers, if any, were among those who returned in 1919 and 1920. They were truly ex-soldiers or servants, their wives and children.

The old Fon of Guzang in Moghamo had what seemed an unusual experience. His son referred to him as an old German man and a soldier. After the war, the Fon and his brother had a farm on Fernando Po. All was reportedly left in the hands of the brother when the Fon returned to the mainland. The brother died on Fernando Po. Martin Lynn wrote from Queens College, Belfast, in April 1987 that he wondered "if many of the interned remained on Fernando Po after 1919. That would make an interesting study."[14] It was reported that about five hundred Cameroonians decided to remain on the labor-starved island when repatriation took place in 1919.

The treatment of missionaries and mission property, especially in the details brought out in this book, deserves more study. Without that harsh treatment would the internment on Fernando Po and the impact of those years for the Catholics have carried the gospel to the most isolated villages of Cameroon? And as for the Protestants, would there have been the quick development of local leadership in the absence of European missionaries?

Conclusion

Following from that topic one that needs to be explored is the influence the returning Protestant Cameroonians had on their local communities. Except for the report that the camps had a Protestant church and that Primitive Methodist missionaries on the island led Sunday services I found no evidence of an organized effort similar to that of the Catholics to evangelize in the camps. A number of facts were in favor of the Catholics. The island itself was nominally Catholic, and so Spanish missionaries helped the few German priests who accompanied the refugees. The German Catholic missionaries were able to remain on the island because they were employed to help with administration of the camps. In their free time they devoted themselves to evangelization. Most if not all German Protestant missionaries had been sent back to Europe. In addition, the Catholic Mission benefitted from the presence of the paramount chief Atangana of the Beti, a Catholic. He even had a Catholic church built in the camp set aside for many chiefs of Kamerun.

There may be other reasons. It may also be that the experience was of great importance to the other denominations as well.

About the North West Region and an area where my interest in German Kamerun began in 1965, an article appeared on 23 February 2017 on the website of the Mill Hill Missionaries about the village of Fonfuka.

Fonfuka is a subdivision in Bum, miles away from a good road at Fundong. The legacy of German Kamerun may nearly be forgotten elsewhere, but the contribution of some of its missionaries on Fernando Po lives on.

A young missionary, Ugandan Tiberius Vuni of the Mill Hill Fathers, as they were known in British Cameroons, the same missionary society that came to the Cameroons in 1922, when the German Pallottines and Sacred Heart Missionaries were not allowed to return, was appointed to Fonfuka. The Catholic community in the remote village of Fonfuka in the North West Region of Cameroon has a distinguished pedigree.

> It was founded nearly one hundred years ago, in 1919 to be precise, by a returnee from the island of Fernando Po, situated off the coast of Cameroon. Many Cameroonians serving in the German colonial army in different capacities were interned there after defeat in World War I. A significant number of them became Christians and turned into activists when they returned to their regions of origin after the war. The little church built by this lay missionary in Fonfuka still stands. However, the seed sown in those distant days has now come to fruition.[15]

A pioneer of the camps of Fernando Po where a German missionary had instructed him to bring what he had learned about Jesus back to his people was Augustine Kiyouh.[16] He was joined by a Baptist ex-soldier from the camps, Joseph Mammadu, who began a Baptist church in the same area.

Augustine was a Bum man from Saff whose parents came to settle in Fonfuka where he grew up. During World War I he was taken with other young men from the area to serve in the German army. He was interned on Fernando Po and came back to Fonfuka with four other men in 1919. There were two other Catholics, Thomas Ngwang and a man known as Martin. There was also a Baptist ex-soldier called Joseph Mammadu and a non-Christian, Corporal Adamu. Of the Catholics only Augustine took his faith seriously and started a small community of believers in his family compound. It was in his hut that the Catholic church started in Fonfuka beginning with a Sunday service and prayers.

At about the same time, Joseph Mammadu began a Baptist community, not in his compound, but on Bum land. As a result many people referred to the Catholic church in Fonfuka as Kiyouh's church because the community was associated with his family compound.

One of those first Catholic Christians of the Fonfuka community founded by Augustine was Ferdinand Ngong. Father Hermann Gufler, a Mill Hill Missionary from Tirol, met him forty years ago. Ferdinand, he writes, "was a lovely old man, short in stature.... Whenever I went to Fonfuka from Nkambe to say Mass there, usually every month, he was always the first person to come and greet me." Fr. Gufler remembered a story from those visits. It was about "a tree [that] had fallen down near Fonfuka... which then 'stood up again on its own' and some 'miracle water' which appeared next to the place where the tree stood. People would go there to collect or drink that water. Pa Ferdinand came to ask me whether as a Christian he could collect some water too which was held to be medicinal."[17]

Ferdinand became one of the first Catholics to marry in the Church, to a woman named Magdalene Fuah. He died on 31 May 1978. From those very early years the Fonfuka church, with roots in the camps of Fernando Po, became a small and serious Catholic Christian presence in Bum, witnessed in the lives of Cameroonians like Ferdinand and Magdalene.

"Dogged perseverance and an open eye for God's presence in all manner of situations, in particular in the local culture, have helped Fr. Vuni to bring to life the seed sown long ago."[18]

These are a few of the topics that need much more study, but what would be most enlightening might be to return to the many villages throughout Cameroon and recall the seed of community sown long ago by the ex-soldiers of German Kamerun and Fernando Po.

Appendix 1

Testimony of Cameroonians

The testimony of Cameroonians who contributed to this story of German Kamerun is reproduced here. It is hoped that their words will enrich our understanding of the past and at times inspire us with examples of endurance, courage, generosity, and adventure: common denominators of the human experience.

One of the priorities of our field research was not only to tell a story of German Kamerun but also to preserve from anonymity the unique lives of many who have lived that past. Their testimony and their life histories told by those who knew them are considered to be an important contribution to any search to understand a Cameroon grassfield's history. They spoke in their local language, strong English, and sometimes Pidgin.

Stephen Nchumuse[1]

In Memfu Stephen remembered one woman, Magdalena, who had gone to Fernando Po.

> My father was the Fon of Nseh and my mother Kimlole who was an Nso princess. I was born in either 1910 or 1911. . . . When the Germans came there was war and this compound was burnt so we left and went to Ndu and others went to the forest at Ngomba. We left from here because we were running from the Germans. By that time I was a child and they ran with me on the back. The Germans had burnt this compound because of the war. When the war was over we were asked by the Fon of Nso to come back. Many people had been killed by the Germans . . . (when they were here) a road was dug going from Nso to Mbam village and then to Banyo. The person who dug the road was called Mekanjo. He was a German. The road this way was dug toward Sop in Nkambe. When the road was dug the German priests came. Father Leonard, Rev. Brothers and Sisters came and started a mission at Nso. They asked the Fon to give children to be learning in the school. The Fon sent messages to the villages requesting people to send their children . . . my father sent me to the German school at Shisong. We were taught in German. All those who were with me have

died. They include Moyuy, Ngeh, Job, Ndregha, Moke. and Mbou. There was also Ngendewan from Kishong. There was one girl but I have forgotten her name. There were nine of us.... When all the fathers went away we left Shisong and dispersed to our various places.

Some who went with the fathers [missionary priests] came back baptized. They had studied enough "book." One of them was Paul Tangwa. When the German priests left Shisong the catechist was Michael Wami. His wife was Elizabeth Yadi, who just died recently. Paul Tangwa had gone away with the fathers.

From here there was one girl who had gone to Fernando Po. Some people went there as carriers and died there. None of them came back as already baptized Christians. The woman who went to Fernando Po went there because her husband was recruited and taken there as a soldier. The name of the woman was Magdalena and her husband was Michael Wedren. They did not become Christians.

Stephen was baptized in 1922. In 1927 he became a catechist and was sent to Mbou in Njottin to start the church.

John Nchari

John Nchari of Tabenken was a young boy when he met German missionaries. Later he met with Bishop Vieter of the Catholic Pallottine Missionaries in Douala. It was September 1988 when the parish priest led me to his compound. It was night and he was on his bed, the room lighted by a bush lamp, with some friends and family crowded around as he spoke about his youth.[2]

> When I was a small child I went to Mbiami and followed the Germans. I worked with one district officer at Bamenda before going to Douala with him. The DO was called Hauptman Menji. I was his houseboy and steward. The DO later left Douala because he said he wanted to go to his own country. I was left in the Catholic Mission with one bishop (Vieter). There were three fathers in the Catholic Mission.
>
> I was sent to the German school and reached class four. Then when a father was to go to the grassfields the bishop said that I should follow him and come here and be his boy and be helping him.
>
> At Douala I was only a schoolboy but I was fed by the mission. I learned doctrine by the time I was at school but only got my baptism when I came to Banso. We traveled by train and reached Nkongsamba and then trekked through Nchang to Bamenda.
>
> When I reached Bamenda I saw the DO. The bishop sent two fathers here and I was given to them by the bishop. They were Fathers Edmond and Leonard. At Nso I was staying with them in the mission at Shisong. I

was there with Peter Wami.... Before the German missionaries left they had given my own baptism. We were twelve who first got baptism. Wami was baptized at Douala but I was baptized at Nso....

Some of the people who came from Fernando Po were John Bansi and Dominic Borri. They were baptized at Fernando Po.

Christianity was often carried to the population in the interior by local people, like the plantation worker Patrick, or the man from Tabenken, John Nchari.

Matthew Lekomu Fobang of Bali-Nyonga

Daniel Ntah remembered his father, Matthew Lekomu Fobang, and his service in the Kamerun army.[3] His father was from Paila Quarter in Bali-Nyonga. His first wife was Basanban of Tikali Quarter and his second wife was Mantan of Nted Quarter. He had nine children. When his was a young man he did not become a soldier at first but went down to work on a plantation at Victoria. When he returned he decided to join the German soldier troops. He saw his colleagues at home dressed and moving as soldiers and so he was anxious to join them. He joined at Bali and went to Bamenda for training. Afterward he went to Nchang and to Ngaoundere where he stayed for many years doing guard duty.

When the English captured Buea in the first war it was thought that they could never reach Yaoundé. The Bali soldiers began as infantry under the instruction of Fon Galega. They were caught by the English people and taken to Fernando Po. My father married while he was a soldier at Ngaoundere. His wife stayed with him until he sent her home before they were captured. He was a private in the army. The English took them to Victoria and then by launch to Fernando Po. At Fernando Po he went to the Catholic Church. He learned his doctrine in German. "Pa could pray throughout his life in German."

> My father never learned a trade at Fernando Po. He never did any other thing than farming.... He managed to join the army because they said they wanted soldiers and since the first Germans who came here said Bali should join because the Bali had helped them so much showing them the road and helping them to overcome the problems they were having. So plenty of Bali people were encouraged to join the army.

When he was a soldier he traveled to many places and rose to corporal. "He said that by the time they were at Fernando Po there were a lot of mosquitoes and that there was too much food. There were so many of them and there were no places even to stay." The people of Fernando Po used to supply them with food "and kept them well." They were told that "they shouldn't be afraid of war because it wouldn't go there. He never attended school."

Peter Vewesse[4]

In 1988 Peter Vewesse remembered the return to the mainland and his journey home to Babanki Tungo in 1919.

According to Vewesse, Cameroonians left Fernando Po in companies, one after the other. His group was the last to go in 1919, in company number 9. The chief of Babanki Tungo did not send anyone to meet them at the coast, and so when they arrived in Douala "the government sent soldiers who came and collected us and we were put on the train at Bonaberi. We traveled to Nkongsamba from where we trekked for twelve days before arriving here," in Babanki Tungo.

When they reached home they were taken to the chief's palace. At first only his relatives came to welcome him and later others from the village. "As I reached they were surprised and very happy. There were so many people who had returned from Fernando Po." Like many others he came back with only the clothes on his back. On the island he "was never paid and so had no cargo." Only one other villager, Cellilous, for whom he had worked, should have had something, but he too came back as poor as Peter.

Peter had attended school at Fernando Po, and when he returned he continued to attend school at Kumbo for about two years.

Eventually he learned bricklaying, but first served as a "chinda," or servant, in the palace of the chief. Later he left and went to Dschang to stay with Alois Mukom, who had been a clerk with the Germans and knew German "book." Mukom was a catechist and had attended the German school at Einsiedeln. When he returned home, people began to attend doctrine in his compound. "One Thaddeus Njua began to teach doctrine at Alois Mukom's compound.... Later we... were teaching doctrine at the old mission."

Godfred Buma[5]

Not only did Godfred Buma of Bali-Nyonga know about Fernando Po, he was born there in 1919. His father was Mission Ngwesodong of Bali-Nyonga and his mother was from Yaoundé. Her name was Akemesa of Njemin.

> I was born about 1919 on Fernando Po. My father was called Mission Ngwesodong and my mother was Akemesa. My mother came from Njemin Yaoundé.
>
> So when the war was strong on the Germans and when they saw they could be defeated, they ran to Fernando Po... so it was at Fernando Po that I was born. As I was delivered all the Bamenda people who were there said it was better to look for a very good name to give to this newborn baby which would be an indication that by the time they were at war they did a good thing like delivering a child. Every Bamenda man was asked to propose a name, but the Bali people said that, although the names people

proposed were good, it were better such a name be in Bali talk. So at last my name was given as Buma, that is Buma Langmia, meaning a child who has been born inside the gun during war time.

When the war ended, the soldiers were brought to Douala, and then my father took me and we passed through Bamenda. When we reached Bamenda it was reported to the DO that they were returned German soldiers. When he came back he went to Bamenda and obtained a license in 1921 to possess a "Dane gun." By that time the English were already in Bamenda. They told me (that we returned) if not in 1920 in 1921.

I was carried on the head. At Naka village they were showing me to the people. They even did that at the palace.

He described the palace houses with grass roofs and that the place could be seen from Bamenda. Where a grandstand is now "the Germans had built a certain zinc house with burnt bricks. People could stand there and see Bamenda." When they arrived, "the followers [younger siblings] of my mother, elders, and some of her family members followed (from Yaoundé) and came to Bamenda, asked directions to Bali-Nyonga, and came here. By the time they arrived we had gone to the farm, and when Bali people heard they were from Yaoundé they thought it might be that they came to take back my mother." So they refused to help them and later sent a message to call his mother from her farm. "Then those people went back without seeing my mother...."

"When I grew and was a boy and was going to the farm my father joined the meeting of ex-German soldiers at Fonkwa's house. My father would carry me there and show me to the people...." The ex-soldiers were happy to hear his name again and be reminded that he was born on Fernando Po. They "had gone to the war as good people" and were not ashamed of what they had done. "I was the second child born to my mother. My elder was a girl who died. She was also delivered at Fernando Po. This was the story my father told me of how he was there."

When his father was in the army he traveled to many places and rose to the rank of corporal.

Buma went to the Native Authority School in about 1927. "I never completed because I left and went with my aunt, Elizabeth Jangmi, to Enugu. She had married a Nigerian soldier, David Tanwen. I only passed class one."

Peter Ndango Fonkwa[6]

Peter Ndango Fonkwa was born in 1855 at Bali-Nyonga. He was the brother of Fon Galega I, son of Gwanolbe, who came from Nigeria. Fonkwa was in the Fon's army of Galega I about 1890 and joined the German army and served in the First World War as a sergeant. He was a prince. His first wife, Nsang

Mafojo, was born in 1876. Both he and his wife were moving during the war with the Germans. He was such a great man in the army that both his wife and he were being carried from Bamenda to Fernando Po by the villagers guided by German soldiers between 1910 and 1918. He ceased to be a member of the German army in 1918. He returned home and settled at Kufat, and after his brother's death in 1941 while he was Fon on the throne he took over and left Kufat for their father's compound at Munung. He gave part of his compound to the Catholic Mission, where a school was opened in 1942. Then the late Fon gave the present site of the Catholic Mission to which the school was transferred in 1955 by Mr. J. N. Lafon. According to his grandson he presented the school with one of the trumpets he was using in the army.

Thomas Nyakom[7]

Thomas Nyakom was one of the relatives of Pa Musang Fotabeng Moses of Bali. Nyakom had gone to Fernando Po following the Germans.

> He told me that when they reached Fernando Po war had never come there, because it was a "free town" where "war" was never fought.... At Fernando Po they only stayed and did nothing and were happy that God had helped them. They were hidden there instead of fighting the war.... When he returned we were happy because God had made him go and stay where there was no war.

Nyakom never married a woman from Fernando Po as some had. "When he returned he was not a tailor or anything." By the time he came back,

> he was already old. He was not baptized there but here. It was Mr. Villhauer (a pioneer Basel missionary who returned after World War I) who used to make church services here at every place.... He had come after the war and was advising people not to be fighting and that God alone made man and God doesn't accept that they should be spilling "peoples' blood."

The Fon of Guzang[8]

Fon John Ngendop Mbayaseh of Guzang in Moghamo and his brother, Kobi Mba, remembered their father but were not clear about his connection with Fernando Po. Guzang is a Moghamo village a few miles from Bali-Nyonga.

In a 1988 interview the Fon said he was born in 1930 at Guzang. His mother was a princess from Bali.

> My father was an old German man. He was a German soldier. He went to the army and when the English sent the Germans away he became a

"chain man" (with the railway). They constructed the railway from Kribi to the east of Cameroon. Before that he stayed in Fernando Po for some years. He had a farm there but one thing was that when coming back he left all things and books over there to a brother who later died there.

The Fon referred us to his brother, Kobi Mba John. "He can say more about my father. I was outside working and as such know little about him." Kobi Mba John was the secretary of his father, the old Fon.

My father was a great man in those days because he was able to speak English. And so the Germans took him and he was working with them. He first left from here and went to Victoria. From there he went to Douala. From Douala to Kribi and from there to Yaoundé and because of a misunderstanding when he was not paid, he left from Yaoundé to Douala. From Douala he went to Fernando Po where he had his farm. He also worked at Abbas Bay as a head man. Then he owned a farm there too. In 1922 [*Was this a second trip?*] he left from Douala to Fernando Po. He helped the Germans carry their things to the ship. He was not a prisoner there. He was there as a headman. He had a small place there for himself. As he came back, as a prince, his brother was made a Fon, then he was made the assistant of the Fon and later Fon. He had learnt to construct roads. When he was installed here as Fon the first thing he did was to construct the road from here to Batibo. The first motor arrived here on 8 July 1948 due to his hard work.

Pius Mbasong of Guzang[9]

Pius Mbasong knew about the local men who had been captured and taken to Fernando because he heard about them from eyewitnesses.

I was born here at Guzang in 1895. By the time I was born there were no maternities here. My father's name was Mbasong and my mother was Matani. She came from Bamenong (Anong) and got married to my father.

I was caught and sent to a German school in the Basel Mission. The headmaster of that school was Dr. Villauer. Later I left the school and was home working and helping my father. That was in 1918.

Some of the people who left here as German soldiers were Samson Bonyam, Bah Wacham, Lekomu. Lekomu was a Bali man. There was also Talai.

When the English came and drove the Germans right to Garoua they were captured and taken to Fernando Po as war prisoners. The English people had come through Tiben, passed through Guzang, and then the

Germans ran to Bamenda. By the time they reached Bali-Nyonga they burnt Bali chief's palace saying that Bali were the people who gave refuge to the Germans. Then they passed to Bamenda and from Bamenda they went to Banyo. From Banyo they went to Ngaoundere and from there to Garoua, and it was there they were captured and taken to Fernando Po. I knew all these things because I heard them from others. From 1916 to 1919 these men were on Fernando Po and they were working there. By the time they were coming back they were paid. I don't know the amount of money that they could have been paid. Others married women from Fernando Po. Some of them were baptized as Catholics. They stayed well because they came back very healthy. It was the government that went and brought them back. It was Fon Gallega who sent people to collect them on the road as they were coming back.... All those who went to Fernando Po had joined the army. As they came back they stayed in their compounds and were doing their business. Some had learnt a trade and came back here and were doing that work, while others came and were farmers.

When they returned they formed a certain meeting called the "meeting of German soldiers." When one of them died they would find bamboo and on it they would put a red feather so that if he had killed a person in war all that would finish. At that time the Fon of Bali was his own governor....

Doh David Longwa Gwangwa[10]

David Gwangwa of Balikumbat on Ndop Plain knew the names of some who returned from Fernando Po. David was born in 1902. His father was Gwangwa and his mother Kahwe. His grandfather was from Samba in Nigeria. As a child he helped to farm groundnuts and maize. In 1923 he went to Government School Bamenda and finished standard six in 1932. In 1942 he married Celine Titi. They had six children.

He remembered that Mathias Sopu returned a Catholic from Fernando Po.

There was also Peter Yella, who had been a servant. John Dinga was a railway driver who was baptized and married at Shisong. There was also Marcus Gopse.

John Dinga returned to join together Catholics at a place behind the big market. The first catechist was from Bafouchu. Then for some years a man called Barnabas, from Santa, I think. In the early years there was no official catechist. Another was John Sambert. Ferdinand, a Bikom man, was also catechist.

Achillous Taboli[11]

Achillous Taboli of Tabenken remembered the Germans and some of the people who came back. "I was born and saw the Germans before they went. . . . When I grew up I had seen the Germans by the time they came to the people to dig the road from Bamenda to Banyo. When the Germans went and the English came and said they never wanted to hear German again, all the German schools were closed. I never attended the German school. They also said doctrine should be taught in Pidgin English. It was the government which gave those orders. . . . Some of the people who got baptism at Fernando Po before coming here included John Kibo, Ndum Marcus Mbori, John Chifu, and Daniel Mbei. They told me that at Fernando Po before they were baptized they had a general examination because they had no time to ask questions one by one. When they were at Fernando Po, because there was no more war, the only thing they did was to teach the catechism and divide food and eat.

John Kibo came home with a wife.

> She was an Ewondu girl from Yaoundé whom he had married during the war time. . . . When John came back he never stayed and later on went to join the English soldiers. He left Bamenda for Calabar, Port Harcourt, and then to Abuja. The wife whom he brought from Yaoundé died in the sea. She never delivered. . . . All of them who were baptized at Fernando Po were strong Christians.

The Fon of Kom, Michael Njiniboh II[12]

At his palace in Laikom, Fon Michael talked of seeing those who returned from Fernando Po.

> Some of them included Peter Njam, Njah Njoh, Francis Fontamamoh, James Ngongbong, Peter Jaff, Joannes Usibom, Francis Ndelai, Felix Mbe, Lucas Nsombi, Kangjum, Michael Tim, and Joannes Achi. Contract Ntoh Chiko, Peter Mbang, Thomas Mboyong Honyoh. Most of these people are dead. . . . Njah Njoh had returned from Fernando Po with Mary who was his wife. She died without delivering children.

Thomas Lambe[13]

Another eyewitness was Thomas Lambe of Babungo.

> I was born, according to my mother, soon after my father left here to be a German soldier. When the soldiers were returning she told me to go to meet them. I trekked to Bamunka (Ndop) and met them. They were

blowing a trumpet. Then I stopped and was afraid and when I was shown to my father he gave me a bottle of water and a bag to hold and we came right here. There were many Babungo people there, but I was too small to know them. There was my father, Ngoh Tubeko, Nsemboh, Nchangwa and Ngwebong Nchangwa.... My father went into the army when the Germans came. He was given by the chief. He told me that they were selected from the palace and sent to Fernando Po.... There was one man called Nazarius who came back with a wife.... My father used to go to Bamenda with Timobo an ex-German soldier. One day he went outside the house and fell there, and when he was brought in he died.

Augustine Kunke[14]

Augustine told the following story at Babungo with a fine description of the arrival of returnees.

My father was with the Germans. He was an army man and they went to Fernando Po. He came back with a woman, but she died and didn't deliver children. She was a woman of Fernando Po and not Yaoundé. She was thin. When they were coming they were in uniform and there was a commander who was giving orders to them. They were blowing a trumpet by the time they were coming back. When they were passing, everybody stood by the side of the road to see them, and they passed directly to the palace. At the palace the chief came out and greeted them and ordered them to go back to their homes because he told them when they were going to go and come back and as everyone had returned they should all scatter and go to their various homes.... They brought nothing to the chief but just went to report. None came back with any trade. They came and just stayed like that.... Those who had that church at first were people who came from Fernando Po.

Aloysius Ngong[15]

Aloysius, a native of Wombong in Kom,

saw the German soldiers come back. We were at Njinikejem. My mother had prepared fufu, and when we reached Baingo we met them. They were blowing a trumpet when they came. They had sent notice that they were coming. There were many of them. My uncle was one Nke.

My brother was on Fernando Po. He told me that before they went there the chief had given them to the Germans and they took them and trained them at Bamenda from where they were taken to Fernando Po. He stayed away for six years. He took baptism at Fernando Po. By that time there was no church here. So when he went to Fernando Po he was baptized. There were many of them who left from here.

He then added something extraordinary:

> When they reached there the Germans said that they should kill the chief of Fernando Po but they couldn't. [This may be connected with the conflict between the Bubi and the Spanish government.]
>
> One of those returnees brought a woman of Fernando Po called Maria Bih. The man who brought her was only remembered as "Max."
>
> When my brother came back they often had a meeting in my compound of the German soldiers. They used to pray in German. They had a hut and made prayers every day. I can still make a short prayer in German which I learnt from that meeting.
>
> When one of the soldiers died all of them would join. Now all have died. They never had any other special thing. . . . They used to be very strong Christians.

Sergeant Nkette[16]

In August of 1988, at his Bali-Nyonga home, Paul Nketi, a son of a former German soldier, spoke about his late father, who was known as Sgt. Nkette. He was among those who served in the Kamerun army. There was no record of his internment after being made prisoner. Rather, from his record, he was coopted into the Nigerian police.

"Nkette Nchig," Number 1162, in his official record, joined the German army at Douala in 1908. He was first stationed in Soppo and then went to Koussari in the Garua area. Returning to Douala and then to Soppo again, he was a "lance corporal" at the outbreak of World War I. During the war he went with the German forces to Nssanakang near Mamfe, and then retreated with the Germans to Bamenda and Nso, where he was made prisoner and taken to Douala.

His service to German Kamerun was recognized by the German government in September 1966 when he was given a bonus of 60,000 cfa. His service to the Nigerian Police Force in the Cameroons Province under the League of Nations Mandate is interesting. According to his discharge certificate, Number 4205, "H Kette Nchig" enlisted at Douala for service in the Southern Police Force on 9 January 1915, soon afer the fall of the town. He served as a police officer in Southern Cameroons for "18 years 8 months," rising to the rank of "first-class sergeant." He voluntarily retired in 1933 and died on 27 October 1966. He drew a pension of 20 pounds, 13 shillings, and 8 pence for more than thirty years. His son remarked that at his death celebration in December 1966, a "keg of gunpowder" was used.

Sergeant Nkette in Bali-Nyonga dress, from a photograph in Paul Nketi's home. © O'Neil, 1988.

Although he also fought in the Kamerun army he was awarded the "Allied Victory Medal" of 1915!

Stephen Doyi[17]

Stephen, of Mantum in Bali, was the grandson of Sgt. Nkette.

Before he took me he was already a policeman and had been a German soldier. He was caught and taken to Ekom and then became a soldier. But when the English people later came he was made a policeman. It was under him that I grew. He is the father of Alois and Paul Nketi. When he was in Mamfe he was a sergeant there. He used to work in the office. It was from the police work that he retired and was obtaining a pension.

That pension only stopped when he died. He was not a Christian. It was his first wife who was a Christian.... This photo on the wall with somebody wearing a cap made of elephant hair is Fon Galega II.... My grandmother, called Anastasia, was wife of the late Sgt. Nkette. She was the first to be baptized here.... Gwane was another German soldier who had returned from Fernando Po. I don't know whether he was baptized or not. When he came back he was just in his compound. The name of his sister is Manong.

Mama Monica Njeke[18]

Mama Monica, of Njenka in Bali-Nyonga, was "born during the German time. My brother was Paul Sabi. We were from one father. Our mother was Tita Ngame. I got married earlier. My brother used to do farming and plant coffee. I know of one German called "Lambaka" who came here. My brother Paul Sabi left from here and went with the Germans. When he was coming back he came with a woman called Anna. She has died. They had children. One was Musa and the other Anchi. His wife was a white woman he brought from Germany. Musa had gone back to Germany."

When her brother returned,

> he built his own house and got married to another woman. He was a baptized Catholic Christian at Fernando Po. At Fernando Po he was a soldier. Before my brother died, there had been only one child, Emilia, who remained.
>
> He did nothing but farming because when he returned he was already old and as such was unable to do anything again.

When he returned from Fernando Po, "he was taken to be a very good man and people were happy because he had come back. Indeed he came back with nothing because all his things were stolen on the ship. It was our father who used to care for him."

John Fomukong[19]

Not everyone, as we have seen, was a "German soldier." According to his son Pius, John Fomukong received professional training in nursing by the Germans and even traveled to Germany. This Bali man also spent time on Fernando Po during World War I. His son Pius was born at Soppo in 1922. His mother was Clara Enaga. He remembered stories of his father who had left Bali during the German time and gone to Buea. At Buea he attended school and later was trained as a nurse. He said that he had been baptized in Europe where he was trained in nursing. "He was even called *Doctor* by the people." "Before Zintgraff came (in 1889) my father already went to the coast. As he went to the coast people thought that he was dead, but one day a white man brought him home. This is what he told me."

He came back during "the English period and he was made to work in a hospital and was even made the head of that hospital. Under the British he was transferred to Bamenda and then to Buea again. Later he was sent to Calabar and then to Abakaleki in Nigeria. It was at Calabar that I started class one of primary school."

His father was "a Catholic Christian, and he was baptized in Europe. He married my mother in 1922, in Soppo, Buea. At Fernando Po he was a war doctor. He used to tell us how they suffered at the front and how people were forced to carry war equipment. He died in Nigeria while he was working there."

When his father was posted to Nigeria "he left me with one Martin Georges in Bamenda. This was in 1931." He stayed with that nurse in Bamenda for sometime before going to Nigeria.

Before his father died in 1961, Pius returned home to care for his grandmother and other family members. After finishing school he had gone to Missellele and was working there as a mail runner from Missellele to Tiko with the CDC. He had married, but "that woman later died."

Patrick Timneng[20]

The grandson of Michael Timneng of Kom remembered some of the stories his father had told him about Fernando Po.

> Let me try to remember his stories. Most of the Bamenda people went there as soldiers, of which my father was one. He was there first as a house boy to a German soldier and later became a soldier. They all prayed in the German language. He was the only one who was a bit literate.
>
> All the Kom people who got baptism came home along with him. Those I can remember that came with my father were: Johannes Ngongmbong, Johanes Mbenglii, Ambrose Foinambu, Johanes Achi, Francis Fointama, Peter Joff, Peter Jobain, Thomas Mbuyongha, and Moses Chianange. None of these mentioned is living.
>
> When they came home, my father, being a bit literate, gathered them in his house for prayers. Gradually there were some catechumens, and they all thought to have a place to build a small bamboo church at Njinikom, where the present weekly market is. Papa Michael Timneng's mother died many years before him. I never saw his father. He grew up with his uncle Nkeh, who later on traveled to Fernando Po as a pagan and got baptized there. When he came home he continued with the uncle Nkeh, and Nkeh, Nicholas, later got baptized before he died.

As he brought the Christian faith from Fernando Po he assembled the people in Wombong village for prayers and religious services. Later a plot was acquired at Njinikom Sailah from where it transferred to the present place. During that time he suffered a lot of tortures and imprisonments from the then Fon Ngam, who did not like Christianity.

I do not know about the escape with the Germans to Spanish territory unless I contact some older persons. Generally they loved the stay there on Fernando Po. They were cordial with the Germans.

Abraham Tituwan[21]

At the time the first Germans came to Bali-Nyonga, Abraham's father was a servant to the Fon. His name was Ngoh Sama, and it was he who took Dr. Zintgraff from Ashong.

> All these things were told to me by my father. Also the chief gave his daughter, Tangi Madomia, who got married to Dr. Zintgraff. When explorer Eugen Zintgraff was leaving, the woman remained and died here.... Some people were German soldiers, including Ndadasi Decomu. They told us how they suffered in the war and they had gone to Fernando Po. By the time they returned some of them were farmers, traders, and those who were old just stayed at home while their families cared for them.

Nsegala Dominic Gwendinga[22]

Dominic Gwendinga was born at Bali-Nyonga in 1926. It was his grandfather who told him stories like one about the arrival of the first white man (Zintgraff), when "the Fon blew a horn." It was his father who went to Fernando Po, but it is not clear he went with the retreating Germans in 1916 or on his own. "My grandfather told me that it was through laborer work that my father went to Fernando Po.... When my father returned from Fernando Po he was a rich man.

He returned with two iron boxes.

> My grandmother told me that they were brought by my father from Fernando Po and that he also came with two sewing machines (one hand and one foot machine). By then in Bali they never used to sew clothes ... so it was that my father came and introduced (sewing machines) so that they could use a machine and sew clothes. And he used to sew only the clothes for the chief.... I don't have anything belonging to my father nor to my grandfather. They died and left many widows with me, and they are like water and all is on my head. They are at Basel there [a place in Bali town], and if we go there you will see so many people like water.

Lucy Diagah[23]

Lucy Diagah of Bali-Nyonga was the daughter of Christian Nyangmia and Mary Kamah.

> My father had been to Dschang. I don't know how he managed to go there.... He was a catechist there during the German time.... He had gotten married to one woman from that Dschang side, and I think the woman died. I saw the meeting which was organized here by all those old German soldiers who had returned from Fernando Po. They used to go there, contributed some money like a "njange" (a traditional savings and loan meeting), ate and drank wine.

Bernard Njangmia[24]

Bernard's father was Christian Njangmia. He had been

> born in Bali and then he attended the vernacular school which was here. Because he was very clever the Fon of Bali-Nyonga selected six of them and sent them to the German school at Sasse ... at Sasse they were baptized in 1913. They never completed that school course because of the 1914 war. The students were sent out. He came here because the Germans were going away and all were sent to various missions to help. He was sent to Mbouda and Bawanjo, where he was working as a classroom teacher and also as a catechist at the same time.

Clement Takwa[25]

Clement knew Daniel Lanjoh, who was trained by the Germans, but was not sure if he had been to Fernando Po.

> We used to move all around here and saw planks because by then everywhere there were forests. The person who taught me this saw work was the late Daniel Lanjoh.
>
> It was Daniel Lanjoh who came and introduced Christianity to me. Daniel Lanjoh had heard that the Germans were at Bamenda, and he went there. There he learnt that sawyer work and Christianity, and when he came back he introduced it to us.

Benedict Jaff[26]

Some people left from here to Fernando Po as soldiers and have already died and I can't remember them again. When the war ended and the Germans left and those people came back, some of them worked as messengers at the Nso palace. Clement Takwa was one of them.

I can't remember when I was born but remember that by that time we were running from the Germans. I ran by myself and I think I was about three years of age.

Nicholas Waneh[27]

Nicholas Waneh of Bafmeng was a "very small boy in German time," but he remembered a Bum man, Peter Njam, at the village of Mbonkesu, who was a "soldier for the Germans." He was, according to Nicholas, a sergeant major, "tall and very fat and wore a khaki uniform." Nicholas continued: "He brought the church from Fernando Po." After staying at Njinikom, he came to be a farmer in Mbonkesu village. Later he became a catechist and, at some point, a polygamist. "He died long ago," killed by a leopard. The animal was catching goats and attacked him. "After three days he died." Whether he was really a "soldier" one cannot know.

Agathe Koigni

A Dutch Mill Hill Missionary, Ben Beemster, was on mission among the Tikar in the Adamawa Region of Cameroon from 1974 to 1984. He met Agathe Koigni and wrote her story. He was impressed that she was a Christian "who evangelized a whole village—not as a catechist but by her witness as a Christian housewife." Twenty years later he updated his studies and broadened his research on the Tikar. The following is taken from his story of Agathe.[28]

> Agathe Koigni was among the thousands who ended up on Fernando Po in 1915. Agathe was born in Bandam, a village near Bankim. Bankim was near a road from the north to Kumbo, where Agathe stayed as a young woman. She lived with a soldier called Marcus Ntem. At Kumbo they began to attend catechism classes in the Catholic Mission. When the war came, the soldiers and their dependents were taken prisoner. They were marched from Kumbo through Tikar and Fulani country to Gashaka. From there they finally reached the coast of Nigeria, where they were transported to Fernando Po. In the island camps they continued their catechumenate and prepared for the sacrament of marriage. The Sacred Heart Missionaries had a solution, the "sixa," from the word sister, to help women prepare for married life. In 1917 there were 33 women in the group. In 1918 there were 203. Agathe was baptized on the island and later became, according to Fr. Beemster, the first Tikar Christian.

APPENDIX 2

Stories of Kamerun and Fernando Po

The following are short stories. They are a combination of imagination, personal experience, real events, and people.

Ngoh Sama

Germany had annexed the coastal area of Cameroon in 1884 and only four years later was extending its influence over a wider and wider area of the interior.

To reach what us now the North West Region of Cameroon the German explorer Eugen Zintgraff had worked out a plan to set up a line of stations from the coast to the high plateau beyond the escarpment that divides the forest from the grassfields. The Germans were attracted by some of the principle trading commodities and the potential manpower of the area and wanted to by-pass local traders. The aim was direct trade to German companies at the coast and away from rival trade routes to the Benue and Calabar.

Many times I walked the paths of Bamessong (Ashong) and Bali-Nyonga (Bali), where elders told stories of the arrival of the first recorded European, the explorer Zintgraff.[1] Guided by his interpreter, Muyenga, a slave of King Manga Bell of the Duala, Zintgraff and a group of 100 Lagosian and 75 Liberian Vai carriers, trailed by hostages from a clash with a local chief along the way and captured grassfield slaves, arrived at Ashong on 12 January 1889. Zintgraff wrote about his journeys to this area in his 1895 book *Nord Kamerun*.

Ngoh Sama had almost completed his journey from Bali-Nyonga as he began the climb to the heights of Bamessong. Once at the top he moved along the ridge. Before he entered the high grass he turned. It was dry season, and the country was covered with a harmattan haze. In the rainy season, Bamessong, perched above the massive forest, was often covered with a damp, cold mist.

He could not see very far, but he knew that on clear days during the rainy season the view of the country was very beautiful. Bamessong was one of the highest villages in the area. Looking east he might see signs of Pinyin village. North were the rolling grassfields and to the southwest were the great forests of West Africa. On other visits he often sat below the market on a grassy hilltop and looked across miles and miles of the forest canopy below the escarpment.

He passed through the first compounds as he descended the rocky path towards the Fon's (chief's) compound. Children were excited. They ran about singing like weaver birds of what they had seen. Until they were finally driven away by elders, they gathered at the Fon's palace near the path down into the forest, a quarter called Enwen. The news of what they saw emerge from the forest had reached the Fon of Bali-Nyonga. An unknown "thing with skin like fire," a stranger had appeared in Bamessong along with 175 carriers. The Fon had sent Ngoh Sama to investigate.

By the time Ngoh reached the compound and greeted the people hundreds of men had arrived from neighboring villages. There they found the carriers of the stranger. The locals, even an armed group from Pinyin village, miles away, stood or squatted silently. Ngoh completed his greeting to the Fon and was led to a small hut in the compound. Sitting outside on a stool, surrounded by the curious, was a peculiar figure. It was a man with redden skin with a beard and clothing he had not seen before. Most of the local men were at a distance, unsure of what or who the visitor might be. Fearful himself but remembering his mission he approached.

It was the German explorer Eugen Zintgraff who had left the coast for the interior of Kamerun in December 1888.

This was the first recorded encounter between a European and Africans in the interior grassfields of Cameroon.

Ngong

On mission in Bafmeng in the North West Region, one night elders told stories about the arrival of Christianity in their country. Pa Ngong's story was one of them. This also happened on a visit to Djottin Mission as well, where similar stories were told. Here I imagine the night one boy's heart was moved by the words spoken about Jesus. His very words are true and from one witness. "My heart went out to there," as he listened to the story of Jesus. The story is fictitious but based on the words of real people.

> It had been a fearful time in the country. His father and many other men had been taken away to work as porters for the Germans, who often passed through the village. Others had gone to work on plantations at the coast and were never heard from again. There was starvation and sickness. Everyone was affected. And then the quarrels began over chieftaincy succession followed by accusations of witchcraft and the terrible sasswood ordeal. No one was safe. Evil was everywhere.
>
> One night two men returned from the coast. Their families rejoiced. They came with stories of life on the plantations and near the sea.

The next evening Ngong and his friends heard singing. It was coming from a small hut in the chief's compound. The village head had given it for the use of the men who returned from the coast. The boys made their way to the hut and looked through the small window. A few people were seated around a fire in the middle of the floor. The faces of others could be seen in the shadows. One of the men, who now called himself Patrick, read from a book in the language of the Germans. He stopped and sang a song they had never heard before. Then he began to speak about Jesus.

The words touched Ngong's heart. Instead of the death and fear of witchcraft that had filled the village he now heard about Jesus and his words of peace and kindness, love and forgiveness. Ngong's life was never again the same. He was determined even at his young age to learn more. In time he was baptized. Later he was a catechist for many years in his own country.

Mathias Anong

Prior to World War I, neither Christianity nor education had been firmly established at Widekum village. That was accomplished in part through the efforts of a man who had been interned with the Germans on the Spanish island of Fernando Po. The man's name was Anong, a member of the Fon of Widekum's family.

Anong was born in Widekum about the year 1895. Sometime in 1912 there was a meeting at Widekum village between the German civil administrator of the Mamfe District stationed at Ossidinge on the Cross River, and the military officer in charge of the Bezirk, or station, at Bamenda.

Captain Adametz came to the village from Bamenda to meet Dr. Mansfeld of Mamfe. Mansfeld had taken over the district after the murder of his predecessor. His nickname among the people was "Dr. Mamfe."

Anong was only a small boy when he first saw Hauptman (Captain) Adametz. One day he was in his father's farm at Widekum village. His father was the village head. The drums began to talk about the arrival of two white men. He had seen white men before. Widekum village had a market on the path between Ossidinge and the escarpment to the grassfields. German soldiers, messengers, traders, missionaries, and many carriers often passed.

Anong dropped his hoe and ran along the river bank toward his father's compound. There he saw the two Germans. Captain Adametz was the district officer at the Bamenda Fort. "Dr. Mamfe," as Mansfeld was called, was his counterpart in Mamfe-Ossidinge. They were meeting at Widekum to decide on the boundary between the two districts, between Ossidinge and Bamenda.

Adametz was laughing and Anong heard him say through an interpreter that "everyone in the forest"—the forest covered most of Ossidinge district—"wants to be a chief." Anong learned later that it was true, almost every village had a "chief," whereas in the grassfields, groups were large and made up of many villages, all under one chief, or Fon.

It was probably on that visit that the Captain arranged with the old chief, the Fon of Widekum, to take Anong with him to Bamenda. After the meeting, as the visitors relaxed and shared some cooked plantains and bush meat and drank palm wine, Anong saw Adametz speaking with the chief and gesture toward him. That night his father told him that he was to join the Captain's group in the morning. Adametz was taking him to the Bamenda fort. He was going to be a houseboy to the Germans.[2] He was to be trained to help in the kitchen and to "pass chop," that is to wait on the Captain's table. Anong was nicknamed "Ma Kanju."

And so began a journey that was to determine his life, not unlike that of many other young boys and men. At Bamenda station he was put with a Duala man who was the Captain's cook.

The young Anong traveled with Adametz when he went to Yaoundé, but most of his time was spent at the Bamenda station. When the war began in 1914 he followed the German officer to meet the British attack from Nigeria at Nsanakang on the Cross River, and at Mamfe. When the Germans retreated from Bamenda in October 1915 Adametz wanted Anong to return to his home in Widekum. He refused, and instead he followed the Germans. Later they retreated from Maroua, Banyo, and finally Yaoundé. He witnessed the fighting that took place between the British, French, and Belgian soldiers. Anong then followed the Germans across the border into Spanish territory. In 1916 he was among the thousands interned on the island of Fernando Po. It was there while a prisoner at a camp near Santa Isabel that he began to attend the Catholic Church and became a catechumen. While on the island he also attended classes at the German school completing to class two.

His instructions for baptism were given in Ewondo, the language of the Yaoundé people in the camps, by the Pallottine missionaries who were among the internees. Anong was finally baptized on the 24 February 1919. He chose the name "Mathias."

Padre Carlos, Catholic Missionary to Fernando Po

As the ship passed along the west coast of Africa Padre Carlos remembered the description by Francis Xavier three hundred years earlier of a great becalmed sea where it seemed Francis and his Portuguese shipmates would be stranded forever. No longer dependent on the winds and current, he leaned over the prow in the twilight hours watching the ship cut through the water. Startled flying fish were leaping into short flight before falling back into the sea. He spent much of his time talking with the crew and other travelers, and reading. At one point he was able to borrow a fishing pole and dropped a baited hook among the large fish that trailed behind when the ship slowed and neared a port. He was never successful.

On board the ship were other missionaries. They were all members of a congregation founded by Archbishop Anthony Claret. All were headed to the new mission vicariate in the Gulf of Guinea. What he had read or heard about tropical Africa slowly became a reality for the passengers. One day to the east he saw the outline of a mountain rising near the coast. It was an active volcano in what had become German Kamerun. And then to the south appearing out the mist, the first peaks of his assignment, the island of Fernando Po. He thought: What a long way from his beautiful Catalonia and strolls on La Rambla of Barcelona.[3]

Catholic missionaries only came in the second half of the nineteenth century to Fernando Po. They came after the work of the Baptists was interrupted by a renewal of Spain's interest in West Africa.

Njeke

Njeke is a woman who was interviewed in 1988. Some of the details of her story are imagined and draw on the experiences of other women who followed their men into Spanish territory in 1916. Njenka Quarter is part of the town of Bali-Nyonga on the road to Bamenda in the North West Region of Cameroon.

Njeke sat in the hut feeding a fire at the center of the floor with dry reeds she had collected along the seashore. She was thinking of her childhood at Njenka quarter in Bali-Nyonga. As a small girl she went to the farm with her parents, collected firewood, and sometimes prepared food for the family. As she grew she began to farm on her own. All that changed one day when she was given to her husband, Ngoro. She was not sure but she thought Ngoro had paid her dowry in brass rods. Of course a woman could not know the amount paid on her head. For her it was a surprise. She was just told one day that Ngoro was her husband. He had been a trader and then found work with the Germans. When she left the village to follow him she could never have imagined that a few years later she might find herself in this strange place near Bata where people were dying of starvation. That evening she heard a rumor when collecting water at the stream that many would soon be crossing the sea to an island. No doubt her husband, Ngoro, would be among them because he was a soldier.

Akenji Mbah

Among the stories collected in the 1980s, this one is told of a young man from the North West Region who had learned carpentry and was now using his trade to build and maintain the camps of the internees on Fernando Po.

> He was fortunate. Most of his countrymen were in the forest clearing bush for farms or constructing roads between the camps and the shoreline. Although he found the heat and fevers of the island oppressive he was glad to be alive after seeing so many die of starvation on the German retreat to Spanish territory first on the mainland and later during the first months on the island.
>
> Akenji Mbah's home was a small village near Pinyin in the Bamenda grassfields. Some years before the war, his uncle returned from the coast to visit his father. He asked that Akenji return with him to help in his kitchen. It was a custom for extended family to benefit from the success of its members. His father decided that he would serve his uncle but also have opportunity to go to one of the white man schools and learn a trade. In his home village there was a small school, but it only taught in the local language. Bali-Nyonga had a "German school," managed by Dr. Villauer, a Basel missionary, which accepted some pupils who had completed at the village schools. Mbah never had chance to attend.
>
> Along with his uncle and many others he set off one bright morning at the beginning of the rainy season of 1910. They traveled through familiar villages and open country down the old escarpment road to the forest, through a German outpost called Tinto, where there was a telegraph station. Locals named the place "Tinto Wire" after the telegraph line that extended through the forest from the coast to the station.
>
> Finally they reached a plantation near the town of Victoria. All was new to him, especially the climate, and the rows of palm and rubber trees. He marveled at how neat the rows of rubber trees were, as each leaned forward to catch the sun. What was familiar was the sight of many faces he recognized. There were so many men from his country. Some had wives and families. At the plantation his uncle was an important man, an overseer. He was responsible for a gang of workers from Bali-Nyonga who cleared bush and sometimes planted oil palms. He was greeted by his uncle's wife, a Bakweri woman with a beautiful smile and kind disposition.
>
> After some months, Mbah was apprenticed to a friend of his uncle to learn carpentry. The custom was that his uncle paid a fee to the carpenter who brought Akenji into his workshop. There were other boys learning work too. The apprentice did all the tedious jobs: cleaning up the workshop, carrying in planks from the bush, planing wood, everything, including cooking sometimes for their master, the carpenter. He was

given a small allowance each month during the three years he remained with the master. Finally he was given a "book," a letter from the carpenter to say that he had completed his training, along with a few simple tools to help him begin to work on his own.

It was then that he was employed by the Germans to put up simple housing for their people. He worked on building the military camp at Banyo. He began by making door and window frames and shutters. In a short time, with the help of the German officer in charge of the carpentry workshop, he was able to make furniture—tables, chairs, and beds. By the time the war came, and he retreated with the Germans, he was known for his skill at making furniture. He only needed a picture, a sketch, or sometimes only a description. But often people brought a sample to imitate. On the island over the first months there was a desperate rush to provide shelter for thousands. As camps were laid out there was a need for hospitals and dispensaries, and the more permanent quarters of the officers. Some of the plantation land they had been given had buildings to be repaired. He joined others in that work.

Now each day when the camp awoke he headed for his workshop, a long thatched shed with strong, heavy work benches. As the months passed, supplies began to reach them from Europe, and among the shipments were excellent tools for the carpentry workshop. Among the officers one stood out for his kindness, Captain Harttmann. On this day, as his mind wandered, he planed hardwoods for making furniture for a new hospital that was being constructed near his camp. One of the "doctors" was also a Christian missionary, a Catholic priest. When he was not at the hospital he and several others gave instructions to catechumens in a makeshift church, which he could see from his shed. Mbah had gone there too. He hoped to be baptized and had already chosen his name. It would be Philip.

Felix Tita, the Teacher

Schools were opened in the camps for any who were interested. Among the internees were former school teachers in Kamerun. Here is one.

One afternoon, on his way back from Santa Isabel to the camp, he saw one of his old pupils from the vernacular school near Bare. The young man worked in the kitchen of the veterinary doctor. He had not been a good student and soon was so distracted that he left to carry his father's bag from place to place. But on this day he was very enthusiastic and appealed to the teacher to resume his lessons in the free time he had each day. The old teacher missed his work and showed some interest. But how? I have already asked my master if there was a school somewhere in the camps. He in turn might talk to Capt. Harttmann, a German officer who had been organizing a workshop that even had European tools for skilled craftsmen to use. He could help find a place and a time when a school could open.

A Story of Michael Timneng

Before the repatriation the missionaries gave final instructions to the catechumens and newly baptized. Among them was Michael Timneng of Kom. This piece is based on what was remembered by his family in 1988 and published in a Mission magazine in the United Kingdom.

During a 1988 visit to the compound of Michael Timneng (also known as Michael Tim), one of the men interned on Fernando Po, a son remembered the story of his father. Timneng was well known as one of the returnees from the island who helped to plant the Christian church in his own tribe and become an "agent of change" in the traditional society of his homeland. Hearing his story and seeing some of the very books in German a missionary handed him gave me much to think about over the years since that evening in Wombong village. In 1996 I wrote small article for a Catholic fundraising magazine for the missions. Using the facts of the story he told, the story describes the final day on the island before he and his comrades returned to the mainland.[4]

It was 1919. The place was a humid clearing in a plantation camp on the island of Fernando Po. A bearded European in a yellowing cassock looked up from the prayer book in his hands and above the rows of dark muscular men lined up in front of him. He searched across the sea for the hazy outline of the Cameroon coast and the heights of volcanic Mt. Cameroon.

The Africans before him that morning were from the mainland. They represented many tribes and small villages of the former German Kamerun. They were part of the thousands of Cameroonians who had been interned with the retreating Germans during the First World War and transported to the island which was then under neutral Spanish control. Among them were some Christians and many catechumens. Among the Germans there were missionaries. The small chapels and catechumenates in the camps became a training ground for an army of Catholic Christians who when they returned to their homes would play an important part in the evangelization of their country.

The day was one of farewell. The Africans were to be carried back to the mainland; the Europeans were preparing to leave for Europe.

The priest paced up and down a line of men from the Bamenda grassfields. He drew some small books in German from his bag: a catechism, a prayer book and the Sunday epistles and gospels. Finally he stopped next to a young man named Tim, who was from a group of people called the Kom. He announced to all of the men that they were to be responsible for bringing the Good News about Jesus to their own people. "Take these books," he said. "Teach your people what is found in them. If you don't, God will know."

Timneng and others are remembered to be among the founders and early supporters of many Catholic communities in Cameroon.

Maria

This is a story of one woman who left the island where she was born and traveled to Kom in the grassfields. Jacqueline de Vries writes that along with the 400 ex-soldiers who returned to Kom there were 170 women. A man named "Max" is said to have returned with a Fernando Po woman called Maria.

Maria was born and baptized on Fernando Po by a Spanish missionary before World War I. She attended a school run by missionary sisters but left after only two years. Now she was married to a Cameroonian who had come to the island with the Germans. With her husband she embarked on a great adventure. It took her first to the mainland at Douala with her husband, Njah Njoh, in 1919, and then to his home in the highlands of Cameroon. It was a most difficult trek through the thick forests and up the escarpment from Tinto Wire to the grassfields. She thought of the story of Jesus on Calvary as she struggled with her loads up and into open country. She was part of a long column of men, women, and children. The forest began to open up as they emerged, following a slippery track cut deep by many years of use by people and cattle and heavy rains. They marched into open country and cooler air, past an abandoned German outpost and barracks for a few messengers and soldiers. She knew the names of many from Kom country from her two years in the camp on Fernando Po. Three more days of walking and they began to ascend again, up and through a gap in the surrounding hills. Then she saw her new home, laid open before her. Her husband pointed in the distance to a high place where they would end their journey, in Kom.

Notes

Preface

1. Daniel J. O'Leary, "Evolution and the Holy Spirit," in *Treasured and Transformed* (Dublin: Columba Press, 2014), 154–55.
2. Ibrahim K. Sundiata, *From Slavery to Neo-Slavery: The Bight of Biafra and Fernando Po in the Era of Abolition, 1827–1930* (Madison: University of Wisconsin Press, 1996), 19.
3. Jacqueline de Vries, "Catholic Mission, Colonial Government and Indigenous Response in Kom, Cameroon," *African Studies Centre*, Research Report 56/1998 (Leiden, The Netherlands), 22.
4. The estuary is home to the Cameroon ghost shrimp, which periodically irrupts into dense swarms. At these times, people catch huge quantities, eating the females or drying them for later use, and making a fish oil from the males. See Lipke B. Holthuis, "Callianassa turnerana," Netherlands Biodiversity Information Facility.
5. This hope is seen in the testimony of missionaries, the administrators, and Cameroonians. The plan worked. The Versailles treaty failed. Kamerun was taken from Germany and divided between Britain and France. For some, "civilization" was set back while colonialization continued.
6. Cameroon Mountain is 13,345 ft. (4,095 meters). It last erupted in 2000.
7. As a story took shape it expanded into more than the history of German Kamerun and World War I and what Catholic Christians experienced, especially in the North West Region. It is also about the planting, growth, and survival of the Christian gospel aided by many missionaries, both Protestant and Catholic. The island of Fernando Po was important in that experience because it was a place where internment led to the preparation of many to return to their villages as catechumens or baptized Christians.
8. Jim O'Connell, *A Life to Live* (Dublin: Columba Press, 2015).
9. Missionary Edith Dynan, a Holy Rosary Sister, wrote to the author from Nigeria in 1986 and 1987 about the Cameroonians interned on Fernando Po during World War I. She was aware of some of the documents concerning 1916–1919 and met people who had been there. In Sister's last letter she wrote that if a study was not undertaken soon the story "would go unrecorded forever, and that would be something precious to lose."

Introduction

1. Harry R Rudin, *Germans in the Cameroons, 1884–1914* (New Haven: Yale University Press, 1938), Introduction, 17. One translation by Arnold Vehoeven is: "I am a boy from Kamerun the German colony; Prince Bismarck left no work undone to make its conquest be." In 1932 Rudin interviewed many in Cameroon who had been educated by the Germans. He spoke with three Cameroonians, and one of them began, for no good reason, to quote this schoolboy poem of old Kamerun. "He happened to be the schoolboy who wrote the orginal!" In 1985 Professor Rudin welcomed me to his home in Hamden, Connecticut. At the time he was retired from Yale University. It was the same Harry Rudin who, in 1931, wrote a doctoral dissertation about Imperial Germany's colonial administration in Africa. There was a view put forward at the Ver-

sailles Peace Conference that "Germany's procedure in her colonies had been open to grave criticism, and that on moral grounds, as well as for political reasons, her retention of them could scarcely be justified." In the Foreword (p. 11) of his book *Germans in the Cameroons*, he came to a different conclusion. "I realize that there were evils in Germany's administration of her colonies; but fundamentally these evils are neither greater than nor different from those existing in any other colonial system. My own conclusion is that German's colonial accomplishments in thirty short years constitute a record of unusual achievement and entitle her to a very high rank as a successful colonial power, a view quite different from that reached in 1919."

2. There are various spellings of Cameroon: There is German *Kamerun*; French *Cameroun*; Spanish *Camarones*; Portuguese *Camaroes*; and British *Cameroons*."

3. A. Victor Murray, *The School in the Bush: A Critical Study of the Theory and Practice of Native Education in Africa* (London: Longmans, 1929). Professor Rudin gave this book to the author in 1985.

4. During World War II the ship SS *Wahehe* was captured by the Royal Navy off Iceland in 1940 and its name changed to *Empire Citizen*. On 3 February 1941, it was sunk by German U boat 107 while part of a convoy between Liverpool and Rangoon, Burma. Seventy-eight died and only three survived.

5. Robert L. Tigor, "Recollections of Robert O'Collins," *Northeast African Studies* 11, no. 1 (2004–2010): 141–44. Harry Rudin had a long career at Yale University, where he was regarded as the history department's primary scholar in European diplomatic history. He was also among the first to promote African history, "advising a growing group of Ph.D. candidates studying the history of Africa, a coming and important field at the time." Students gave Professor Rudin the nickname "Black Harry," presumably because of his gloomy countenance, "but he was in fact a cheerful teacher and scholar and one of the favorites of graduate and undergraduate students alike."

6. Antonio M. Carrasco, *Orden en Rio Muni* (Madrid: De Librum Tremens, 2011). See also "Orden en Rio Muni: La Guinée espagnole a l'heure de la Grande Guerre," 4 January 2014, *Association France-Guinée Equatorial*. The monument is made of basalt stone and about four meters in height. It is on the site of an old military cemetery where eight Germans and hundreds of Cameroon soldiers of the "German colonial guard" are buried. They had died not in combat but due to tropical sicknesses and exhaustion during their internment on the island from 1916 to 1919.

7. Stephanie Trouillard, *France 24*, 14 February 1915, "La Guinée equatorial à l'heure de la Grande Guerre," Deutsche Botschaft Malabo, Rede von Botschafter Rainer Munzel anlasslich des Volkstrauertags. Trouillard, a journalist for *France 24*, wrote about the forgotten memorial to the *Schutztruppe* of Kamerun. According to Trouillard it was erected in 1922 by the "pro-German Spanish governor." The governor in Santa Isabel in 1922 was Angel Barrera Luyando, the same governor who was there during the war.

8. Correspondence, Rainier Konrad Munzel, 7 May 2015: "Many thanks for your email and for your interest in the fate of the German soldiers here in EG." According to Ambassador Munzel no soldiers were buried in Spanish Rio Muni on the mainland. The refugees retreating from Kamerun remained there for eight weeks before transportation to Fernando Po. Elsewhere the number of German graves is given as eight.

9. The name *Askari*, or soldier, was used in the vernacular in East Africa to refer to indigenous units of the regular army. The name was then extended to all native soldiers. See also Rémy Porte, *The Conquest of the German Colonies* (St. Cloud, 2006); the book is in French: Rémy Porte, *La conquête des colonies allemandes: naissance et mort d'un rêve impérial* (St. Cloud [Hauts de Seine], ed. 14–18). Also W. O. Henderson, *German Colonial Empire, 1884–1919* (London: Routledge, 1993).

10. Helmuth Stoecker, "Loyalty to Germany in Cameroon, 1914–1930," in Kuma Ndumbe, ed., *Africa and Germany from Colonization to Cooperation, 1884–1986* (Yaoundé: Editions Africa Venir, 1986), 330ff.

11. In 1984 a German banker was sent by the West German government to East Africa to give back-pay to some 350 old solders who had served in the German colony. Of the 350 who turned up at Nwanza only a few were able to show certificates of service issued in 1918. Some brought pieces of their old uniforms as proof they had served in the Askaris. The banker had an idea. "As each claimant stepped forward, he was handed a broom and ordered in German to perform the manual of arms. Not one man failed this test." *New York Times*. See Byron Farwell, *The Great War in Africa, 1914–1918* (New York: W.W. Norton, 1989), 387; Charles Miller, *Battle for the Bundu: The First World War in German East Africa* (London: Macdonald and James, 1974), 333.

12. The name "Cameroons" by itself was usually applied only to the environs of the Cameroon, or Wouri, River. It referred mainly to the group of chieftancies or towns along that river. The word Duala was used to refer to the people of that area and Douala to the town. Kamerun was the name given to the German colony that ceased to exist during World War I. See Shirley Ardener, *Eye-Witnesses to the Annexation of Cameroon, 1883–1887* (Buea: Ministry of Primary Education and West Cameroon Antiquities Commission, 1968). Editor's notes.

13. Mr. Mukom had been a teacher, a politician, and later a prominent figure in the international credit union movement.

14. Abba Saliou, "From the Battlefield to Cemeteries and Reinstatement: A Trajectory of Soldiers during the First World War in Cameroon, 1914–1916," Conference, *Africa and the First World War*, Lisbon, July 11–12, 2013. Abstract.

15. Ian McCall, *Sweet Pass Kerosene, Nigeria: A Personal History* (Eyemouth: Cross Border, 2011), 122.

16. Erich Student, *Kameruns Kampf, 1914/16*, vol. 22 (Berlin: Verlag Bernard & Graefe, 1937), 334.

17. See Hew Strachan, *The First World War in Africa* (New York: Oxford University Press, 2004), 184: "Annexation and retention remained the dominant European motivation in the war in Africa. . . . Germany's African claims resided not in the preservation of land but in the unity of the Schutztruppen themselves."

Chapter 1

1. Ardener, *Eye-Witnesses*, 1.
2. Buea Archive: No. AB20, original file no. 1454/1925, "Assessment Report on the Mogamaw and Ngemba Areas, 1925," Bamenda Division, 11 no. 61.
3. By mid-1884 there was a complete reversal of Britain's position. German traders increased in number. The senior staff of the Baptists was brought to their lowest point by ill health and death. In five years the Baptist Missionary Society was gone.
4. Bruce Fetter, ed., *Colonial Rule in Africa* (Madison: University of Wisconsin Press, 1979), 7.
5. The other participants were Austria-Hungary, Belgium, Denmark, Spain, Sweden, Norway, Italy, The Netherlands, Russia, Turkey, and the United States.
6. From the South African website for Kasie Economics: The Berlin Act was an important change in international affairs. It created the rules for "effective occupation" of conquered lands, ensuring that the division of Africa would take place without war among the European powers. Through the Berlin Act, the European powers justified dividing a continent without considering the desires of the indigenous peoples. While this appears extremely arrogant to us now, it seemed to them to be the obvious extension of their imperialism. The Berlin Conference is one of the clearest examples of the assumptions and preconceptions of this era, and its effects on Africa can still be seen today. The arbitrary boundaries the Europeans imposed often divided an ethnic group and also brought enemies under the same government causing strife that still

exists today. The boundaries of present-day Africa were largely determined at the Conference. Not everyone agrees with the importance of the the Berlin Act. While some historians of the era agree that it gave the legal and political framework for the partition of Africa, others think its importance has been grossly exaggerated, that it was even a failure. One points out that the "scramble" for Africa had already begun before Berlin. See Matthew Craven, "Between Law and History: The Berlin Conference of 1884–85 and the Logic of Free Trade," *London Review of International Law* 3, no. 1 (2015): 31–59.

7. Robin Hallett, *Africa since 1875* (Ann Arbor: University of Michigan Press, 1974), 43, 47: The decade of the 1880s was the "scramble for Africa." Political claims by the major powers in Europe were made to parts of Africa "in most of which they had shown no previous interest." Germans feared being forced out of trade along the coast by the French, who were imposing "protectionist tariffs" in areas where Europeans had previously traded freely.

8. Halett, *Africa*, 44–45.

9. Victor T. LeVine, *The Cameroons from Mandate to Independence* (Berkeley: University of California Press, 1964), 15–43.

10. Rudin, *Germans,* 256ff. During the time of the German colony the supply of ivory, which was limited, was eventually exhausted. Palm products usually were second or third in value among the exports from Kamerun. They came from the central part of the colony and were used in Germany to make soap and candles. Like ivory, palm oil was brought to the coast by local traders who traded for it with natives in the interior. There were many problems connected with palm products. A major one was the method local people used to harvest kernels especially the practice of cutting down palm trees to produce their palm wine.

11. Rudin, *Germans,* 157: "This firm was organized in 1837 and began its trading operations in West Africa in 1849. It was not until 1868 that its first trading station was established in the Cameroons." Adolf Woermann succeeded his father in 1880 as president.

12. Hallett, *Africa*, 448; Ardener, *Eye-Witnesses,* 19–20.

13. Hallett, *Africa*, 448–53.

14. Rudin, *Germans,* 45.

15. Hallett, *Africa*, 449; Stoecker, *Kamerun,* 259

16. Ardener, *Eye-Witnesses,* 23ff. One can read the account of these events in Ardener's study. It is of special interest because of the splendid sources she uses, the "eye-witnesses" of the title.

17. LeVine, *Cameroons,* 23.

18. Hallett, *Africa*, 449.

19. LeVine, *Cameroons,* 23.

20. LeVine, *Cameroons,* 25.

21. Rudin, *Germans,* 58–59.

22. LeVine, *Cameroons,* 261n.20: "The elements of the *Basler Evangelische Missionsgesellschaft*, which established themselves in Kamerun, represented the Stuttgart branch of the society. It was one of the several missionary bodies asked by the German government to take over the work and property of the English Baptists.

23. Hallett, *Africa*, 450.

24. LeVine, *Cameroons,* 26; See also Rudin, *Germans,* 110–12, and 226n21.

25. Rudin, *Germans,* 195: "Both figures are so small that it is ridiculous to assert that the Germans militarized their colony. The fact is that Germany adhered quite loyally to the provisions of the 1885 Act of Berlin...."

26. Margaret Field, *The Prime Minister's Lodge Buea* (Buea: Ministry of Primary Education and West Cameroon Antiquities Commission, Government Printer, 1969, 2nd ed.).

27. Hallett, *Africa*, 451; Rudin, *Germans,* 147.

28. LeVine, *Cameroons,* 28.

29. Rudin, *Germans,* 16.

30. Hallett, *Africa*, 452: Von Puttkamer is remembered for his connection with the Schloss at Buea "which he built for his mistress, a cabaret dancer from Berlin"; about this story that Von Puttkamer built the place for his mistress, Paulina, an opera singer from Berlin, Field writes that the "legend" is a "delightful fiction." It is true that there was a countess who stayed with him from time to time. See Field, *Minister's Lodge*, 11.

31. This was the result of the Second Moroccan Crisis. French troops occupied the city of Fez on 21 May 1911. In March opponents of the sultan had staged an uprising and the sultan asked for French help to restore order. The German Foreign Secretary sent the cruiser *Panther* to anchor in the harbor of Agadir on the Atlantic coast and encouraged local resistance to the French. Britain supported France, as did Russia. Austria-Hungary did not help Germany. So reluctantly Germany agreed to recognize a French protectorate over Morocco in return for territory in Africa. Kamerun received what was called Neu-Kamerun.

32. LeVine, *Cameroons*, 30, 113: The expropriation of Douala land was not legally cleared up until 1952: The Douala villages of Bell, Akwa, Deido, and Mbassa were to be moved from the waterfront to new sites several miles into the interior and a model city built. The German government offered 90 pfennigs per square meter. The Duala wanted 3 marks and refused to sell. One town was constructed, New Bell.

33. Norman Aste Horner, "Protestant and Roman Catholic Missions among the Bantu of Cameroon" (Ph.D. thesis, Hartford Seminary, 1956), 23ff.

34. Horner, "Missions," 25.

35. See Adam Hochschild, *Bury the Chains: Prophets and Rebels in the Fight to Free an Empire's Slaves* (New York: Macmillan, 2005): review in *The Guardian*: "... brings us the story of one of the most successful episodes of human rights activism relating how ... a small group of men (and one woman) took on the vested interests of state, church and big business—and won." The most tireless worker was Thomas Clarkson, with the help of the Quakers, "the only religious group to campaign wholeheartedly against the trade."

36. Hochschild, *Bury the Chains*, 348–49; the Slave Emancipation Act of 1833 saw full freedom after a set period of time. On 1 August 1834, all children under age six were to work as unpaid apprentices to former masters. Finally the enslaved in the British Caribbean were freed as of midnight 31 July 1838.

37. There is a story that the extraordinary happened. When Clarke and Prince left for England to give their report, lightning struck the mast of their ship during a storm leaving them to drift to the West Indies and Jamaica. When the Jamaicans met the pioneers, some of the freed slaves wanted to join the mission. One was Rev. Joseph Merrick, the pastor of a parish at Jericho, who joined them on their return to England and later back to Africa.

38. Sundiata, *From Slavery to Neo-Slavery*, 66.

39. Werner Keller, *The History of the Presbyterian Church in West Cameroon* (Victoria: Presbook, 1969), 1–3, 47ff.

40. Paul R. Dekar, "Jamaican and British Baptists in West Africa, 1841–1888," *Missiology* 29, no. 4 (October 2001): 433–47.

41. Martin Lynn, "The Creoles of Fernando Po," *Journal of African History* 25 (1984): 250ff.

42. The Primitive Methodist Church grew from Wesleyan Methodism in the early nineteenth century. The movement came from open-air prayer, or Camp Meetings. The most famous was held at Mow Cop on the border of Saffordshire and Cheshire, in May 1807. Its founders were Hugh Bourne and William Clowes. The Primitive Methodists put great emphasis on the role of lay people. Women were allowed to be ministers. Followers were sometimes called "Ranters" because they often sang in the streets. In 1812 the movement took the name the Society of the Primitive Methodists. At first it was a home and colonial missionary organization. In the 1840s there was a reorganization of the conference and support was encouraged for overseas missions. In 1843 the annual reports were published under the name of the Primitive

Methodist Missionary Society. Missionaries had already gone to the United States in 1829 and then to Canada. In 1844 they went to Australia and New Zealand. The first missionaries sailed for Africa in January 1870 and settled on Fernando Po. An English ship visited Fernando Po. Captain Robinson and ship's carpenter Hinds were Methodists. After they left, the Methodist home mission sent out two missionaries, Rev. R. W. Burnett and R. W. Roe. Soon they had a group of fifteen in Santa Isabel. Some were connected with the Baptists who had left, or were new arrivals from the African coast. Soon the work spread to San Carlos Bay and Banni. In both places the missionaries established cocoa farms. Some younger members bought farms with the help of the mission. Despite the discouragement of the climate and the obstacles put in "the way of the native converts" by the Spanish Jesuits, the missionaries reported that "some progress has been made and the church gathered." See Jurg Schneider and Vilaro Guell, "Fourteen Views of Fernando Po to Save the Colony," *Photo Researcher* 21 (April 2014): 38–52. When the first missionaries arrived they were welcomed by a small group of people. One of them was Elizabeth "Mamma Job," a freed slave. The first services were held in her house. She was a pillar of the church and was credited with raising around one hundred orphans before her death in 1896. See John R. Pritchard, "My Primitive Methodist Ancestors," myprimitivemethodists.org.uk.

43. See Edwin Ardener, *Kingdom on Mount Cameroon: Studies in the History of the Cameroon Coast, 1500–1870* (Oxford: Berghahn Books, 1996).

44. Charles W. Weber, *International Influences and Baptist Mission in West Cameroon* (Leiden: E. J. Brill, 1993), 20ff.

45. Emmanuel Aloangamo Aka, "Joseph Merrick, Alfred Saker and the Foundations of Christianity in the Cameroons, 1844–1876" (Yaoundé, 1987). E. A. Aka credits Merrick and the date 1844 for the foundation of the Christianity in Cameroon. He wants "to underline Merrick's importance in Cameroon history, in which Saker has been credited with the achievements of Merrick."

46. Ardener, *Eye-Witnesses*, 9.

47. Dekar, "Jamaican and British Baptists," 447.

48. Ardener, *Eye-Witnesses*, 9.

49. Sundiata, *Slavery*, 66.

50. Weber, *Baptist Mission*, 2; Ardener, *Mount Cameroon*, 50.

51. "Annual Public Meeting of the Baptist Missionary Society," Exeter Hall, Wednesday, 30 April 1862, 5, Yale Library.

52. Weber, *Baptist Mission*, 3.

53. Ardener, *Eye-Witnesses*, 11.

54. "English Baptist Missionary Society," *Missionary Herald* 76 (June 1880): 282.

55. Weber, *Baptist Mission*, 4.

56. Dekar, "Jamaican and British Baptists," Conclusion.

57. Keller, *Presbyterian Church*, 10ff.

58. Emmanuel Akyeampong, "Introduction to Visual Interpretation of the Basel Mission Archive Photo Project," Basel Mission Archive website, www.bmpix.org.

59. F. E. Stoffler, *The Rise of Evangelical Pietism* (Leiden: E. J. Brill, 1965).

60. Mark A. Noll, "Pietism," *Elwell Evangelical Dictionary* (Grand Rapids: Baker Books, 1984, 2001).

61. Akyeampong, "Basel Mission Archive Photo Project."

62. Keller, *Presbyterian Church*, 14.

63. Horner, "Missions," 35.

64. Weber, *Baptist Mission*, 6ff.

65. Horner, "Missions," 26.

66. Horner, "Missions," 46ff.

67. Horner, "Missions," 49.

68. Rudin, *Germans,* 372.

69. Marienberg today is a small town along the road between Yaoundé and Douala. On 6 October 2015, the German ambassador to Cameroon, Holger Mahniche, made a visit. Marienberg, according to a German Embassy newsletter, is a place of pilgrimage and a symbol of German/Cameroon relations.

70. Horner, "Missions," 50.

71. *The Tablet,* December 2, 1893, 902, "African Catholic Missions, the First Mission Sisters in Cameroon."

72. Arnold Vehoeven, unpublished notes on Ossidinge mission.

73. Herman Skolaster, *Die Pallottiner im Kamerun* (Limburg: Lahn, 1924), 218. Hermann Gufler translated sections of Skolaster's book into English in the early 1980s. He retired to Absam, near Innsbruck, Austria, after more than fifty years on mission in Cameroon.

74. Rudin, *Germans,* 372.

75. Arnold Vehoeven has written about the beginnings of the Sacred Heart Mission in Kamerun in "Birth of Adamawa Prefecture," 2012, private circulation.

76. Anthony Ndi, *Mill Hill Missionaries in Southern West Cameroon* (Nairobi: St. Paul Press, 2005), 23.

77. Skolaster, *Pallottiner,* 218.

78. Philippe Laburthe-Tolra, "Christianisme et ouverture au Monde, Cameroun 1845–1915," in *Revue française d'histoire d'outre-mer* 75, no. 279 (1988): 207–21.

79. Keller, *Presbyterian Church,* 47.

80. Weber, *Baptist Mission,* 22–3.

81. De Vries, "Catholic Mission," 32–33.

Chapter 2

1. Strachan, *First World War in Africa,* viii.

2. See Mahon Murphy, "Prisoners of War and Civilian Internees Captured by the British and Dominion Forces from the German colonies during the First World War," Ph.D. thesis (London School of Economic and Political Science, 2014).

3. Joannes Emonts, *In Steppen-und Bergland Inner-Kameruns* (Aachen, 1927). Translation by Arnold Vehoeven, 2011.

4. The most useful study of World War I in Cameroon is Strachan's *First World War in Africa.* Other books on WW I are John Keegan, *The First World War* (New York: Vintage, 2000); David Stevenson, *1914–1918: The History of the First World War* (New York: Penguin, 2005); Hew Strachan, *The First World War* (New York: Penguin, 2014); Hew Strachan, ed., *The Oxford Illustrated History of the First World War* (New York: Oxford University Press, 2014); Barbara Tuchman, *The Guns of August* (New York: Ballantine, 2004).

5. Mary Evelyn Townsend, *The Rise and Fall of Germany's Colonial Empire, 1884–1918* (New York: Macmillan, 1930), 270, in Murphy, "Prisoners of War."

6. Strachan, *First World War in Africa,* 12.

7. Strachan, *First World War in Africa,* 20–21; 20n.: Strachan explains that the "basic premises of German strategy … have almost entirely eluded English-language authors.…"

8. Strachan, *First World War in Africa,* 54–55.

9. Strachan, *First World War in Africa,* 57.

10. Emonts, *Inner-Kameruns,* 308.

11. Emonts, *Inner-Kameruns,* 309.

12. H. C. O'Neill, *The War in Africa and the Far East, 1914–17* (London: Longmans, 1918), 43.

13. Strachan, *First World War in Africa,* 16–17.

14. Englebert Mveng, *Histoire du Cameroun* (Paris: Presence Africaine, 1963), 347: There is a photograph of stacks of weapons left by troops as they entered Spanish territory in early 1916.

15. W. O. Henderson, "The Conquest of the German Colonies, 1914–18," *History* 27, no. 106 (September 1942): 97–160.

16. Strachan, *First World War in Africa*, 32

17. Keller, *Presbyterian Church*, 47.

18. Keller, *Presbyterian Church*, 47ff.; Murphy, "Prisoners of War," BA, R1001/3991: William Bell, Rudolf's uncle, was in Lagos, Nigeria, at the start of the war and helped recruit guides, spies, and pilots for the British.

19. Rev. W. Stark, ed., "The Martyrdom of the Evangelical Missions in Cameroon, 1914," *Reports of Eyewitnesses* (Berlin: Steglitz, 1915); Pastor Stark, pamphlet, 8/15.

20. It is important to note with W. Roger Louis that "nearly the entire body of Allied (British and French) political and colonial literature 1914–1920 was ... devised to create a climate of 'whatever happens, these Colonies can never be returned to Germany.'" See W. Roger Louis, *Great Britain and Germany's Lost Colonies, 1914–1919* (Oxford: Clarendon, 1967), 116.

21. Frederick Quinn, "An African Reaction to World War I, The Beti of Cameroon," *Cahiers d'études Africanes* 13, no. 52 (1973): 722–31.

22. *The Continent* 45 (November 12, 1914): 1560 (Presbyterian Church in the USA, 156 Fifth Ave., New York).

23. Skolaster, *Pallottiner*, 266.

24. Murphy, "Prisoners of War," nn. 25, 26. See also Kenneth Orosz, "The Dwarf, the Goetzen and CS Forester's African Queen," 30 June 2016: "Public awareness of the African theatre in the Great War stems largely from C. S. Forester's 1935 novel *The African Queen*, and its subsequent 1951 film adaptation. Long thought to have been inspired by British activities on Lake Tanganyika, Forester's novel more closely resembles events in Cameroon where German missionary Alphons Hermann attempted to sink HMS *Dwarf* using homemade torpedoes."

25. Murphy, "Prisoners of War," 101.

26. Murphy, "Prisoners of War," 52.

27. Skolaster, *Pallottiner*, translation, 4.

28. Weber, *Baptist Mission*, 20ff.

29. Horner, "Missions," 63ff.

30. *The Cameroon Diary of Lt. Arthur Lees, 1914–15* (London: Mandaras, 2010), ii.

31. "World War I and the Fight for the American Mind," New York Public Library, Exhibit to August 15, 2015.

32. See "Correspondence relative to the alleged ill-treatment of German subjects captured in the Cameroons," HM Stationary Office, London 1915, 47 pages; Stark, "Martyrdom of the Evangelical Missions," 40-44.

33. Murphy, "Prisoners," 145. Mahon Murphy mentions complaints also found in "Stark" and "Correspondence."

34. See Helga Bender Henry, *Cameroon on a Clear Day* (Pasadena, CA: William Carey Library, 1999). The author is the daughter of Carl and Hedwig Bender. She was born in Soppo in 1915. The book is more than a biography of the Benders. It is also a contribution to the history of Christian missions in Cameroon.

35. Stark, "Martyrdom of the Evangelical Missions."

36. "Correspondence, alleged ill-treatment of German subjects," London, 1915.

37. Today it is spelled "Yabassi."

38. Skolaster, *Pallottiner*, translation, 7.

39. "The Soldiers Burden," in Harry's Africa website, http://www.kaiserscross.com/188001/home.html.

40. The *Appam* was captured by the German SMS *Moewe* on January 15, 1916. The *Appam*

was on its way from Senegal to Liverpool. The four British officers and thirty British sailors were taken prisoner. In addition twenty Germans, including three women, were freed. All went onboard the *Moewe*. The Germans also took sixteen boxes of gold and one million marks. The *Appam* was ordered to Newport News in the United States as a prize of war. Captain Nicolaus Dohna's *Moewe* was one of the most noted German warships of WW I. The *Moewe* was an armed merchant ship that ran the blockade and roamed the shipping lanes of the Atlantic.

41. Skolaster, *Pallottiner*, 11.

42. Captain John Fitzhandinge Paul Butler, The Kings Royal Rifle Corps attached to the WAFF, was awarded the Victoria Cross for his bravery on November 17, 1915, and a later action near the Ekam River on December 27.

43. Maj.-Gen. Charles Dobell, Cameroons, March 1, 1916. Army Dispatch, Cameroons Campaign, War Office, 31 May 1916. Gazette No. 29604.

44. The Pioneers were a labor corps formed in 1917 that employed British troops and an estimated 10,000 Africans, and thousands of others during World War I. In 1939 it became the Royal Pioneer Corps, made up of combatants who were used for light engineering work.

45. Dobell, *Despatches*, 1916, War Office.

46. Skolaster, *Pallottiner*, 15

47. Robert John O'Neil, "A History of Moghamo 1865–1940, Authority and Change in a Cameroon Grassfields Culture" (Ph.D. thesis, Columbia University, 1987), 166–78; interview, Nicholas Nde, Widekum, 16/6/84.

48. Keller, *Presbyterian Church*, 49.

49. Keller, *Presbyterian Church*, 47–54.

50. Emonts, *Inner-Kameruns*, 402.

51. See "*In Wartime*, from Kumbo to Home via Captivity," in *Herzens Jezu, 1916/1917*; Aloys Huppertz, *Deutsche Herz-Jesu-Priester in Kamerun (1912–1915)* (Kaisersesch: Peter Sesterhenn, 1992).

52. Emonts, *Inner-Kameruns*, 309ff.

53. Emonts, *Inner-Kameruns*, 401.

54. Huppertz, *Herz-Jesu-Priester*. Father Ben Beemster's notes and translation (pp. 149–74).

55. Beemster, Notes.

56. Quinn, "Beti," 725.

57. Sundiata, *Slavery*, 125. Sundiata gives a total of 24,000 refugees, including European officials, African troops, and their family members.

58. Skolaster, *Pallottiner*, 23ff.

59. Akinjide Osuntokun, *Equatorial Guinea–Nigerian Relations, the Diplomacy of Labour* (Ibaden: Oxford University Press, 1978), 27.

60. Helmuth Stoecker, "Loyalty to Germany in Cameroon, 1914–1930," University of Humboldt, Berlin, in Kuma Ndumbe, ed., *Africa and Germany from Colonization to Cooperation, 1884–1986* (Yaoundé: Editions Africa Venir, 1986), 330ff.

61. Skolaster, *Pallottiner*.

Chapter 3

1. General Charles Dobell, *Despatches*, 1916.

2. Sundiata, *Slavery*, 19.

3. *European War, Information Quarterly* (April 1916): 38: Estimates of the number retreating into Rio Muni were "900 Germans and 14,000 colonial troops." Erich Student described the retreat to the border in more detail. On 6 February von Hagen's detachment crossed near Mayo in the east. In the west Hädicke, Adametz, and Liebe crossed near pillar IV. The same day a rearguard of the 9th company beat off the French north of the Ntem River. On 7 February

the French were at Ngoa. To the south on 9 February Rammstedt walked into Spanish territory near boundary pillar VI, Dickmann near V, and Engmall near IV. On the 9th, von Gossler's detachment, the 4th company, still blocked the road at the last German place before the border at Banjassa. On the 14th the French tried to occupy the place. With the last cartridge, the 4th company left Cameroon. See Erich Student, *Kameruns Kampf, 1914/16*, vol. 22 (Berlin: Verlag Bernard & Graefe, 1937), 332ff.

4. Sundiata, *Slavery*, 19.

5. Ardener, *Eye-Witnesses*, Appendix C, 86: Woermann to Eduard Schmidt, Hamburg, 6 May 1884.

6. Sundiata, *Slavery*, 34n1: for a list of his sources; Osuntokun, *Guinea–Nigerian Relations*, 1–35.

7. Osuntokun, *Guinea–Nigerian Relations*, 4.

8. Sundiata, *Slavery*, 8.

9. Sundiata, *Slavery*, 9: Their Pidgin English was called "Pichi" or "Pichinglis" and before that Fernando Po Creole, an offshoot of the Krio language of Sierra Leone. Today it is the language of Malabo, along with Spanish on the island of Bioko.

10. *Missionary Herald*, BMS London, copied by Gilbert Schneider, secretary, NAB Heritage Center, Sioux Falls, SD.

11. Sundiata, *Slavery*, 10.

12. Osuntokun, *Guinea–Nigerian Relations*, 14–19.

13. Basil Davidson, *Africa in Modern History* (London, Allen Lane, 1978), 33.

14. In 1893 Mary Henrietta Kingsley arrived. She signed on to become a palm-oil trader in West Africa. She was not only a merchant but also a scientist.

15. Sundiata, *Slavery*, 15–29.

16. Sundiata, *Slavery*, 298–99: ADM/137/28, Lt. de Vaisseau, Commandant Boissarie to Captain Fuller, March 8, 1916.

17. Miquel Vilaro I Guell, "Rio Muni en el contexto de la I Guerra Mundial," in *Hispania Nova, Revista de Historia Contemporaenea* 12 (2014): 14–21.

18. Murphy, "Prisoners of War," 142–49.

19. Interview, Paul Neaka, Ashong, October 28, 1984.

20. D. José Vincent, *Una Obra de Colonizacion Alemana en Fernando Poo* (Madrid, 1919).

21. Strachan, *First World War in Africa*, 21.

22. Louis, *Great Britain and Germany's Lost Colonies*, 9.

23. Carlos A. Font Gavira, *Los Alemanes del Camerun, Implication de Espana en la Gran Guerre, 1914–1918*, 2014; also in *La Gaceta de Guinea Ecuatorial* and the academic blog of Fundacion sur Africa, "Los Internados del Camerun," 19 September 2016.

24. Gavira writes that 875 Germans went on to Cadiz while 6,047 Cameroon soldiers with 4,550 wives and 440 children, along with 4,088 servants stayed on Fernando Po. Madrid was in favor of returning all the Cameroons to Cameroon but accepted their commitments as a neutral country and granted asylum until the end of the war. The British Admiralty estimated that there were around 200 officers, 12,000 indigenous troops, including their wives and children, and presumed there were around 5,000 carriers attached to the troops.

25. *The New York Times*, 14 February 1916, "More Kamerun Refugees."

26. Jacqueline de Vries, "The Internment and Repatriation of German-Cameroonian Soldiers in Fernando Po, 1916–1919," The Internationational Network for the Study of the Great War, *Africa and the First World War*, Lisbon, July 11–12, 2013, abstract.

27. Vincent, *Una Obra*.

28. Since you are especially interested in Fernando Po, I am sending you another photo that shows twelve sisters (white habits) together with one sister of another congregation (black habit). They arrived in two groups of six each, by the end of November and beginning of Decem-

ber 1914. They stayed with Spanish sisters at Basilé for several weeks. In February and in March 1915 they left for Limburg in two groups. Another group of four Sisters came to Basilé for about three weeks, in January / February 1915. A few months after the departure of all these sisters, two other groups arrived: one group of three sisters by the end of 1915, and another group of five sisters in January 1916. They stayed on Fernando Po until May 1916 and left together for Limburg. The other six sisters out of 30 reached home without passing Fernando Po. From Sr. Adelheid Scheloske SAC, Provincial Archivist, 16 August 2017.

29. Amber Murry, "Narratives along the Chad-Cameroon Oil Pipeline," *Geography and the Environment* 8, no. 1 (2015): 44.

30. Osuntakun, *Guinea–Nigerian Relations*, 299n3: C.O. 583/46/26618, Lugard to C.O., 18 May 1916; Armand Annet, *En colonne dans le Cameroun: notes d'un commandant de campagnie 1914–1916* (Paris: Editions René Debrasse, 1949), 120: Annet gives the number of German troops as 6,000 and other Cameroonians as 8,000, mostly Jaundes under Chief Atangana. But there is little agreement over the numbers of those who crossed into Spanish territory and those who there were transferred to Fernando Po. See LeVine, *Cameroons*, 262n24; Wilhelm Kemner, *Kamerun* (Berlin: Freiheits-Verlag, 1937), 77: Kemner claimed to be citing a Spanish Internment Report of 31 January 1917, which gave the total crossing the boundry as 70,000. It was broken down into 5,621 soldiers, 4,354 wives, 980 "attached persons," and 560 children, plus 16,000 porters. He also gives the number of 3,000 grasslands chiefs and their retinue. The rest, about 40,000 persons, were from the Yaoundé area. All except 15,000 (Europeans and persons connected with the military) were returned to the Cameroons. The 15,000, according to Kemner, were interned on Fernando Po.

31. Murphy, "Prisoners of War," 53.

Chapter 4

1. Huppertz, *Herz-Jesu-Priester*, 139. Mill Hill Missionary Arnold Vehoeven translated sections of Huppertz's book, including Schuster's letter, from the German. Father Vehoeven writes on 30 December 2017: "The letter from Conrad Franz Xavier Schusster (*sic*) appeared in the Sacred Heart Fathers' bi-monthly magazine: *Das Reich des Herzens Jesus*. It was in the issue of November and December 1912 under the rubric: Aus den Missionen. The letter was titled Im Gefangenenlager auf Fernando Po.—In the prison camp on Fernando Po by Pater Conrad Schusster, and was on pages 137–43."

2. Vincent, *Una Obra*, 13ff.: Unless noted otherwise most of the information about the camps on pages 89 to 98 of this book is found in Vincent's *ABC* articles. Several photographs of the camps are from the collection of the German colonial officer Hermann Harttmann (1885–1953). His colored slides are in the Linden Museum, Stuttgart, Germany.

3. Gavira, *Los Alemanes*.

4. Dobell, *Despatches*, 84.

5. Jide Osuntakun, "Anglo Spanish Relations in West Africa during the First World War," *Journal of the Historical Society of Nigeria* 7, no. 2 (June 1974): 291–301.

6. LeVine, *Cameroons*, 33.

7. Sundiata, *Slavery*, 125

8. The influenza pandemic of 1918 has been called the most devastating in world history. The estimates for deaths around the world are from twenty to fifty million people. It has also been called the "Spanish flu," not because it began there but because during the war Spain was able to report more freely on it. There were an estimated eight million deaths in Spain alone.

9. Interview with Pius Fomukong, Bali-Nyonga, August 5, 1988.

10. Vincent, *Una Obra*, 6: This is an example of the propaganda that often filled Vincent's articles. Repeatedly, the Spanish governor general, D. Angel Barrera, and the Spanish officials

in charge of keeping guard in the encampments expressed their admiration for all this work. On their visits they witnessed that despite all the hard work, the German discipline and training have not suffered and that "a true companionship joined the black soldiers with their white masters."

11. Quinn, "Beti," 722–31.

12. Philippe Laburthe-Tolra writes that Lt. Dominik, the chief of post at Yaoundé, took some boys, ten to fifteen years of age, to stay at Kribi. One was Martin Tabi and the author, his cousin, Karl Atangana. Bishop Vieter decided to send Tabi and Atangan with Brother Jager to the interior. Martin Tabi was guide and interpreter. He became the first head catechist at Mvolye. He led an exemplary life of *riguer*. He was always faithful to the memory of the Germans, refusing to later collaborate with the French. As for Atangana he became the interpreter and right-hand man of Lt. Dominik. As a Catholic he was founder of the Congregation of St. Joseph, a valuable asset of the Catholic missionaries. Of the "Frères Coadjuteurs," Laburthe-Tolra compares their training as artisans at Yaoundé with that of the Baptist mission in Douala. As for Atangana, who died in 1943, when someone asked Catholics why they were Christians they would answer, "Parce que Atangana la dit."

13. See also G. Nerin, *La ultima selva de Espana* (Madrid: Los Libros, 2010).

14. Huppertz, *Herz-Jesu-Priester*; Schuster, "Prison Camp on Fernando Po," 137–92. Translation by Fr. Arnold Vehoeven.

15. C. Schuster, "In the Prison Camps on Fernando Po," *in* Huppertz, *Herz-Jesu-Priester*, 159.

16. *Catholic Encyclopedia* 17:306. He began to study for the priesthood at Solsona in September 1870. At thirty-one years of age he was appointed apostolic prefect of the missions of Guinea. In September 1890 he left for West Africa on the steamer *Larache*. By October 19, he could see Fernando Po "with its 9,000 foot peak." They arrived in Santa Isabel and climbed the "Cuesta de las fiebres" (hill of fevers). It was a reminder of how dangerous the climate was and how many missionaries had already died. In seven years, eighteen had died, most of them victims of fever, and all of them between twenty-five and thirty years of age. The new prefect encouraged all the missionaries to open boarding schools in each mission and to provide meals. To do this he had the help of Conceptionist missionary sisters. In 1909 he helped to found the Auxiliaries of the Missions, an institute for African sisters, now known as the Missionary Sisters of Mary Immaculate.

17. Huppertz, *Herz-Jesu-Priester*, 172–73; see the text of Reich's 1920 letter.

18. Huppertz, *Herz-Jesu-Priester*, 246ff. Two other letters are quoted written to Sr. Oda in Germany from Santa Isabel. One is from Maria Mande and her busband, dated 9 January 1918. "If the good God helps then we shall see each other again in our Grasslands." The other, dated 8 September 1917, is from Anna Ngum, also with her husband in a camp. "Thank you for all the good you have done for me in Kumbo.... We hope that when there is peace once again, we will meet again."

19. School of Oriental and African Studies, London: archives: Primitive Methodists, Mision Metodista, Santa Isabel, Fernando Poo, West Africa, December 18, 1916. All other reports for the years 1916–19 are missing. Dr. Mark Faulkner writes about the archive: Although there is little about the pastoral care of the internees there is "quite a bit of anti-Catholic sentiment." The Methodists refer to "the Priests" and lament pitch fights between the youth in their camp and the Catholic youth. Indeed, the Catholics do appear a little provocative—opening an outstation just down the road from the Methodist mission. Also there is a nice letter to HQ assessing the relationship between Methodists and the state. They suggest that this is cordial although the governor cannot be too friendly as this will incur the wrath of the church and, it was noted, all the officials are under the "thumb of Rome."

20. Vincent, *Una Obra*, 33–34.

21. Vincent concludes his reports with a letter sent to the Peace Conference: 37/8/9, Peti-

tion to King Don Alfonso XIII to intervene at the Peace Conference, signed by "K Atangana of the Banes and Jaundes; Adgia Lifida of the Mohammedans and 117 other chiefs."

22. Huppertz, *Herz-Jesu Priester*, 142–47. This translation of the story of the missionaries imprisonment and trek through Nigeria was done by Fr. Ben Beemster.

23. Huppertz, *Herz-Jesu-Priester*, 139.

24. Gavira, *Los Alemanes*; Eduardo Gonzalez Callejo, "El Internamiento de los colonos alemanes del Camerun en la Guinea Espanola, 1915–1919," *Endoxa*, Series Filosoficas, 37 (2016): 223–36, Universidad Nacional de Educacion a Distancia, Madrid; Miguel Villaro, *La Internacion de la Schutztruppe* (Madrid: Letras de Autor, 2016); Sergio del Molino, *Soldados en el Jardin de la Paz* (Zaragoza: Las Tres Sorores, 2009).

25. Peter Vewesse, Babanki Tungo, September 16, 1988.

Chapter 5

1. Huppertz, *Herz-Jesu-Priester*, 184.

2. Victor Julius Ngoh, *The Untold Story of Cameroon Reunification, 1955–1961* (Limbe: Presprint, 2011), Introduction. See also Victor Julius Ngoh, *Southern Cameroons, 1922–1961: A Constitutional History* (Aldershot: Ashgate, 2001); Bongfen Chem-Langhee, "Southern Cameroons Traditional Authorities and Nationalist Movement, 1953–1961," *International Journal of African Historical Studies* 16, no. 4 (1983).

3. Secretary of the Paris Missionary Society, 1919, in Richard V. Pierard, "Allied Treatment of Protestant Missionaries in German East Africa in WWI," in *African Journal of Evangelical Theology* 12, no. 1 (1993): 72, 74.

4. C. José Cordero Torres, *Geografia Historica de Isla de Fernando Poo* (Madrid: Institute de Estudias de Africanas, 1947), IX. "Repatriacion de los internados de Camerones, 1919–1920."

5. De Vries, "Internment and Repatriation," abstract.

6. Ngoh, *The Untold Story*, 1.

7. At the end of this book Appendix 1 has the transcribed testimony of some informants.

8. Margaret MacMillan, *Paris 1919* (New York: Random House, 2001), 98–106.

9. LeVine, *Cameroons*, 31–38.

10. See Jan-Bart Gewald, "Mbadamassi of Lagos: A Soldier for King and Kaiser, and a Deportee to German South-West Africa," *African Diaspora* 2 (2009): 103–24. Quoted in Murphy, "Prisoners of War."

11. Stoecker, "Loyalty," 331: "the military operation in East Africa, which lasted until the end of the war and those in Cameroon were later seized upon by pro-imperialist German historians and publicists to create the myth of 'our loyal' native solders and faithful Africans ... legend soon became a standard argument of German colonial propaganda.... The alleged 'loyalty of the natives' to Germany during the 1st World War [was] cited time and again as proof of the Reich's 'achievements as a colonizing nation' and in support of its claim to colonies in Africa. The myth had, in fact, been invented by Gen. Von Lettow-Vorbeck, former governor of East Africa ... in peace negotiations with Russia in December 1917 ... rejected Bolshevik demand that colonial people ... granted right of self -determination ... arguing inter alia 'that the alleged faithfulness displayed by the natives' towards their 'German friends had been evidence of their attachment and resolve to stay with Germany under all circumstances.'"

12. Herbert Purschel, *Die Kaiseriche Schutztruppe für Kamerun, Gefuge und Aufgabe* (Berlin, 1936), 67, 114.

13. See Pierard, "Allied Treatment," 4–17. Pierard also notes that early in the war the Germans also arrested British missionaries and exploited their African converts for labor and as carriers (porters).

14. Secretary of the Paris Missionary Society, 1919, in Pierard, "Allied Treatment," 72, 74.

15. Ndi, *Mill Hill Missionaries*, 27; John P. Jordan, *Bishop Shanahan of Southern Nigeria* (Dublin: Elo Press, 1971), 67.

16. Correspondence of Johannes Stöckle to the author (December 23, 1997). Johannes was in Cameroon with the Basel Mission before World War II. He returned to Cameroon after the war and devoted himself to the preservation of the culture and language of the Bali people. One title is *Traditions, Tales and Proverbs of the Bali-Nyonga* (Cologne: Rudiger Koppe Verlag, 1994).

17. Horner, "Missions," 92.

18. The Paris Evangelical Mission Society appointed Chaplain Allégret and three others to help him. There was Bergeret, a former missionary in New Hebrides and New Caledonia; Ochsner de Coninck, retired from the Basuto Mission; and Missionary Christol of Zambesi. See Henry, *Cameroon*, 83.

19. Keller, *Presbyterian Church*, 50.

20. Keller, *Presbyterian Church*, 47–59. About "secret societies" see Malcom Ruel, *Leopards and Leaders* (London: Tavistock, 1969).

21. Horner, "Missions," 72ff.

22. Marcus Garvey was a Jamaican-born political leader. He was also a journalist and the publisher of the *Negro World* in New York and a promoter of the Pan African Movement. He founded the Universal Negro Improvement Association. His Black Star Line promoted a return to Africa of the diaspora. See Colin Grant, *Negro in a Top Hat: The Rise and Fall of Marcus Garvey* (New York: Oxford University Press, 2008).

23. LeVine, *Cameroons*, 111–12.

24. Weber, *Baptist Mission*, 32.

25. Weber, *Baptist Mission*, 31–35.

26. Horner, "Missions," 81–83.

27. Horner, "Missions," 94.

28. Horner, "Missions," 93.

29. Campling's successor was Peter Rogan. Rogan landed at Victoria on 4 December 1925. He retired from Cameroon in 1962. In 1949 he ordained the first Cameroonian of the British Cameroons, Fr. Aloysius Wankuy.

30. Correspondence of Anthony Ndi to the author (28 May 2014).

31. Bernard Booth, *Mill Hill Fathers in West Cameroon: Education, Health and Development, 1884–1970* (University of Ottawa: International Scholars Publications, 1995), 51–52.

32. Ndi, *Mill Hill Missionaries*, 55.

33. Elizabeth Chilver, "Native Administration in West Central Cameroons, 1902–1954," in *Essays in Imperial Government* (Oxford: Blackwell, 1963), 119.

34. Jacqueline de Vries, *Catholic Mission, Colonial Government and Indigenous Response in Kom (Cameroon)* (Leiden: African Studies Centre, 1998), 35ff.

35. De Vries, *Catholic Mission*, 39: Timneng was considered a very powerful person by one informant: "Today I am a Christian but I still do not trust Timneng, because his strength was not only the church. He was a wizard, stronger than the Fon, stronger than all of us put together."

36. De Vries, *Catholic Mission*, 37

37. Strachan, *First World War in Africa*, Introduction, 8–10.

38. "Different Visions? Postcards from Africa by European and African Photographers and Sponsors." In *Delivering Views: Distant Cultures in Early Postcards*, ed. C. Geary and Virginia Lee-Webb (Washington: SIP, 1998), 147. Postcards became very popular with the rise of photography as a means to bring evidence of missionary work overseas. Christraud Geary writes that with the rise of physical and cultural anthropology in the middle of the nineteenth century photography became one way to document all aspects of life under colonial rule and "postcards helped to encode images of Africa" that appealed to the "Western imagination."

39. *Buea Archives*, 8 September 1917, Confidential, E/171/1917, divisional officer Bamenda to Resident, British Cameroons.

40. *Buea Archives,* 27 June 1923. Hawksworth to divisional officer, extract: 965/23.
41. Strachan, *First World War in Africa,* 184.
42. John C Barrett, "World War 1 and the Decline of the First Wave of the American Protestant Missions Movement," *International Bulletin of Missionary Research* 39, no. 3 (July 2015): 122–26.
43. Interview with Daniel Ntah, Bali-Nyonga, 6 March 1988.

Conclusion

1. Interview with Daniel Ntah, about his father, Matthew Fobang.
2. George N. Njung, "West Africa," *International Encyclopedia of the First World War* (Ann Arbor: University of Michigan, 2014), online.
3. Fons Eppink, Mill Hill Missionaries website, http://www.millhillmissionaries.co.uk/author/fons/, 22 February 2016.
4. Elizabeth Chilver, "Paramountcy and Protection in the Cameroons: The Bali and the Germans, 1883–1913," in *Britain and Germany in Africa,* ed. P. Gifford and W. R. Louis (New Haven: Yale University Press, 1967), 479–511.
5. Ralph Austen, "Mythic Transformation and Historical Continuity: The Duala of Cameroon and German Colonialism, 1884–1914," in *African Crossroads* (Oxford: Berghan Books, 1996), 63–64.
6. Rudin, *Germans,* 420.
7. Edwin Ardener, The "Kamerun Idea," *West Africa,* June 6 and 14, 1958; Willard Johnson, *The Cameroon Federation* (Princeton: Princeton University Press, 1970).
8. LeVine, *Cameroons,* 31–38
9. *New York Times,* 11 February 2017, A7.
10. Fides News Agency, Rome, 9 March 2017.
11. O'Neil, "A History of Moghamo," 122; Rudin, *Germans,* 310; *Deutsche Kolonialblatt* no. 23 (1904): 698–702: "Uprising in Anyang."
12. Strachan, *First World War in Africa,* 21.
13. George N. Njung, "Soldiers of Their Own: Honor, Violence and Conscription in Colonial Cameroon during the First World War" (Ph.D. dissertation, University of Michigan, 2016).
14. Martin Lynn, Queens College Belfast, correspondence with the author, April 1987.
15. Eppink, http://www.millhillmissionaries.co.uk/author/fons/.
16. Tiberius Vuni, correspondence with the author, 27 February 2017.
17. Hermann Gufler, correspondence with the author, 28 February 2017.
18. Eppink, http://www.millhillmissionaries.co.uk/author/fons/.

Appendix 1

1. Interview with Stephen Nchumuse, Memfu, 12 September 1988.
2. Interview with John Nchari, Tabenken, 13 September 1988.
3. Interview with Daniel Ntah, Bali-Nyonga, 6 March 1988: As a child Daniel moved with his father, "carrying his bag," and worked in the family garden near the compound. He was born in Nted Quarter in 1917 and had two sisters from the same mother: Ndanted and Bisona. He stayed at home until 1929 when went to the Basel Mission Vernacular School. Daniel's grandfather, the father of Fobang, was Tandap, and his mother was Malungu. Fobang also served his father by carrying his bag wherever he went. When Eugen Zintgraff came to Bali in 1889, "he was still young, about twelve years of age. He was very familiar with life in the town."
4. Interview with Peter Vewesse, Babanki Tungo, 16 September 1988.
5. Interview with Godfred Buma, Bali-Nyonga, 9 February 1988.

6. Interview with his grandson, 5 August 1988.
7. Interview with Pa Musa Fotabeng Moses, Bossa, 25 May 1988.
8. Interview with Fon Ngendop and Kobi Mba, 5 August 1988.
9. Interview with Pius Mbasong, Guzang, 6 August 1988.
10. Interview with Doh David Longwa Gwangwa, Balikumbat, September 1988.
11. Interview with Achillous Taboli, Tabenken, 13 September 1988.
12. Interview with Michael Njiniboh II, Fon of Kom, Laikom, 20 September 1988.
13. Interview with Thomas Lambe, Bubungo, 18 September 1988.
14. Interview with Augustine Kunke, Babungo, 18 September 1988.
15. Interview with Aloysius Ngong, Wombong, Kom, 19 September 1988.
16. Interview with Paul Nketi, Bali-Nyonga, 26 August 1988.
17. Interview with Stephen Doyi, Mantum, 10 August 1988.
18. Interview with Mama Monica Njeke, Njenka, Bali-Nyonga, 5 August 1988.
19. Interview with Pius Fomukong, Njenka, Bali-Nyonga, 5 August 1988.
20. Interview with Patrick Tim, Wombong, Kom, 3 March 1988. Patrick Tim repeated a story about all of the Kom soldiers coming home early because the Fon had died. "The German captain was not happy to miss this group, but the death of Fon Yuh forced him to release them and they never returned." Fon Yuh died in 1912, so it is a story that may be mixed up with another. "Had it not been their Fon (Yuh) did not die they would not have come home earlier. They respected their usual tradition which today is not as before. No one cares now whether the Fon dies or not."
21. Interview with Abraham Tituwan, Kopin, Bali-Nyonga, 12 August 1988.
22. Interview with Nsegala Dominic Gwendinga, Bali-Nyonga, 23 August 1988.
23. Interview with Lucy Diagah, Bali-Nyonga, 23 August 1988.
24. Interview with Bernard Njingmia, Bali-Nyonga, 3 August 1988.
25. Interview with Clement Takwa, Ngonsen, 13 September 1988.
26. Interview with Benedict Jaff, Ngonsen, 13 September 1988.
27. Interview with Nicholas Waneh, Bafmeng, 1 January 1988.
28. Interview with Ben Beemster, "The First Tikar Christian," *Diakonia* 2 (Breda, 1990): 5–10. Not only did Beemster write a splendid account of the life of Agathe but he included a study of the Tikar. It is thanks to his translation from the German of the experience of Schuster and other Sacred Heart missionaries on Fernando Po that we know of their life in the island camps.

Appendix 2

1. Bamessong today is Ashong; Bali-Nyonga is Bali.
2. For descriptions of Mamfe and Dr. Mansfeld and others, see Fr. Arnold Vehoeven, "Apatha Hill, Catholic Church in Mamfe Diocese, 1912–2012," no. 3 F, Mill Hill Missionaries, Bamenda, *Cameroon,* private circulation.
3. Rev. Henry Roe described arriving at Fernando Po in 1870 (Henry Roe, *West African Scenes: Descriptions of Fernando Po* [London: Elliot Stock, 1874]). He was traveling on the ship *Mandingo* out of Liverpool. After twenty-six days at sea they see the island on Monday, 21 February 1870, at 3:30 am. "We glide gently in full sight of land on our right." Fernando Po is reached. He first sees the foam on the shore and then the palm trees. At 4 am the *Mandingo* sails into Santa Isabel harbor. On land ahead they see "eight lights" to guide them. The ship's canon is fired to announce the arrival of the British mail. Almost at once the ship is surrounded by boats and canoes of the local people.
4. Robert O'Neil, "Evangelisation" (London: The Little Way Association, no. 43, 1996), 20–21.

Select Bibliography

Books

Ardener, Edwin, *Kingdom on Mount Cameroon: Studies in the History of the Cameroon Coast, 1500–1870* (Oxford: Berghahn Books, 1996).

Ardener, Shirley, *Eye-Witnesses to the Annexation of Cameroon, 1883–1887* (Buea: Ministry of Primary Education and West Cameroon Antiquities Commission, 1968).

Austen, Ralph, "Mythic Transformation and Historical Continuity: The Duala of Cameroon and German Colonialism, 1884–1914," in *African Crossroads* (Oxford: Berghahn Books, 1996).

Booth, Bernard, *Mill Hill Fathers in West Cameroon: Education, Health and Development, 1884–1970* (University of Ottawa: International Scholars Publications, 1995).

Carrasco, Antonio M., *Orden en Rio Muni* (Madrid: De Librum Tremens, 2011).

Chilver, Elizabeth, "Native Administration in West Central Cameroons, 1902–1954," in *Essays in Imperial Government* (Oxford: Blackwell, 1963).

———, "Paramountcy and Protection in the Cameroons: The Bali and the Germans, 1883–1913," in *Britain and Germany in Africa*, ed. P. Gifford and W. R. Louis (New Haven: Yale University Press, 1967).

Emonts, Joannes, *In Steppen-und Bergland Inner-Kameruns* (Aachen, 1927).

Field, Margaret, *The Prime Minister's Lodge Buea* (Buea: Ministry of Primary Education and West Cameroon Antiquities Commission, Government Printer, 1969).

Fetter, Bruce, ed., *Colonial Rule in Africa* (Madison: University of Wisconsin Press, 1979).

Gavira, Carlos A. Font, *Los Alemanes del Camerun, Implication de Espana en la Gran Guerre, 1914–1918*, 2014.

Hallett, Robin, *Africa since 1875* (Ann Arbor: University of Michigan Press, 1974).

Henry, Helga Bender, *Cameroon on a Clear Day: A Pioneer Missionary in Colonial Africa* (Pasadena, CA: William Carey Library, 1999).

Hochschild, Adam, *Bury the Chains: Prophets and Rebels in the Fight to Free an Empire's Slaves* (New York: Macmillan, 2005).

Huppertz, Alois, *Deutsche Herz-Jesu-Priester in Kamerun (1912–1915)* (Kaisersesch: Peter Sesterhenn, 1992).

Johnson, Willard, *The Cameroon Federation* (Princeton: Princeton University Press, 1970).
Jordan, John P., *Bishop Shanahan of Southern Nigeria* (Dublin: Elo Press, 1971).
Keller, Werner, *The History of the Presbyterian Church in West Cameroon* (Victoria: Presbook, 1969).
Krieger, Milton, ed., *Victor LeVine's Shorter Cameroon Writings, 1961–2007* (Bamenda: Langaa, 2015).
LeVine, Victor T., *The Cameroons from Mandate to Independence* (Berkeley: University of California Press, 1964).
Louis, William R., *Great Britain and Germany's Lost Colonies, 1914–1919* (Oxford: Clarendon, 1967).
MacMillan, Margaret, *Paris 1919* (New York: Random House, 2001).
McCall, Ian, *Sweet Pass Kerosene, Nigeria: A Personal History* (Eyemouth: Cross Border, 2011).
Molino, Sergio del, *Soldados en el Jardin de la Paz* (Zaragoza: Las Tres Sorores, 2009).
Mveng, Engelbert, *Histoire du Cameroun* (Paris: Presence Africaine, 1963).
Ndi, Anthony, *Mill Hill Missionaries in Southern West Cameroon* (Nairobi: St. Paul Press, 2005).
Ngoh, Victor Julius, *The Untold Story of Cameroon Reunification, 1955–1961* (Limbe: Presprint, 2011).
Osuntokun, Akinjide, *Equatorial Guinea–Nigerian Relations, the Diplomacy of Labour* (Ibaden: Oxford University Press, 1978).
Porte, Remy, *La conquête des colonies allemandes: naissance et mort d'un rêve imperial* (St. Cloud [Hauts de Seine], ed. 14–18).
Purschel, Herbert, *Die Kaiseriche Schutztruppe fur Kamerun, Gefuge und Aufgabe* (Berlin, 1936).
Rudin, Harry R., *Germans in the Cameroons, 1884–1914* (New Haven: Yale University Press, 1938).
Skolaster, Herman, *Die Pallottiner im Kamerun* (Limburg: Lahn, 1924).
Stoecker, Helmuth, "Loyalty to Germany in Cameroon, 1914–1930," in Kuma Ndumbe, ed., *Africa and Germany from Colonization to Cooperation, 1884–1986* (Yaounde: Editions Africa Venir, 1986).
Strachan, Hew, *The First World War in Africa* (New York: Oxford University Press, 2004).
Student, Erich, *Kameruns Kampf, 1914/16*, vol. 22 (Berlin: Verlag Bernard & Graefe, 1937.
Torres, C. José Cordero, *Geografia Historica de Isla de Fernando Poo* (Madrid: Institute de Estudias de Africanas, 1947).
Townsend, Mary Evelyn, *The Rise and Fall of Germany's Colonial Empire, 1884–1918* (New York: Macmillan, 1930).
Vincent, D. Jose, *Una Obra de Colonizacion Alemana en Fernando Poo* (Madrid, 1919).

Vries, Jacqueline de, *Catholic Mission, Colonial Government and Indigenous Response in Kom (Cameroon)* (Leiden: African Studies Centre, 1998).
Weber, Charles W., *International Influences and Baptist Mission in West Cameroon* (Leiden: E. J. Brill, 1993).

Articles

Ardener, Edwin, "The 'Kamerun Idea,'" *West Africa* (June 6 and 14, 1958).
Callejo, Eduardo Gonzalez, "El Internamiento de los colonos Alemanes del Camerun en la Guinea Espanola, 1915–1919," *Endoxa*, Series Filosofoficas, 37 (2016): 223–36, Universidad Nacional de Educacion a Distancia, Madrid.
Barrett, John C, "World War 1 and the Decline of the First Wave of the American Protestant Missions Movement," *International Bulletin of Missionary Research* 39, no. 3 (July 2015): 122–26.
Craven, Matthew, "Between Law and History: The Berlin Conference of 1884–85 and the Logic of Free Trade," *London Review of International Law* 3, no. 1 (2015): 31–59.
Dekar, Paul R., "Jamaican and British Baptists in West Africa, 1841–1888," *Missiology* 29, no. 4 (October 2001): 433–47.
Henderson, W. O., "The Conquest of the German Colonies, 1914–18," *History* 27, no. 106 (September 1942): 97–160.
Laburthe-Tolra, Philippe, "Christianisme et ouverture au Monde, Cameroun 1845–1915," in *Revue francaise d'histoire d'outre-mer* 75, no. 279 (1988): 207–21.
Lynn, Martin, "The Creoles of Fernando Po," *Journal of African History* 25 (1984): 250ff.
Noll, Mark A., "Pietism," *Elwell Evangelical Dictionary* (Grand Rapids: Baker Books, 2001).
Pierard, Richard V., "Allied Treatment of Protestant Missionaries in German East Africa in WWI," in *African Journal of Evangelical Theology* 12, no. 1 (1993): 4–17.
Quinn, Frederick, "An African Reaction to World War I, The Beti of Cameroon," *Cahiers d'études Africanes* 13, no. 52 (1973): 722–31.
Stark, Rev. W., ed., "The Martyrdom of the Evangelical Missions in Cameroon, 1914," *Reports of Eyewitnesses* (Berlin: Steglitz, 1915).
Sundiata, Ibrahim K., *From Slavery to Neo-Slavery: The Bight of Biafra and Fernando Po in the Era of Abolition, 1827–1930* (Madison: University of Wisconsin Press, 1996).
Tigor, Robert L., "Recollections of Robert O'Collins," *Northeast African Studies* 11, no. 1 (2004–2010): 141–44.
Vries, Jacqueline de, "The Internment and Repatriation of German-Cameroonian Soldiers in Fernando Po, 1916–1919," The International

Network for the Study of the Great War, *Africa and the First World War*, Lisbon, July 11–12, 2013, abstract.

Dissertations

Horner, Norman Aste, "Protestant and Roman Catholic Missions among the Bantu of Cameroon" (Ph.D. thesis, Hartford Seminary, 1956).

Murphy, Mahon, "Prisoners of War and Civilian Internees Captured by the British and Dominion Forces from the German Colonies during the First World War" (Ph.D. thesis, London School of Economic and Political Science, 2014).

O'Neil, Robert John, "A History of Moghamo 1865–1940, Authority and Change in a Cameroon Grassfields Culture" (Ph.D. thesis, Columbia University, 1987).

Archives

School of Oriental and African Studies, London: Archive, Primitive Methodists.
National Archive Annex, Buea, SW Region, Cameroon.
Archive, Mill Hill Missionaries, Heritage Center, Freshfield, UK.
Archive, Bernard Fonlon Center, St. Thomas Major Seminary, Bambui, NW Region, Cameroon.

In Addition

A recent book published in Spain by Dr. Vilaro I Güell tells the story of the internment using archival sources unavailable for this book. The achievement of Spain and Governor Barrera in maintaining her neutrality in Spanish Guinea during WW I while giving asylum to thousands of German soldiers and their retinue is important to the historiography of Spain in colonial Africa. We can add and also for the Cameroon.

In one of the final paragraphs of his book he writes of Governor Barrera who reported to the ministry of state in October 1919 about the "disinternment" of the German internees in the Spanish territory. "In total there were returned to the land 18,342 internees, 44,837 bundles of luggage and 2,643 animals."

Vilaró i Güell, Miquel, *La Internación de la Schutztruppe: La Guinea Española en la Gran Guerra* (Barcelona: Letras de Autor, 2016).

Index

ABC, the Spanish newspaper, 82–84
Akwa, Chiefs of, 14
Allegret, Elie, 116
American Baptists, 105
American Presbyterian Mission, 29, 118
Ardener, Edwin, 127–28
Ardener, Shirley, 7, 11,
Arnett, Resident, 7
Atangana, Paramount Chief Charles, 67–68, 94–98, 105, 108, 130
Ayameken, village of, 80–82
Ayermich, General Joseph, 42, 86, 101

Babanki Tungo, xiv, 4
Bali-Nyonga, 5, 64
Bamenda, xvii, 5, 64
Baptist Missionary Society, xvii, 9, 12, 19–26,
Barrera, Governor Angel, 79–82, 101, 108
Basel Mission, 12, 26–29, 66, 105, 116–17
Bata, 82–86
Bell, Rudolf Manga, 16–18, 47
Bender, Carl, 39, 53, 118
Berlin Conference, 8
Beti, 96–98
Bimbia, 10, 22
Bintner, William, 123–24
Bioko, xiv–xv
Bismarck, Chancellor, 10
Booth, Bernard, 120–23
British Administrators, Problems with, 122–24
Buchner, Dr., 11
Buea, 13–14, 55–56
Buma, Godfred, 109

Cameroon, Republic of, xiv
Chacon, Don Carlos, 21, 77
Claretians, 98–99, 101–2
Chiefs, Colony of, 94–96
Chilver, Elizabeth, 121
Christian missions, 18–39
Clarke, John, 20
Coll, Pedro Armengol, 98, 103
Condominium, 107, 111

Dernberg, Bernard, 15
Dobell, General Charles, xiv, 49, 54, 58–59, 62, 111–12
Douala, xvi, 7, 22, 49–50
Douvry, Pere, 116, 119
Dschang, 60–63
Duala, 9, 16

Ebermaier, Governor, xiv, 16, 42, 52, 72, 86–87, 97, 102, 124
Eboko, Nanga, 84–85
Emonts, Joannes, 43, 65
Eppink, Fons, 127
Equatorial Guinea, 84–85
Evangelization in the camps, 98–100,
Evangelization continues, 115–25

Fatherland, The, 54
Faulkner, Mark, xi
Fernando Po, xiv, xvii, 4–5, 48, 57–58, 62, 68–70, 104
Flags of Kamerun, 16
Fobang, Matthew, 106, 125–27
Fonfuka, 131–32
Forgwe, Primus, xi
Forkwa, Benard, xi
Fuller, Alexander, 22

Fuller, Joseph Jackson, 22–23

General Act of Berlin, 19
German Baptist Missionary Society, 29, 52–53, 118
German Missionaries, xvii, 26–30
Glum, Governor Otto, 16
Gossner Society, 30
Guell, Miquel Vilaroy, 80–82

Hewett, E. H., 10–11
Hoegn, Karl, 35, 116, 119
Holy Spirit Missionaries, 119
Huppertz, Alois, 65–66, 107

Imperial Protection Force, 3
Internment, 49–50, 54
Internment camps, 82–86, Chapter 4

Jamaica, 19–20
Johnson, Thomas Horton, 22–23

Kamerun, xiv–xviii, 1–2, 8
Keller, Werner, 39, 64, 117
Koigni, Agathe, 5, 149
Kolonialamt, 5
Kom, 121–24
Kribi, 58

League of Nations, 112–13
Lees, Lt. Arthur, 52
Legacy, German, 113–14
LeVine, Victor, 113–14, 128
Lloyd James, xi
Lock Priso, 7, 12
Logue, Peter, xi
Loyalty, Kamerun, 114–15
Luciano, Miriam, xi
Lynch, Hollis, xi
Lynn, Martin, 21, 130

Malabo, 2
Mandate, 112–13
Merrick, Joseph, 22
Military Camp, 87–94
Mill Hill Missionaries, xvi, 113, 119–20, 131

Milner-Simon Agreement, 112
Modi Din, Pastor, 116
Moghamo, xvii
Monument, Malabo, 2
Mora, 67–68
Mukom, Aloysius, 4–5
Mukom, Benedict, 4
Munzel, Ambassador Ranier, 2
Murphy, Mahon, 40, 81, 114

Nachtigal, Gustav, 7, 11
Ndi, Anthony, 113, 119
Neaka, Paul, 82
Neu Kamerun, 15–16, 112
New York Public Library, 52
Ngoh, Victor Julius, ix, 107, 111–12
Njinikom, xvi
Njung, George, 127
Nkwen village, 120–21
North West Region, xiv, 18, 120
Ntah, Daniel, 127

Obelisk, 2
O'Brien, Thomas, xi
O'Connell, James, xvii
O'Leary, Daniel, xiii

Pallottine Missionaries, 4, 31–35, 66, 85, 99, 103ff., 116, 119
Pallottine Missionary Sisters, 32, 34, 85
Paris Missionary Society, 107, 117
Picot partition, 111–12
Polizeitruppe, 13–14
Presbyterian Church from the United States, 48–49
Primitive Methodists, 22, 48, 77, 99–100
Prisoners of war, 49–50, 65

Quinn, Frederick, 97–98

Rememberance Day, 2
Repatriation, 107 ff.,
Repatriation, Cameroonians remember 109–10
Rio Muni, xv, xvii, 67–69, 74–86

Index

Rohde, Reinhold, 67
Roman Catholic Missions, 30–39
Rudin, H., xi, xiv, 1, 127
Ruxton, Major, 113

Sacred Heart Missionaries of Sittard, 35–39, 43ff., 66, 99–102, 116
Saker, Alfred, 22–25
Same, Lotin, 117–18
San Carlos, 96
Santa Isabel, 78, 87ff.
Schools, Camp, 98–100
Schuster, C., 87, 99–104
Schutztruppe, xiv–xviii, 2, 13, 42–45, 55, 62–65, 68–69, 71, 99, 110, 114–15, 124, 128–30
Scramble for Africa, 1, 8
Seitz, Governor Theodore, 15
Seized mission property, 115
Shanahan, Joseph, 115–16, 123
Short Stories, 150–58
    Anong, Mathias, 152–53
    Carlos, Padre, 153–54
    Maria, 158
    Mbah, Akenji, 155–56
    Ngong, 151–52
    Njeke, 154
    Sama, Ngoh, 150–51
    Timneng, Michael, 157–58
    Tita, Felix, 156–57
Skolaster, 56–57, 61–63
Soppo, xvi, 3, 14
Spain, xiv, 66, 70, 74–79, 87–88, 101–2, 106
Spanish Muni, 62
Stockle, Johannes, 116
Stoecker, Helmuth, 114
Strachen, Hew, 40, 124
Student, Eric, 52
Sundiata, Ibrahim, xiii, 21,

Testimony of Cameroonians, 133–49
    Buma, Godfred, 136–37
    Doyi, Stephen, 144–45
    Fobang, Matthew Lekomu, 135
    Fomukong, John, 145–46
    Fonkwa, Peter Ndango, 137–38
    Gwangwa, David, 140
    Kunke, Augustine, 142
    Lambe, Thomas, 141–42
    Mbasong, Pius, 139–40
    Mbayaseh, Fon John Ngendop 138–39
    Nchari, John, 134–35
    Nchumuse, Stephen, 133–34
    Ngong, Aloysius, 142–43
    Njeke, Monica, 145
    Njiniboh II, Fon Michael, 141
    Nkette, Sergeant, 143–44
    Nyakom, Thomas, 138
    Taboli, Achillous, 141
    Vewesse, Peter, 136
Time of Trial, 39, 64
Timneng, Michael, xvii, 5, 110, 121–22, 146–47
Togo, 44

United Native Church, 117–18

Verdzekov, Paul, xi
Versailles, Treaty of, 6, 111–12, 124
Vewesse, Peter, xiv, 4–5, 105
Victoria, 9, 12, 22, 24–25
Vieter, Heinrich, 32–34
Vincent, Jose, 82–84
Vries, Jacqueline de, xiii, 39, 121–22
Vuni, Tiberius, 121–22

West Africa Frontier Force, 55
Woermann, Adolf, 9–10
Wouri River, xiv

Yaoundé, 63, 67–68

Zimmerer, Governor Eugen, 13
Zimmermann, Karl, 42, 72, 102
Zintgraff, Eugen, 13

Hamden, Connecticut, 1985. The author with Professor Emeritus of History, Harry Rudin, Yale University, author of *Germans in Cameroon*.

Praise for
Under the Gun

I wish to commend Rev. Fr. Robert O'Neil for his very successful production of *Under the Gun*. It is a succinct but very illuminating analysis of Cameroon history during World War I. But first he provides a welcome background to the war by his story of the Imperial German Colony of the Kamerun since 1884.

He then proceeds with his main themes: missionary activity and World War I in the Cameroons; the internment as refugees of German soldiers and their Cameroon cohorts on the off-shore island of Fernando Po, and the return of Africans to the mainland in 1919 and 1920.

The two appendices based on Fr. O'Neil's interviews with Cameroonians have also enhanced the value of the book.

Readers of *Under the Gun* will be well rewarded.

Hollis R. Lynch
Professor Emeritus of History (West African)
Former Director of the Institute of African Studies
Columbia University

About the Author

Robert O'Neil, a priest and member of the Mill Hill Missionaries, was born in Bridgeport, Connecticut, USA. He holds a PhD in History from Columbia University in New York. Ordained in July 1965 at Westminster Cathedral by Cardinal Heenan, he spent his first years on mission in Cameroon, West Africa. He is the author of *Cardinal Herbert Vaughan, Mission to the British Cameroons* and *Mission to the Upper Nile*. For nineteen years he was an assistant at St. Mary's Parish on the Lower East Side of Manhattan. He resides at the Mill Hill residence in Hartsdale, New York.

About the Publisher

The Crossroad Publishing Company publishes Crossroad and Herder & Herder books. We offer a 200-year global family tradition of books on spiritual living and religious thought. We promote reading as a time-tested discipline for focus and understanding. We help authors shape, clarify, write, and effectively promote their ideas. We select, edit, and distribute books. With our expertise and passion, we provide wholesome spiritual nourishment for heart, mind, and soul through the written word.

www.ingramcontent.com/pod-product-compliance
Lightning Source LLC
Chambersburg PA
CBHW020737230426
43665CB00009B/462